T0274731

"There can be little doubt that Western cu   ie
central problems are metaethical and conc   )-
logical foundations for the existence and _____   y.
Adam Lloyd Johnson's stunning book strikes at the very heart of the matter by
presenting a rigorous, well-structured defense of his uniquely trinitarian solution to these problems, along with a deep analysis and evisceration of the leading
rival—Erik Wielenberg's Godless Normative Realism. Johnson leaves no stone
unturned, his research is exceptional, and his topic and treatment of it are first-
rate. I very strongly recommend this book."

—J. P. Moreland,
Distinguished Professor of Philosophy,
Talbot School of Theology, Biola University

"Adam Lloyd Johnson's *Divine Love Theory* develops a theistic trinitarian metaethical theory and engages critically with my own secular metaethical approach.
Johnson's theory builds in innovative and insightful ways on the theistic framework put forward by Robert Adams in his modern classic *Finite and Infinite Goods*
(Oxford University Press, 1999). Johnson makes a compelling case that incorporating specific elements of the Christian doctrine of a triune God into an Adams-
style framework for ethics yields a stronger view. In making this case, Johnson
follows Adams's lead in drawing connections between work in theology and work
in contemporary analytic metaethics. Work that does this successfully is rare, and it
is a particular virtue of Johnson's manuscript that it does so. Johnson also engages
extensively and critically with my own work, particularly my book *Robust Ethics*
(Oxford University Press, 2014). Indeed, Johnson represents the most careful and
extensive critique of my work that I've encountered. Perhaps unsurprisingly, I do
not agree with all of Adam's objections to my position, but there is certainly much
here with which I (and others attracted to my general approach—an approach
shared by, for example, Derek Parfit, Russ Shafer-Landau, Michael Huemer, and
David Enoch) must contend. Overall, then, *Divine Love Theory* is an important
and original contribution to the ongoing contemporary debate between theists and
nontheists over the foundations of morality. It is a work that will be of interest to
theologians and philosophers alike."

—Erik Wielenberg, Professor of Philosophy, DePauw University

"Johnson's book is very well-done and very helpful to the reader; I love the historical overview. Also, his Evolutionary Debunking Argument against Wielenberg's
position is really good. Lastly, I found the part on imaging the obedience in the
Trinity as a basis for the obligation to obey God creative and interesting."

—William Lane Craig, Professor of Philosophy,
Talbot School of Theology and Houston Baptist University

"Adam Lloyd Johnson's *Divine Love Theory* is one of the finest works on the subject that I have read. Johnson's scholarship is comprehensive, from patristic theology to some of the most recent work in analytic philosophy of religion. He invariably defends the best positions, navigating skillfully between implausible extremes, and his arguments are first-rate. He skillfully defends Robert Adams's Christian Platonism and Plantinga's evolutionary argument against naturalism, and he provides us with a state-of-the-art critique of Erik Wielenberg's atheistic moral realism, on both metaphysical and epistemological grounds. Johnson demonstrates the relevance of recent debates about the Trinity to the problem of theistic metaethics. I endorse this book enthusiastically."

—Robert Koons,
Professor of Philosophy,
University of Texas at Austin

"This is no run-of-the-mill or garden-variety book; it is really superlative work and a cut above, in my estimation. It is written beautifully, argued cogently, and researched thoroughly. It is also on cutting-edge topics. He offers a trinitarian metaethic that sports numerous strong explanatory features, and contrasts it with a leading secular ethical account, namely, that of Erik Wielenberg's. For some years I have worked in the area of theistic ethics, but my own work has for the most part been confined to a defense of Anselmian theology. Anselm himself believed both in the God of classical theism and the distinctively Christian God—my own work has been largely delimited to the former. By employing distinctively Christian resources of trinitarian theology, Johnson has extended the work to something beyond generic theism to something specifically Christian. This is vitally important and a fascinating project. Repeatedly, this work generates fresh, solid insights that comprise genuine contributions to the literature. The way, for instance, he used trinitarian theology to give a finer-grained account of Robert Adams's theistic adaptation of a model of moral obligations was genuinely perspicacious—and it's just one of many examples of his innovation that could be adduced."

—David Baggett,
Professor of Philosophy,
Houston Baptist University

"Dr. Johnson's book, *Divine Love Theory* will be of interest to anyone engaged in philosophy of religion and ethics. He provides a good historical overview and then takes on one of the most formidable contemporary atheistic proposals for grounding objective morality within atheism, the so-called Godless Normative Realism of Erik Wielenberg. Johnson's own proposal is a refreshing and insightful address that is often missed in the moral debate of mere theism: trinitarianism. *Divine Love Theory* is at once more consistent with the largest theistic population, Christians, but also provides greater explanatory power over competitors, theistic and atheistic alike. Breadth of consideration includes interaction with various positions like Natural Law, Divine Will, and Divine Command Theory. Of other importance is the consideration of other objections to Wielenberg's bloated ontology and also Johnson's nice up-to-date discussion of evolutionary debunking arguments relative to moral epistemology. I commend this important and insightful piece in the historical and contemporary debate concerning God and morality."

—Corey Miller,
President of Ratio Christi

"*Divine Love Theory* is a unique contribution to scholarship because it focuses on the specifics of trinitarian theology as a way of responding to an atheist critique of theistic metaethics, while articulating how the central insights of his theory are available to both classical and social trinitarians. More specifically, Johnson argues that his 'trinitarian moral theory' is a more plausible explanation for objective morality than atheist Erik Wielenberg's 'godless normative realism,' by (i) defending the former from criticisms by the latter, and by (ii) developing metaphysical and epistemological objections to the latter. In addition, Johnson defends his chosen theory from possible objections which are independent of Wielenberg's criticisms. The strength of the argument lies in how Johnson adds more theological detail (the Trinity and relations of intratrinitarian love between the persons) to an extant account of moral goodness (Robert Adams's divine nature theory) and shows how this addition answers questions raised by atheists. In addition, the argument is particularly sensitive to contemporary evangelical debate about 'eternal functional subordination' within the Trinity, articulating a version of trinitarian metaethical theory which sidesteps this recent controversy."

—Greg Welty,
Professor of Philosophy,
Southeastern Baptist Theological Seminary

"Yes, evangelical churches today affirm their belief in the trinitarian nature of God. It is in our doctrinal statements and occasionally in our language. But so what? In a season of self-help teaching from many of our pulpits, the doctrine of the Trinity has been benched for more practical theology. Yet, it is in the wonder and mystery of the trinitarian nature of God that many of our most beloved beliefs are rooted. The trinitarian nature of God is at the center of what defines the love and life for which our souls long. For this reason, I was excited to explore Adam Lloyd Johnson's presentation of the trinitarian nature of God as the basis for morality in this age of moral turmoil. Adam writes with the mind of a scholar and the heart of a pastor. Put your thinking cap on. It is well worth the effort."

—Bryan Clark,
Senior Pastor,
Lincoln Berean Church

"I wish to add my enthusiastic endorsement for Adam Johnson's *Divine Love Theory*. Johnson's fresh and original version of the moral argument for the existence of God appeals to an essentially *Christian* concept of God, thus arguing that certain salient features of our moral experience are best explained by appeal to the triune God and the ultimacy of love as shared among the persons of the Trinity. The argument thus goes beyond, say, my own attempt to ground the dignity of persons in the 'personhood' of God but leaving open the question of the number of 'persons' involved in that grounding. This central feature of the argument, combined with Johnson's assessment of one of the more promising recent attempts at a secular grounding of morality (i.e., Erik Wielenberg's *Robust Ethics*) will likely spur discussion in new directions."

—Mark Linville,
Senior Research Fellow,
Faulkner University

Divine Love Theory

HOW THE TRINITY IS THE SOURCE AND FOUNDATION OF MORALITY

ADAM LLOYD JOHNSON

RATIO
CHRISTI
BOOKS

KREGEL
ACADEMIC

Because God is a Trinity of three divine persons loving one another, I believe we image God the brightest when we love God and one another. I dedicate this book to my wife, Kristin, because she helps me, a selfish brute, see the beauty and joy of selfless loving relationships. In this way she images God to me.

CONTENTS

Part 1: Moral Theory

What's This Disagreement All About?
A Rich History

Godless Normative Realism
A Broad Array of Moral Theories

The Question at Hand
My Primary Argument
A Theological and Apologetic Approach

Part 2: Divine Love Theory

The Importance of the Trinity
Moral Value in the Divine Love Theory
Moral Obligation in the Divine Love Theory

Objection 1: Concerns with Loving Relationships Within the Trinity
Objection 2: Concerns from Divine Will Theorists
Objection 3: Concerns from Natural Law Theorists
Objection 4: Concerns with God's Will Being Arbitrary
Objection 5: Concerns with Platonism

FOREWORD

It is an exciting time for moral apologetics. Work on theistic ethics and versions of the moral argument for God's existence has experienced a major resurgence in recent years. Deductive, inductive, abductive, natural-signs-theoretic, and confirmation variants of moral arguments have been advanced using the technical machinery of analytic philosophy. Correlatively, a whole range of theistic metaethical accounts have been delineated and defended—from natural law approaches to divine command theories, from divine motivation to divine desire accounts, from divine will to divine motivation analyses, and more besides.

The common chord struck by so many of these diverse approaches has been the nagging suspicion and principled case for an ineliminable dependence of morality on theism. Into this burgeoning literature Adam Lloyd Johnson's significant contribution, *Divine Love Theory,* is a welcome addition, augmenting and supplementing many prior approaches and occasionally breaking prior paradigms. It is eminently worthy of a seat at the table. Johnson has done an admirable job here of laying out a fresh variant of theistic ethics, assigning primacy to the love of God as illumined by the perichoretic relationship featured in trinitarian monotheism. This makes the project cutting edge and superlative, featuring a metaethics that sports numerous strong explanatory features and entails among other things that God's commands are not arbitrary but a function of God's desire for us to enjoy the deepest aspect of reality: the love of the Trinity.

Johnson's book adds important texture to the recent work extolling and explicating the explanatory benefits of Anselmian theology in the realm of ethics and metaethics. Anselm himself was both a proponent of greatest being theology and distinctively Christian theology. In that vein, Johnson has extended the work of moral apologetics to something beyond generic, thin, or bare theism to something thicker and specifically Christian. The idea of using distinctively trinitarian resources in this way makes for a fascinating project generative of fresh, solid insights that comprise genuine contributions to the literature. If something in even the vicinity of his argument goes through, it pushes in the direction of classical theism, generally, and Christian theism, specifically, providing a robust account of a range of important moral phenomena, likely a better explanation than the salient alternatives on offer.

A luminary from the history of the moral argument, John Henry Newman, spoke of the ampliative function served by special revelation. Unapologetically tapping into specifically Christian theology arguably yields important dividends. The way, most centrally, Johnson uses trinitarian theology to give a finer-grained account of Robert Adams's theistic adaptation of a social requirement model of moral obligations is genuinely perspicacious—just one of many examples of his innovation.

The scholarship and research of this extended essay is top-notch, delving deeply into two separate literatures: one in theology pertaining to the Trinity, and another in ethics and metaethics. The range and breadth of Johnson's scholarship is impressive, and the depth of his understanding of both sets of material is fantastic, as is his facility in their interaction, synthesis, and rapprochement. The quality of the case is at a very high level, the writing a thing of beauty, and the result a joy to read. Readers may not agree with every ancillary point along the way, but the central integrating thread of his argument strikes me as fundamentally right. Of this I am sure: the work is not responsibly ignored, and the investment in closely and carefully reading and considering it will be time well spent.

—David Baggett
Houston Baptist University

ACKNOWLEDGMENTS

First, I'd like to thank my Savior, Jesus Christ, for loving me in spite of my failures. I'm often amazed that he would want someone like me on his team as he works to draw people back to the loving relationship with God they were created for. Above all else, I hope this work pleases him.

I'm also thankful to Francis Schaeffer for inspiring me to pursue a ministry of apologetics. I became a Christian when I trusted in Christ as a teenager, but throughout my twenties I had doubts concerning whether Christianity was true. In my late twenties I had a full-blown crisis of faith. Though Schaeffer had passed away many years before, through his books he rescued me spiritually, intellectually, and emotionally. It was at that point that I sensed God calling me to help others the way Schaeffer had helped me. Thus, I began the process of moving away from my actuarial science career to pursue seminary, the pastorate, and eventually my current ministry of teaching and writing.

In fact, there's a sense in which the initial idea for my Divine Love Theory came from reading Francis Schaeffer's work. He pointed out that, according to many atheists, love is merely an accidental chemical reaction that nature "selected" for in the haphazard process of evolution because it led to greater chances of survival and reproduction. However, no one can live out this way of thinking consistently—even the scientist goes home from the lab at night and tells her family she loves them, and she truly means it. We just can't escape

3

the truth that love is real. However, within such an atheistic belief system one must take an irrational leap of faith to believe love is real. Schaeffer contrasted this with Christianity which he argued has a rational explanation for how love can be real. He explained that the love between the persons of the Trinity is the source and foundation of the love we experience because we were created in God's image.[1]

I would like to thank the two seminaries that provided my theological and philosophical education. I spent thirteen straight years—the first few at Southern Evangelical Seminary because of Norman Geisler's influence and the rest at Southeastern Baptist Theological Seminary—working on my master of divinity and doctor of philosophy degrees. These schools are not merely institutions; they're communities of people seeking to grow in wisdom and knowledge so they can glorify God by serving others with the gifts and abilities he has given them. At these schools God blessed me with wonderful friends, knowledgeable teachers, and godly mentors.

In particular, I'm thankful to Dr. Bruce Little for serving as my major professor for the first five years of my PhD program, for helping me think more clearly, and for providing sound advice. I am thankful to Dr. Greg Welty for serving as my major professor after Dr. Little retired, for helping me improve my writing, and for giving frequent encouragement. I'm thankful to Dr. William Lane Craig for agreeing to instruct my independent study PhD seminar and allowing me to work with him for a few years on his debate with Erik Wielenberg and the resulting book about that debate. I'm also thankful for Erik Wielenberg's feedback, suggestions, and friendship as I've engaged him on this topic over the last several years. I'm thankful for David Baggett, who has been a tremendous source of encouragement in my life over the last couple years, spurring me on in this area of moral apologetics. I also want to thank my friend Joel Mohrmann for all the time he spent proofreading the manuscript; beyond fixing my poor grammar and obnoxious misuse of commas, Joel gave valuable feedback in several areas.

Lastly, I would like to thank my wife, Kristin, and my children, Caroline (and her husband Bryce), Will, Xander, and Ray for their patience, support, and love throughout this research and writing process. I don't express enough how much I appreciate my family and the fellowship I enjoy with them.

---

1.   Francis A. Schaeffer, *The God Who Is There*, 2nd Ed., vol. 1, A Christian View of Philosophy and Culture of *The Complete Works of Francis A. Schaeffer: A Christian Worldview* (Wheaton, Ill.: Crossway Books, 1985), 93–107.

PART 1

MORAL THEORY

CHAPTER 1

MORAL DISAGREEMENT

What's This Disagreement All About?

This book is about a specific disagreement over morality between theists and atheists. It may be best to begin by explaining what this disagreement is *not* about. First, it isn't about the morality of a specific action, such as abortion, euthanasia, or lying to Nazis at your front door. Certainly, these are important discussions to have, and there's plenty of disagreement about these topics among theists, among atheists, and between theists and atheists, but that's not the disagreement I'm considering in this book.

Second, this disagreement isn't about whether atheists can be good people. Both sides agree that atheists can, generally speaking, be good, moral people. Of course no one's perfect, but both sides believe that, for the most part, theists and atheists can live good, moral lives.[2]

---

1. The term *good* is being used here in a simple comparative way. As will be discussed in chapter 4, it's an important part of Christian theology that all humans, including all atheists and all

Third, this disagreement isn't about whether atheists can know moral truth. Both parties believe that at least some moral truths are self-evident to all theists and atheists alike. On the atheistic side, Russ Shafer-Landau defends well the notion of self-evident moral principles.[3] He explains that it's "self-evident that, other things being equal, it is wrong to take pleasure in another's pain, to taunt and threaten the vulnerable, to prosecute and punish those known to be innocent, and to sell another's secrets solely for personal gain. When I say such things, I mean that once one really understands these principles . . . one doesn't need to infer them from one's other beliefs in order to be justified in thinking them true."[4] Similarly, many Christians maintain that basic moral truths are self-evident to people because of "the work of the Law written in their hearts" by God (Rom. 2:15).

Fourth, this disagreement isn't about the objectivity of morality. Both sides in this particular debate agree that moral truth is objective. Whether morality is objective is an important topic to discuss and debate, and there's no shortage of folks eager to do so, but that's not the disagreement I'm talking about in this book. On the atheistic side of this debate, Shafer-Landau explains that the purpose of his book *Moral Realism* is to defend "the theory that moral judgements enjoy a special sort of objectivity: such judgements, when true, are so independently of what any human being, anywhere, in any circumstance whatever, thinks of them."[5] Additionally, David Enoch describes objective morality as the position that "there are response-independent . . . irreducibly normative truths . . . objective ones, that when successful in our normative inquiries we discover rather than create or construct."[6]

On the theistic side, C. Stephen Evans agrees with Enoch's description of objective morality and congratulates him for offering the most comprehensive and sophisticated case for objective morality to be found in the literature.[7] Evans notes, "Enoch makes the case for this first by considering a very simple . . . [opposing] view that he calls 'Caricatured Subjectivism,' but he then goes on to argue that the argument generalizes and applies" to many other opposing views.[8] Further, Alvin Plantinga writes, "Moral truths are *objective*, in the sense that they

---

theists, are morally imperfect to one degree or another and thus require God's forgiveness to be reconciled back to a right relationship with him.

3.   Shafer-Landau, *Moral Realism*, 247–66.
4.   Shafer-Landau, *Moral Realism*, 248.
5.   Shafer-Landau, *Moral Realism*, 2.
6.   Enoch, "Robust Metanormative Realism," 21. See also Enoch, *Taking Morality Seriously*.
7.   Evans, *God and Moral Obligation*, 166.
8.   Evans, *God and Moral Obligation*, 167.

are in a certain way independent of human beliefs and desires. It is wrong to torture people for the fun of it, and would remain wrong even if most or all of the world's population came to believe that this behavior is perfectly acceptable, and indeed came to desire that it be much more widely practiced."[9] For example, if everyone in the world took a pill tonight that caused them to wake up tomorrow believing that rape was morally right, that still wouldn't make rape morally right, because the truth "rape is wrong" is an objective moral truth that exists outside us, beyond our attitudes, opinions, and personal beliefs.

Both sides in this disagreement reject the most direct opposing position to objective morality, the idea that morality is subjective. Those who promote subjective morality argue that there is no objective moral truth that exists beyond our personal opinions. If morality were subjective, it wouldn't be legitimate for a person to say that someone else is doing something objectively wrong, because there would be no objective moral truth they could appeal to. In other words, if morality were subjective, it wouldn't be legitimate for someone to say that racism is objectively wrong; all she could say is that she doesn't prefer it. Both sides in the particular disagreement I'm talking about reject subjective morality because they both believe that some things are really right and some things are really wrong, that there are objective moral truths that exist independently, beyond what we think and feel. Both sides agree that morality exists apart from us as objective truth that we can know and understand. This doesn't mean it is always easy to know what's morally true; sometimes it can be quite difficult. But this isn't unique to the realm of moral truth; finite humans face this difficulty in all areas of truth, including science, history, politics, and philosophy.

So what specific disagreement *is* this book all about? My focus here is between theists and atheists who disagree over what is the best explanation for the *existence* of objective moral truth—theism or atheism. What's the best explanation of these objective moral truths? Where do they come from? How can they "exist" out there apart from us? The theists in this disagreement claim God is the best explanation for objective morality. For example, David Baggett and Jerry Walls argue that "the authority of moral obligations needs an account . . . [and] Theism—entailing a loving, perfect God who commands, who knows us better than we know ourselves, who knows truly what is in our ultimate best interest, and who desires the best for us—can, we submit, most effectively provide it."[10]

---

9.   A. Plantinga, "Naturalism," 249.
10. Baggett and Walls, *God and Cosmos*, 290.

The particular atheists in this disagreement argue against this claim that God is the best explanation for objective morality.

Some have quipped that if moral truth is self-evident, then by definition it needs no explanation. In his debate with William Lane Craig, atheist Walter Sinnott-Armstrong claims that if a moral truth is self-evident, then no reason need be given for it. For example, since rape is self-evidently wrong, there's no need to go further and explain *why* it is wrong. He writes, "You don't need to add that humans were made in God's image or that we are His favorite species or anything religious."[11] He argues that a self-evident moral truth doesn't need an explanation, for that's simply what it means to be self-evident. However, those who make such assertions have confused knowing moral truth (epistemology) with the existence of moral truth (ontology). Craig responds simply by making this important distinction and explaining that Sinnott-Armstrong's mistake is to "think that our ability simply to see that rape is wrong implies that no account need be given of why rape is wrong."[12]

The key difference here is between knowing *that* something is wrong and knowing *why* it is wrong. Theists and atheists alike can know something is morally wrong self-evidently, but explaining what actually *makes* it wrong is something else entirely. In other words, people can know *that* morality is objective and *that* rape is wrong without appealing to God, but theists argue that atheists don't have a sufficient explanation as to *why* rape is wrong. This is a more fundamental issue than merely knowing a particular moral truth or that morality is objectively true. It's not necessary to believe in the existence of God to apprehend moral truth, but, so argue these theists, without God's existence there's no foundation for such truths to exist in the first place. Paul Copan writes that atheists "do not have to believe in God to *know* right from wrong . . . [but their explanation of objective morality's] more fundamental level of being—that is, the actual ground or basis . . . —is inadequate."[13]

The summary of this disagreement that I've presented so far has oversimplified the discussion a bit for the sake of introduction. When it comes to this specific disagreement, not everyone on the atheists' side is an atheist and not everyone on the theists' side is a theist. For example, there are theists who have built, or defend, moral models that affirm objective morality but don't include God in any way, thereby implying that God isn't required for the existence of

---

11. Sinnott-Armstrong, "No Good Reason," 34.
12. Craig, "Reason Enough," 69.
13. Copan, "Hume and the Moral Argument," 223, original emphasis.

objective morality. In such cases the person himself or herself isn't an atheist, but their model is atheistic and thus will be so described in this book; instead of atheistic, some may prefer the term *godless, nontheistic,* or *secular.* Clearly such theists, though they believe God exists, don't think that God is the best explanation for objective morality.

Alternatively, there are atheists who believe that *if* morality were objective, then theism would be the best explanation for its existence. For example, Paul Draper argues, "The probability that moral agents exist given naturalism is extremely low, much lower than it is given theism. . . . [There] is the possibility that some 'historical outcomes' like the existence of embodied moral agents are much more probable on theism than on naturalism and hence significantly raise the ratio of the probability of theism to the probability of naturalism."[14] However, these particular atheists reject the existence of objective morality and therefore find no compelling reason to embrace theism. Thus, technically, the specific disagreement I'm considering in this book is between those who maintain God is the best explanation for objective morality, which is mostly but not exclusively argued for by theists, and those who think God isn't the best explanation for objective morality, which is mostly but not exclusively argued for by atheists.

A Rich History

For many centuries before the modern era, most Western thinkers believed that God is the best explanation for moral truth. Though these thinkers agreed *that* God is the ultimate foundation for morality, they disagreed as to *how* he serves as this foundation—for example, by his commands, because of his moral nature, through ideas in his mind, as a moral exemplar, or in creating human nature with a certain purpose (telos). Though they differed on the details, they all agreed that an immaterial and personal God, as the ultimate source of all things, provides a fitting explanation for morality, which itself is both immaterial and personal.

This is not only true of Judaism, Christianity, and Islam (the Abrahamic religions); many ancient Greek philosophers also believed morality has a transcendent source. Some of them, including Plato and Aristotle, even described this transcendent source in similar ways to how the Abrahamic religions described God. The Christian theologian Thomas Aquinas understood Plato's theory of forms as the conclusion of Plato's search for certainty in the face of the constant change we

---

14. Draper, "Cosmic Fine-Tuning," 311.

experience in the physical world.[15] The state of flux we find in the physical world, which includes ourselves, just couldn't provide the objectivity Plato, like many others, assumed must be the case concerning truth, including moral truth. Thus, he posited transcendent universals, which include moral truths, that exist objectively apart from us. He also suggested in the *Timaeus* that a divine craftsman, the Demiurge, employed these universals in making the physical world.[16]

In his celebrated work *After Virtue*, widely recognized as one of the most important works of moral philosophy in the twentieth century, Alasdair MacIntyre calls this predominant view I've described from the premodern era the "classical tradition," which includes Greek philosophy and Christian theism.[17] He often refers to this classical tradition as Aristotelian but regards Aristotle "not just as an individual theorist, but as the representative of a long tradition, as someone who articulates what a number of predecessors and successors also articulate with varying degrees of success."[18]

MacIntyre notes, "Most medieval proponents of this [moral] scheme did of course believe that it was itself part of God's revelation, but also a discovery of reason and rationally defensible."[19] He explains that Aristotle and the New Testament share "a unitary core concept . . . [that] turns out to provide the tradition of which I have written the history with its conceptual unity."[20] MacIntyre argues, "The New Testament's account of the virtues, even if it differs as much as it does in content from Aristotle's . . . does have the same logical conceptual structure as Aristotle's account. A virtue is, as with Aristotle, a quality the exercise of which leads to the achievement of the human *telos*."[21] Plato, Aristotle, and Thomas Aquinas may differ "in a number of important ways," but the "presupposition which all three share is that there exists a cosmic order which dictates the place of each virtue in a total harmonious scheme of human life."[22] MacIntyre even admits, "I became a Thomist after writing *After Virtue* in part because I became convinced that Aquinas was in some respects a better Aristotelian than Aristotle. . . . I had now learned from Aquinas that my attempt to provide an account of the human good . . . was bound to be inadequate until I had provided it with a metaphysical grounding."[23]

15. Doolan, *Aquinas*, 45–46.
16. Plato, *Timaeus* 28a.
17. MacIntyre, *After Virtue*, 52.
18. MacIntyre, *After Virtue*, 146.
19. MacIntyre, *After Virtue*, 53.
20. MacIntyre, *After Virtue*, 186.
21. MacIntyre, *After Virtue*, 184.
22. MacIntyre, *After Virtue*, 142.
23. MacIntyre, *After Virtue*, x.

MacIntyre also provides an extended explanation of how, when this classical theistic tradition was jettisoned in the modern era, various thinkers tried but failed to find or establish a new foundation for objective morality. Without God, how could objective moral truth exist apart from our own ideas and preferences? If there's no fixed point, no absolute standard, and no ultimate purpose for human beings, then how could our moral beliefs be anything more than our personal opinions?

MacIntyre argues that David Hume's proclamation of the is-ought problem, that *oughts* do not follow from what *is*, sometimes referred to as the fact-value gap, "was itself a crucial historical event. It signals both a final break with the classical tradition and the decisive breakdown of the . . . project of justifying morality in the context of the inherited, but already incoherent, fragments left behind from tradition."[24] He explains, "The joint effect of the secular rejection of both Protestant and Catholic theology and the scientific and philosophical rejection of Aristotelianism was to eliminate any notion of man-as-he-could-be-if-he-realized-his-*telos*. . . . The elimination of any notion of essential human nature and with it the abandonment of any notion of a *telos* leaves behind a moral scheme composed of two remaining elements [*is* and *ought*] whose relationship becomes quite unclear."[25] These modern thinkers "reject any teleological view of human nature, any view of man as having an essence which defines his true end. But to understand this is to understand why their project of finding a basis for morality had to fail."[26] In other words, "once the notion of essential human purposes or functions disappears from morality, it begins to appear implausible to treat moral judgments as factual statements."[27]

John Hare similarly critiques modern secular attempts to propose foundations for objective morality based on classical theistic models such as Aristotle's and Duns Scotus's, among others, while at the same time rejecting their theistic assumptions.[28] He notes, "Elizabeth Anscombe (herself a Christian) made this point about moral law in her famous article 'Modern Moral Philosophy' in 1958."[29] In this article she wrote, "It is not possible to have such a [moral law] conception unless you believe in God as a law-giver; like Jews, Stoics, and Christians."[30]

---

24. MacIntyre, *After Virtue*, 59.
25. MacIntyre, *After Virtue*, 54–55.
26. MacIntyre, *After Virtue*, 54.
27. MacIntyre, *After Virtue*, 59.
28. Hare, *God and Morality*, 17.
29. Hare, *God and Morality*, 260.
30. Anscombe, "Modern Moral Philosophy," 5.

MacIntyre further explains that the failure of these modern attempts at finding a new, nontheistic foundation for objective morality led to the birth of subjective morality:

> On the one hand the individual moral agent, freed from hierarchy and teleology, conceives of himself and is conceived of by moral philosophers as sovereign in his moral authority. On the other hand the inherited, if partially transformed, rules of morality have to be found some new status, deprived as they have been of their older teleological character and their even more ancient categorical character as expressions of an ultimately divine law. If such rules cannot be found a new status which will make appeal to them rational, appeal to them will indeed appear as a mere instrument of individual desire and will.[31]

While some modern thinkers claimed their models did preserve objective morality, "what those philosophers in fact provided were several rival and incompatible accounts, utilitarians competing with Kantians and both with contractarians, so that moral judgments . . . became essentially contestable, expressive of the attitudes and feelings of those who uttered them."[32] These irreconcilable contentions led many to the horrifying conclusion that objective morality was merely "a theatre of illusions,"[33] a realization that paved the way for the acceptance, and eventual promotion, of subjective morality.

Friedrich Nietzsche played a large role in promoting subjective morality as he forcefully proclaimed the failure of these modern nontheistic attempts to find a foundation for objective morality. As an atheist, he sensationally declared, "God is dead," but by that he simply meant the idea of God had much less influence on the way people thought than it used to. He's an unlikely ally to theists in this debate because his "critique of modern philosophy, and particularly of modern moral philosophy, comes precisely from his conviction that a genuinely objective moral order . . . would require a God as its foundation."[34] This conviction of his gave "rise to a scathing critique of secular moralists of his day, who believe that they can hold on to an objective morality without God."[35] Nietzsche

---

31. MacIntyre, *After Virtue*, 62.
32. MacIntyre, *After Virtue*, x.
33. MacIntyre, *After Virtue*, 77.
34. Evans, *God and Moral Obligation*, 122.
35. Evans, *God and Moral Obligation*, 122.

sharply ridiculed as naive those who thought "morality could survive when the God who sanctions it is missing!"[36]

MacIntyre similarly argues that Nietzsche wittingly demolished the modern "project to discover rational foundations for an objective morality."[37] He writes, "It was Nietzsche's historic achievement to understand more clearly than any other philosopher . . . not only that what purported to be appeals to objectivity were in fact expressions of subjective will, but also the nature of the problems that this posed for moral philosophy."[38] In Nietzsche's view, the "rational and rationally justified autonomous moral subject . . . is a fiction, an illusion; so, Nietzsche resolves, let will replace reason and let us make ourselves into autonomous moral subjects by some gigantic and heroic act of the will."[39]

Nietzsche isn't the only atheist who has argued that, without God as a foundation, morality could not be objective. In chapter 1, "The Subjectivity of Values," of his book *Ethics: Inventing Right and Wrong*, J. L. Mackie launches his argument with the sentence "There are no objective values."[40] He labels his view "error theory" because he claims that "although most people in making moral judgments implicitly claim, among other things, to be pointing to something objectively prescriptive, these claims are all false."[41] Elsewhere he admits that "objective intrinsically prescriptive features, supervening upon natural ones, constitute so odd a cluster of qualities and relations that they are most unlikely to have arisen in the ordinary course of events, without an all-powerful God to create them. If, then, there are such intrinsically prescriptive objective values, they make the existence of a god more probable than it would have been without them."[42] Mackie argues that belief in objective morality made sense when people believed in God, but since that belief has fallen away, so should the belief in objective morality.[43]

In addition, existentialist philosopher Jean-Paul Sartre writes, "There can no longer be an *a priori* Good, since there is no infinite and perfect consciousness to think it. . . . If God does not exist, we find no values or commands to turn to which legitimize our conduct."[44] Richard Taylor boldly writes that "the modern

---

36. Nietzsche, *Will to Power*, 147.
37. MacIntyre, *After Virtue*, 113.
38. MacIntyre, *After Virtue*, 113.
39. MacIntyre, *After Virtue*, 114.
40. Mackie, *Ethics*, 12.
41. Mackie, *Ethics*, 35.
42. Mackie, *Miracle of Theism*, 115–16.
43. Mackie, *Ethics*, 40.
44. Sartre, *Existentialism and Human Emotions*, 22–23.

age, more or less repudiating the idea of a divine lawgiver, has nevertheless tried to retain the ideas of moral right and wrong, not noticing that, in casting God aside, they have also abolished the conditions of meaningfulness for moral right and wrong as well."[45] He writes also, "The concept of moral obligation is unintelligible apart from the idea of God. The words remain but their meaning is gone."[46] Hare summarizes the situation well: "Since the middle of the twentieth century, there have been several voices within analytic philosophy saying that we need to discard or revise our understanding of the moral law or moral obligation, because it makes sense only against the background of a theistic world-view that 'we' have lost."[47]

Other atheists have said, "No, wait a minute, not so fast. Even if there's no God, it doesn't follow that there are no objective moral truths." These atheists argue that it's a mistake to think that only God could provide the foundation for objective morality. Maybe something else provides the foundation. Or maybe objective moral truth doesn't need a foundation at all. Maybe objective moral truths exist on their own and hence need no foundation. Of particular interest in this line of thinking is the position of G. E. Moore, one of the founders of analytic philosophy.

In his book *Principia Ethica*, published in 1903, Moore claimed that moral goodness was not a natural property such as human pleasure, like the utilitarians maintained, nor was it a supernatural property connected somehow with God.[48] Instead, he argued that goodness is a simple, nonnatural property. Evans explains that ethical nonnaturalists such as Moore "agree with theists that ethical truths cannot be explained naturalistically, but don't necessarily think God plays an essential role in ethics."[49] Moore believed that this understanding of goodness preserved objective morality in that it affirmed moral truths that exist independently of us.

Moore's moral theory was Platonic in that he held that moral goodness, like the number seven, doesn't exist in space and time and isn't accessible to us via our senses.[50] Thus Moore accepted the existence of Plato's abstract objects while denying the theistic aspects of Plato's view.[51] He defended the existence of moral goodness as a nonnatural property via his famous open question argu-

---

45.   Richard Taylor, *Ethics, Faith, and Reason* (Cambridge, MA: Harvard University Press, 1985), 2.
46.   Taylor, *Ethics, Faith and Reason*, 83–84.
47.   Hare, *God and Morality*, 260.
48.   Moore, *Principia Ethica*.
49.   Evans, *God and Moral Obligation*, 8.
50.   Hare, *God and Morality*, 194.
51.   Moore, *Principia Ethica*, 162.

ment. According to Moore, other philosophers had committed what he called the naturalistic fallacy in that they tried to define moral goodness by identifying it with a nonevaluative property such as the "avoidance of pain" or being "commanded by God." However, no matter what nonevaluative property someone claims is identical with moral goodness, it will always be an open question whether that property itself is good. Thus, if a utilitarian claims goodness is the avoidance of pain, it's appropriate to ask whether the avoidance of pain itself is good. Moore argued that the only way to avoid this open question argument is to maintain, as he did, that moral goodness is a separate, nonreductive, indefinable, nonnatural property.

Moore's proposal generated an interesting problem: If moral properties aren't natural, then we can't access facts about morality via our senses. If we can't access facts about morality via our senses, then how can we have knowledge of such properties? In this regard Moore was an intuitionist, in that he claimed we have a unique type of cognitive ability that allows us to know, though not infallibly, if something is morally good or not. He insisted that the best way for us to intuitively ascertain whether or not something, or some situation, has intrinsic goodness is to imagine that nothing else exists at all except that particular thing and then ask ourselves if we would still consider its isolated existence something that's good.[52]

MacIntyre is highly critical of Moore's proposal and argues that it, like all other modern nontheistic attempts to sustain objective morality, failed miserably. He writes, "Moore's readers . . . saw themselves as rescued thereby from Sidgwick and any other utilitarianism as decisively as from Christianity. What they did not see of course was that they had also been deprived of any ground for claims to objectivity and that they had begun in their own lives and judgments to provide the evidence to which emotivism [a form of subjective morality] was soon to appeal so cogently."[53] MacIntyre's historical account is detailed and complex, but, in summary, he chronicles the process of how, when people rejected Moore's Platonism because of its excessive Platonic ontology, his concept of moral intuitionism degenerated into emotivism, the notion that our moral statements are merely the expression of our subjective emotions.[54] He even argues that "wherever something like emotivism is found to flourish it generally is the successor theory to views analogous to Moore's or Prichard's."[55]

---

52. Moore, *Principia Ethica*, 234. This is sometimes referred to as Moore's isolation test.
53. MacIntyre, *After Virtue*, 65.
54. MacIntyre, *After Virtue*, 64–66.
55. MacIntyre, *After Virtue*, 18.

Moore's impact on the philosophical conversation concerning objective morality has been substantial. Shafer-Landau claimed that it's "possible to trace the history of twentieth-century metaethics as a dialectic of positions, each of which takes Moore's tripartite division of theories for granted [naturalism, nonnaturalism, and supernaturalism], and proceeds with its own argument from elimination."[56] What's particularly relevant to the disagreement I'm discussing in this book is that "a brand of moral realism that hearkens back to G. E. Moore has found new life, championed by, among others, Colin McGinn, Russ Shafer-Landau, Michael Huemer, William FitzPatrick, David Enoch, and Derek Parfit."[57] One of these champions, David Enoch, explains that when he first defended this view in 2003, he "claimed the great philosophical advantage of being in the ridiculed minority, putting forward a view many don't think is even worth considering." However, Enoch goes on to say that this view is "now making an impressive comeback," and notes how Stephen Finlay "classifies this as the now dominant view."[58]

In this book I'll compare and contrast my divine love theory with the theory of one of these Moorean champions, Erik Wielenberg, who admits that "G. E. Moore is perhaps the most well-known defender of the sort of non-naturalism I hold" and also notes that this "view has seen something of a resurgence in recent years."[59] The main question I'll seek to answer is this: Which of these two models, my divine love theory or Wielenberg's atheistic moral theory, provides the better explanation for the existence of objective morality?

56. Shafer-Landau, *Moral Realism*, 58.
57. Wielenberg, *Robust Ethics*, ix. See Huemer, *Ethical Intuitionism*; Parfit, *On What Matters*; Enoch, *Taking Morality Seriously*; Shafer-Landau, *Moral Realism*; McGinn, *Ethics, Evil, and Fiction*; FitzPatrick, "Robust Ethical Realism."
58. Enoch, *Taking Morality Seriously*, 6; see Finlay, "Normativity, Necessity, and Tense," 57.
59. Wielenberg, "In Defense," 26.

CHAPTER 2

ERIK WIELENBERG'S
ATHEISTIC MORAL THEORY

Godless Normative Realism

Erik Wielenberg is one of those atheists I described in the previous chapter who disagrees with the notion that the idea of objective morality must be rejected if there is no God. In the last paragraph of his book *Robust Ethics: The Metaphysics and Epistemology of Godless Normative Realism*, he writes that the "ideas that reality includes objective, *sui generis* moral features . . . still have something to be said for them . . . [and] we should not be too quick to abandon these old-fangled notions."[1] Wielenberg has presented a sophisticated philosophical theory in which God is not necessary for objective morality because moral values and duties exist on their own without any foundation. He explains that he has attempted "to develop a coherent view of . . . morality that is both empirically and philosophically plausible . . . [and] to defend a robust approach

---

1. Wielenberg, *Robust Ethics*, 176.

to ethics (without appealing to God or weird cognitive faculties) by developing positive accounts of the nature of moral facts and knowledge and by defending these accounts against challenging objections."[2] He described his view as "godless normative realism," a combination of holding that "robust normative realism is true and there is no God."[3] Thus, his position is that objective moral values and obligations exist, even though God does not. He explains, "Whereas proponents of theistic approaches to moral realism seek to make God the foundation of objective moral truth, I argue that it is at least as plausible to construe objective moral truth as not needing an external foundation at all."[4]

There are three noteworthy features of Wielenberg's theory: its brute ethical facts, its making relationship, and its nonnaturalism. If he's correct concerning the first noteworthy feature, his brute ethical facts, then God isn't required for objective morality because some moral truths exist on their own as necessary facts that need no foundation. He writes, "Such facts are the foundation of (the rest of) objective morality and rest on no foundation themselves. To ask of such facts, 'where do they come from?' or 'on what foundation do they rest?' is misguided. . . . They come from nowhere, and nothing external to themselves grounds their existence; rather, they are fundamental features of the universe that ground other truths."[5]

At times Wielenberg's description of these brute ethical facts makes them sound much like Platonic abstract objects. It can be difficult to describe the precise distinction between abstract and concrete objects because different people draw the line between these two categories at different places. Greg Welty laments that "the abstract/concrete distinction is in disarray, ontologically speaking."[6] Keith Yandell notes that "the concrete-abstract distinction is easier to illustrate by example than it is to state in clear terms," but he suggests that, generally speaking, it is agreed upon that abstract objects, if they exist, are "aspatial, atemporal or everlasting, causally impotent, mindless, and necessarily existing."[7] Paul Gould and Richard Brian Davis also note that "abstract objects are said to be impersonal entities: such things as properties, relations, propositions, numbers, sets, and the like."[8] A key part of the common definition of abstract objects is that they're noncausal; that is, they can't enter into the causal

2.   Wielenberg, *Robust Ethics*, ix.
3.   Wielenberg, *Robust Ethics*, 57.
4.   Wielenberg, *Robust Ethics*, x.
5.   Wielenberg, *Robust Ethics*, 38.
6.   Welty, "Theistic Conceptual Realism," 94.
7.   Yandell, "Response to Scott A. Shalkowski," 155.
8.   Gould and Davis, "Modified Theistic Activism," 51.

chain of events. Concrete objects then, generally speaking, are understood to be objects that can enter into the causal chain of events, which includes both material things such as cucumbers, planets, and electrons and immaterial things, if they exist, such as angels, God, and souls.

Wielenberg often uses Platonic terms to describe his model, referring to moral properties and states of affairs as abstract objects. For example, he writes, "I take it that a fundamental category of existing thing is the category of states of affairs. States of affairs are necessarily existing abstract entities that obtain or fail to obtain."[9] Craig summarizes his position as follows:

> Wielenberg espouses what I have elsewhere called Atheistic Moral Platonism. That is to say, Wielenberg takes moral values and duties to be identical to certain independently existing abstract objects. His view is akin to mathematical Platonism, which holds that in addition to the world of concrete objects, there exists an independent realm of immaterial, causally effete, abstract objects like numbers, sets, and other mathematical entities. . . . Wielenberg wants to affirm the objectivity and even necessity of moral values and duties . . . [and so] must find some transcendent ground. . . . He finds this in Moral Platonism.[10]

Wielenberg admits his view is Platonic in the sense I've described when he states, "If we want to situate my view in the history of philosophy, I think it is very Moorean and it's also Platonic. People sometimes use Platonic like as a type of criticism but I embrace the label."[11]

Proponents of moral theories similar to Wielenberg's also describe their theories in Platonic terms. For example, Shafer-Landau explains that once "we have some reason to try to accommodate moral values in our ontology, . . . we have two alternatives: to identify moral properties and facts with descriptive ones, or to enter a *sui generis* line in our ontological budget."[12] He goes on to provide reasons to reject the first, naturalist alternative in favor of the second, nonnaturalist one. Similarly, Enoch prefers to describe his theory as a form of "robust realism" but notes, "I will not be offended if you call me a Platonist."[13] Later he writes, possibly with a hint of sarcasm, "According to Robust Realism . . . the normative

---

9. Wielenberg, *Robust Ethics*, 36.
10. Craig, "Metaphysics of Morals," 333–34.
11. *Armchair Atheism*.
12. Shafer-Landau, *Moral Realism*, 79.
13. Enoch, *Taking Morality Seriously*, 8.

truths are out there, as it were, in Plato's heaven, utterly independent of us and our motivations."[14]

The second noteworthy feature of Wielenberg's theory is his proposed making relationship in which natural, nonmoral properties are responsible for instantiating moral properties. The importance of this proposal to his model is made clear by his explanation that "the making relation is the cement of the foundation of normative reality."[15] He construes this relationship as a type of causation when he writes, "Whatever moral properties are instantiated are conserved or sustained by various underlying non-moral properties via a robust causal relation that holds between the relevant non-moral and moral properties."[16] Wielenberg summarizes this making relationship well when he responds to this question: What is the source of human moral rights and obligations?

> I propose the following answer: any being that can reason, suffer, experience happiness, tell the difference between right and wrong, choose between right and wrong, and set goals for itself has certain rights, including the rights to life, liberty, and the pursuit of happiness, and certain obligations, including the duty to refrain from rape (in typical circumstances). Having such cognitive capacities *makes* one have such rights and duties. Evolutionary processes have produced human beings that can reason, suffer, experience happiness, tell the difference between right and wrong, choose between right and wrong, and set goals for themselves. In this way, evolutionary processes have endowed us with certain unalienable rights and duties. Evolution has given us these moral properties by giving us the non-moral properties that make such moral properties be instantiated. And if, as I believe, there is no God, then it is in some sense an accident that we have the moral properties that we do. But that they are accidental in origin does not make these moral properties unreal or unimportant.[17]

As with his proposed brute ethical facts, Wielenberg claims this making relationship is brute in that it has no ontological explanation and no foundation external to itself.[18] Though Wielenberg believes this making relationship has always

---

14. Enoch, *Taking Morality Seriously*, 217.
15. Wielenberg, *Robust Ethics*, 38.
16. Wielenberg, *Robust Ethics*, 20.
17. Wielenberg, *Robust Ethics*, 56.
18. Wielenberg, *Robust Ethics*, 37.

existed timelessly and necessarily as a brute fact, moral goodness itself wasn't exemplified until the correct nonmoral properties arose. He explains,

> If a given entity is good, it is good in virtue of or because of certain non-moral properties of that entity. Pleasure, for instance, is good because of the qualitative feel that pleasure has. Persons are valuable, and possess certain rights, because of certain capacities they have—for instance, the capacity to experience pain, and to reason. When an entity possessing the right sort of non-moral properties comes into existence, that entity will also possess the property of being good. When such entities are produced by entities or processes that do not possess moral properties, then value arises from valuelessness. More precisely, in such cases, entities that have the property of being good arise from entities or processes that do not have this property. For example, for many years the universe was devoid of sentient life. Eventually, valueless processes produced beings that could experience pleasure, and, at some point, the first episode of pleasure occurred. At that moment, the property of goodness was exemplified for the first time.[19]

The third noteworthy feature of Wielenberg's theory is that it's nonnatural. He explains that he sides with Moore against reductive naturalists in that "Moore maintains that ethical properties are real and *sui generis*; they are non-natural and are not reducible to any other kind of property."[20] As for his brute ethical facts, he maintains that they are "a fundamental type of property not reducible to or fully constituted by some other type of property. Contra the Thaleans, all is not water, or physical, or natural."[21] Thus he opposes the idea that moral properties are, or can be reduced to, some sort of natural property. As for his proposed making relationship, he claims that moral properties are causally instantiated by "non-normative [nonmoral] properties. While many of the relevant non-normative properties will be natural properties (i.e., properties that can be studied using the methods of empirical science), I wish to leave open the possibility that other sorts of properties can be included in the base properties."[22]

Thus, Wielenberg classifies his theory as nonnaturalism because, though he accepts the causal closure of the physical, he also proposes nonnatural,

---

19. Wielenberg, "Objective Morality," 80.
20. Wielenberg, *Robust Ethics*, 1–2.
21. Wielenberg, *Robust Ethics*, 14.
22. Wielenberg, *Robust Ethics*, 13.

nonphysical properties.[23] Because he maintains that a completed theory of physics is not quite a theory of everything, Wielenberg differs from those atheists that affirm reductive naturalism—that is, the claim that everything can ultimately be reduced to natural physical materials.[24] Therefore it's important to describe Wielenberg properly: he's an atheist with Platonic leanings, but he's not a naturalist. Alvin Plantinga helpfully explains the difference between naturalism and atheism as follows: "Naturalism obviously entails atheism; it is stronger than atheism, however, in that there are varieties of atheism—classical Platonism and Stoicism, for example . . . —[that] it excludes."[25] Wielenberg is an atheist because he doesn't believe God exists, but he's not a naturalist because he rejects the idea that the only things that exist are natural physical materials.

Wielenberg admits that the ontological excessiveness of his nonnatural theory turns away many of his fellow atheists who embrace strict naturalism.[26] However, as noted above, this moral nonnaturalism is becoming more popular. Enoch, another proponent of nonnaturalism, argues that "naturalism—understood as a metaphysical thesis—is false," and "sufficient reason has been given to include irreducibly normative facts in our ontology."[27] He writes, "There are response-independent, non-natural, irreducibly normative truths . . . objective ones, that when successful in our normative inquiries we discover rather than create or construct."[28] Another proponent, Shafer-Landau, explains, "Non-naturalism insists on distinct sets of facts—the moral, and everything else."[29] He maintains that there are "'brute' relations at the bottom-most level of ethics. By definition, there cannot be any deeper, more basic, general, or fundamental justification of the moral-descriptive relation that is claimed to be ultimate."[30] While addressing the hesitancy many have in accepting the existence of nonnatural moral facts, he compares this proposal with a fairly common position in the philosophy of mind: "The sort of nonnaturalism that I find appealing is one that bears a very close structural parallel to certain non-reductionist theories in the philosophy of mind. According to these latter views, mental properties are not identical to physical ones; mental facts are not physical facts; but mental properties are realized by instantiations

---

23. Wielenberg, *Robust Ethics*, 15.
24. Wielenberg, *Robust Ethics*, 15.
25. A. Plantinga, "Naturalism," 251.
26. Wielenberg, *Robust Ethics*, 16.
27. Enoch, *Taking Morality Seriously*, 12.
28. Enoch, "Robust Metanormative Realism," 21.
29. Shafer-Landau, *Moral Realism*, 72.
30. Shafer-Landau, *Moral Realism*, 98.

of physical properties. At least in worlds relevantly close to ours, there would be no mental life without the physical stuff that constitutes it."[31]

Wielenberg explains that he had two goals in writing his book *Robust Ethics*. First, he wanted to defend his theory against various objections. For example, many theists and atheists find implausible his claim that objective moral truths can exist on their own with no need of a foundation. Second, he wanted to critique theistic theories of objective morality in an attempt to show that they don't live up to their claims. He notes that many who defend his type of atheistic model have not engaged with theistic alternatives, but explains that this lack of engagement "might not be problematic if there were no theistic approaches to ethics worth taking seriously or if there were no challenging arguments against the feasibility of secular versions of moral realism. However, there are both worthwhile theistic theories of morality and challenging arguments against secular moral realism, and hence an important part of providing a full defense of robust normative realism is addressing these theories and arguments."[32] The two theists he focuses on most are Robert Adams and William Lane Craig because "Robert Adams's version of supernaturalism as developed in his masterpiece *Finite and Infinite Goods* (1999) is a strikingly subtle and sophisticated God-based approach to ethics. And Craig is perhaps the most forceful contemporary critic of secular approaches to morality."[33] He notes these two theists are connected in that "Craig appeals to Adams's work at crucial junctures in defending his own theistic approach to morality."[34] In this context, Craig has commented that "Wielenberg has emerged as the most important contemporary critic of theistic meta-ethics."[35]

Though theists have argued at length that, compared to atheism, theism provides a more plausible explanation for objective moral truth, further reflection on and articulation of God's relationship to morality is required to answer Wielenberg and other recent critics of the theistic position. Thus, there's a sense in which Wielenberg has provided a useful service to theists by critiquing their theories of objective morality. His critique should spur us theists on to consider more carefully our positions and to provide a fuller explanation of *how* it is that God provides the foundation for objective morality. His work should cause us theists to think more deeply about our position, to recognize problems with our

31. Shafer-Landau, *Moral Realism*, 72–73.
32. Wielenberg, *Robust Ethics*, 41.
33. Wielenberg, *Robust Ethics*, 41.
34. Wielenberg, *Robust Ethics*, 42.
35. Craig, "Metaphysics of Morals," 333.

existing theories and our understanding of them, and to strive to be more precise in our explanations. His critique may help theists recognize some things we've mistakenly assumed, or encourage us to consider more fully our unexplored or ill-considered presuppositions. Answering a critic like Wielenberg may cause theists to reconsider some of the facets of our theories, or it might lead us to a better understanding or articulation of our positions.

It's for these reasons that theists should be thankful for Wielenberg's detailed work in this area. While I'd love to convince Wielenberg that theism is correct, an admirable lesser goal would be to sharpen the theistic position such that Wielenberg and other atheists would understand it better and possibly find it less incoherent and implausible.

A Broad Array of Moral Theories

For the sake of slowly easing in those new to this material, thus far I've oversimplified the discussion and narrowed it down to simply moral objectivism versus moral subjectivism. However, the actual situation is much more complex; there's a plethora of moral positions that have been proposed and defended. While the field of moral theory, sometimes called metaethics, contains a dizzying array of terms, labels, and classification systems, most theorists begin by making a distinction between cognitive theories and noncognitive theories.[36] Below is a list of categories and subcategories followed by brief descriptions.

I. Cognitive theories
    A. Constructivism
        1. Objectivist constructivism
        2. Subjectivism
        3. Relativism
        4. Kantianism
        5. Contractarianism
        6. Ideal observer theories
        7. Ideal agent theories
    B. Realism
        1. Naturalism
            a. Moral functionalism
            b. Cornell realism

---

36. For a more detailed taxonomy of moral theories, see Shafer-Landau, *Moral Realism*, 13–79. For a book-length treatment, see van Roojen, *Metaethics*, especially the helpful flowchart on p. 5.

        2.   Nonnaturalism (sometimes called robust realism)

        3.   Supernaturalism

    C.   Error theories

II.   Noncognitive theories

    A.   Prescriptivism

    B.   Expressivism

        1.   Emotivism

        2.   Plan-expressivism

        3.   Norm-expressivism

All cognitive theories maintain that moral judgments are beliefs that can somehow be true or false, but the different cognitivist positions disagree among themselves as to what makes these beliefs true or false.[37] Noncognitive theories, on the other hand, argue that our moral judgments do not express true or false propositions because ultimately there's nothing that makes them true or false; according to these theories, moral judgments are merely ways we communicate our noncognitive commitments, such as our emotions.[38]

As for different cognitive theories, constructivist theories claim that moral truths are created and fixed through some sort of constructive function undertaken by a person or a group of persons, either actual or idealized.[39] They think moral obligations do have authority and a sense of objectivity but are not constituted by objective facts.[40] In opposition to this, realism is a type of cognitive theory that holds that the moral standards that fix moral facts are real in that they are not made true by their ratification from within an actual or hypothetical idealized perspective.[41] Lastly, error theories agree that moral statements do reflect moral beliefs—hence technically they're a form of cognitivism—but they say that all these moral statements are false because ultimately there is no moral reality.[42]

As for different forms of constructivism, objectivist constructivism says that moral claims are objective in the sense that they require some degree of idealization beyond particular people for the attitudes that construct and thus fix moral truth.[43] Subjectivism holds that morality is constructed out of particular

---

37.   Shafer-Landau, *Moral Realism*, 17.

38.   Shafer-Landau, *Moral Realism*, 5, 19.

39.   Shafer-Landau, *Moral Realism*, 17, 45.

40.   Evans, *God and Moral Obligation*, 8.

41.   Shafer-Landau, *Moral Realism*, 17.

42.   Shafer-Landau, *Moral Realism*, 19.

43.   Shafer-Landau, *Moral Realism*, 39.

individual opinions.[44] Relativism maintains that morality is constructed out of particular social conventions or agreements among particular people.[45] Kantianism proposes that morality is specifically constructed out of a particular person's rational will.[46] Contractarianism claims morality is constructed out of the edicts of deliberators situated in special circumstances.[47] Ideal observer theories propose that morality is constructed by the perspective that a hypothetical ideal observer would have if there were such an ideal observer. Ideal agent theories are similar but instead propose that the hypothetical ideal individual is a participant in moral issues and not merely an observer.

As for different forms of realism, in this context naturalism refers to the belief that moral properties are some type of natural property such that the strict ontology of naturalism can be maintained.[48] In particular, moral functionalism is a form of naturalism that claims moral facts are determined by their function or place in a complex network. Cornell realism argues that moral properties are their own category of natural properties and thus are not identical to, and cannot be reduced to, other natural properties.[49] Nonnaturalism (sometimes called robust realism) rejects the naturalist's claim that moral properties are nothing over and above natural properties, but instead that moral properties are unique nonnatural properties.[50] Lastly, supernaturalism is a form of realism that maintains that God somehow serves as the foundation of morality. The two most common forms of supernaturalism are divine command theory and natural law theory.

As for different types of noncognitive theories, prescriptivism claims that moral statements function as imperative sentences such that when someone says "rape is wrong," they're actually communicating the prescription "do not rape." On the other hand, expressivism maintains that moral statements merely express a person's evaluative attitude. Emotivism, the most common type of expressivism, holds that the evaluative attitude being expressed in moral statements stems from our noncognitive emotions.

Even though, as you can see, there are a host of moral theories, I will not address most of them in this book because my focus here is on a specific disagreement between two types of moral realists. Wielenberg's version of robust

---

44. Shafer-Landau, *Moral Realism*, 17.
45. Shafer-Landau, *Moral Realism*, 17.
46. Shafer-Landau, *Moral Realism*, 17.
47. Shafer-Landau, *Moral Realism*, 17.
48. Shafer-Landau, *Moral Realism*, 19, 55.
49. Shafer-Landau, *Moral Realism*, 63.
50. Enoch, *Taking Morality Seriously*, 4.

realism and my divine love theory are both forms of moral realism; the former is nonnatural and the latter is supernatural. Assuming that morality is objectively real, which of these two theories is the better explanation for the existence of objective morality?

As I explained above, there has been a surge of interest in, and defenses of, nonnatural moral realism. However, there has also been a corresponding increase of those advocating for supernatural moral realism. On the theistic side, sophisticated supernatural moral theories have been developed by contemporary thinkers such as Robert Adams, Robert Audi, C. Stephen Evans, John Hare, Mark Murphy, Philip Quinn, and Linda Zagzebski.[51] Hare explains that his aspiration for his book *God's Command* was for it "to be the next in a recent series of books that have defended forms of divine command theory within analytic philosophy."[52] After noting the series he referred to includes works by Quinn, Adams, and Evans, he says, "No one looking at the discipline in the late 1960s, when I was doing my training, would have predicted the existence of this series. These titles, and others like them, are a manifestation within ethical theory of a much larger shift within the discipline."[53] These two separate conversations concerning moral realism, one mostly involving atheists and the other mostly involving theists, have taken place in parallel, with little engagement between the two groups. My book is unique in that it brings these two conversations together.

---

51. Adams, *Finite and Infinite Goods*; Audi, *Rationality and Religious Commitment*; Evans, *God and Moral Obligation*, 166; Hare, *God's Command*; Murphy, *God and Moral Law*; Quinn, *Divine Commands and Moral Requirements*; Zagzebski, *Divine Motivation Theory*.
52. Hare, *God's Command*, vi.
53. Hare, *God's Command*, vi.

CHAPTER 3

PROPOSING A DIVINE LOVE THEORY

The Question at Hand

Celebrated contemporary philosopher John Searle writes that "for many of us, myself included, the central question in philosophy at the beginning of the twenty-first century is how to give an account of ourselves as apparently conscious, mindful, free, rational, speaking, social, and political agents in a world that science tells us consists entirely of mindless, meaningless, physical particles."[1] The issue I'm considering in this book is how to give an account of an important part of our human experience: objective morality. All moral realists are convinced that objective moral truths do exist, but nonnatural realists and supernatural realists disagree as to what the best explanation is for their existence. How do we decide who's correct?

Advocates on both sides of this disagreement agree that this issue should be evaluated abductively—that is, as an inference to the best explanation. David Baggett, a proponent of theistic moral theories, explains,

---

1.   Searle, *Mind*, 7.

An inquiry into the "best explanation" invokes the process of abduction, a common form of reasoning that distinguishes itself from deduction in a few ways. Most importantly, whereas a deductive argument makes an effort at forging an airtight evidential connection between premises and conclusion, an abductive approach asks, less ambitiously, what the best explanation of the relevant phenomena is. It typically uses criteria like explanatory scope and power (along with plausibility, conformity with other beliefs, etc.) to narrow down the explanation candidates to the best explanation, and warrants, potentially anyway, to infer that the best explanation is likely the true explanation.[2]

Similarly, David Enoch, a proponent of nonnatural moral realism, argues that inference to the best explanation is a viable approach for this issue.[3] He explicitly notes the importance of plausibility when he writes, "The game being played is . . . that of overall plausibility points,"[4] and "the plausibility-points game is comparative: the view that we should endorse is the one that has—when all considerations are taken into account—the most plausibility points overall."[5]

Here's a simple example of how the process of abduction works. Let's say you're a farmer, your crops have produced a harvest ten times greater than you've ever seen, and you don't know why this happened. Your friend Toni comes to you and presents a possible explanation: the weather conditions this year (sun, rain, wind, etc.) were just so perfect that they caused your crops to produce this tremendous amount. Another friend, Lenny, approaches you with an alternative explanation: a local scientist developed a new super-fertilizer and secretly put it on your crops to test its effectiveness. Now you have two explanations to consider. Which one best fits the evidence? It will take some work on your part to fully explore both explanations and see which one is most plausible and best fits the evidence.

This simple farmer example illustrates the process of abductive reasoning, which boils down to an inference to the best explanation. This is the abductive approach I will use in this book to evaluate my theory and Wielenberg's theory. The question I've set out to answer is this: Which theory has more plausibility points, Wielenberg's godless normative realism or my divine love theory?[6]

2.   Baggett, "Psychopathy and Supererogation," 131.
3.   Enoch, *Taking Morality Seriously*, 57–58.
4.   Enoch, *Taking Morality Seriously*, 14–15.
5.   Enoch, *Taking Morality Seriously*, 267.
6.   In this book I don't make a formal "inference to the best explanation" argument, but this style of argument operates at an implicit level throughout this book. For an exhaustive treatment on this form of argument, see Lipton, *Inference to the Best Explanation*.

My Primary Argument

In this book I'll attempt to explain how God is the source and foundation of objective morality. While this proposal, which I'll refer to as my divine love theory, isn't wholly unlike those made by others, it does provide further details that help shed light on the issue and has the potential to answer some of Wielenberg's critiques of theistic moral theories. In particular, I'll argue that the ultimate ground of objective morality is God's trinitarian nature as found in, and expressed among, the loving relationships between the divine persons of the Trinity. I'll then show how this theory is a more plausible explanation of objective morality than Wielenberg's by pointing out the strengths of my theory and the weaknesses of his.

As for the order of this book, in part 2, I'll present my divine love theory as a proposed explanation for the existence of objective morality, respond to several potential objections, and highlight several ways in which my theory is explanatorily superior to Wielenberg's godless normative realism. In part 3, I'll raise a metaphysical objection to Wielenberg's theory: the bloated model objection. In part 4, I'll raise an epistemological objection to Wielenberg's theory: the lucky coincidence objection. Toward the end of both parts 3 and 4, I'll show how Wielenberg has tried to turn the tables by claiming that theistic moral theories also face similar objections. However, in both cases I'll argue that my theory overcomes these objections.

The uniqueness of this book is threefold. First, while many Christians ground objective morality in God's nature, here I specifically propose that it's grounded in the trinitarian aspect of his nature—that is, in the loving relationships between the persons of the Trinity. My divine love theory is similar to Robert Adams's moral theory but includes several adjustments and one large addition. The large addition is that important truths concerning God's triune nature are used to expand Adams's theory in significant ways, shed greater light on the nature of morality, and more clearly show how trinitarian theism provides a better explanation for morality than Wielenberg's godless normative realism. Second, while many have critiqued Wielenberg's theory, several of the critiques I offer in this book are not found elsewhere. Third, this book is unique in that it provides the most extended responses in the literature to Wielenberg's critiques of theistic moral theories, often utilizing truths concerning God's trinitarian nature to build the responses. I'll attempt to show that if God does in fact exist as three persons, then this truth nullifies several of Wielenberg's key criticisms of theistic moral theories.

When it comes to moral theory, over the last few decades Christians have mostly focused on defending the notion that morality is objective, and rightfully so, as the relative morality of postmodernism has been predominant in our Western culture. However, as I showed above, belief in objective morality has made an incredible comeback in the early part of the twenty-first century. This resurgence could be part of Western culture's recent yearning for objective truth in light of what many saw as political truth-spinning in the recent American presidential elections and the European Brexit controversy. Many of those who had promoted subjective and relative truth in the past have awoken to its ills and now herald the importance of objective truth while lamenting what they call our current "post-truth era." Broadly speaking, then, there's greater emphasis on objective truth in our culture right now, of which objective moral truth is but a subset. With moral issues taking the forefront in our society's conversations (abortion, gender identity, same-sex marriage, the use of force by police, racism, etc.), the issue of *how* morality can be objectively real in the first place is especially pertinent.

There are many reasons to be thankful for this revival of objective truth and moral realism. One reason is that it has created an opportunity for Christians to join the conversation and advocate for important truths. However, it does mean that Christians now need to focus less on fighting for objective morality itself and spend more time arguing that God is the best explanation for objective morality. Christians need to move beyond merely fighting yesterday's enemy of relative morality and focus their attention instead on defeating atheistic explanations of objective morality like Wielenberg's.

Christians also need to move beyond merely fighting yesterday's enemy of reductive materialism, the idea that all that exists is the physical material universe, and instead focus their attention on defeating nonnatural atheistic theories like Wielenberg's godless normative realism. While reductive materialism still has plenty of adherents, that position is waning. Top-notch atheist philosophers such as Thomas Nagel and David Enoch have pointed out the weaknesses and absurdities of reductive materialism.[7] While it may be useful to refer to them at times as fellow combatants against reductive materialism, Christians must remember that their positions are also ultimately atheistic and thus are competitors to Christianity.

A Theological and Apologetic Approach

This book is both theological and apologetic. First, it's a theological project in that in chapters 4 and 5, I attempt to explain how God's trinitarian nature provides the source and foundation of objective morality. In this theological

---

7.   Nagel, *Mind and Cosmos*; Enoch, *Taking Morality Seriously*.

part of the book, I'll assume without argument that God exists and the Bible is from him.[8] John Hare expresses the same assumptions at the beginning of his book *God's Command* when he writes, "I myself am a Christian, and I have the conviction that God has spoken decisively in the Scriptures that Christians call 'the Old and New Testaments.'"[9] Therefore, in my attempt to describe reality accurately, in this theological part of the book I'll freely help myself to information from special revelation (Scripture) and also from general revelation (philosophy and human moral experience). The following brief but insightful guideline from Keith Whitfield will direct my theological method: "While Scripture is the primary source of our theology, we recognize that the role reason and tradition play in our biblical interpretation remains fundamental to theological projects."[10] This theological part is also tied to analytic philosophy in the sense that, because I work within this tradition, I'll interact with analytic philosophers to help explicate my theory, and I'll occasionally use the tools of analytic philosophy to understand and defend trinitarian theism.

Second, this book is apologetic because, starting in chapter 6 and continuing through the rest of the book, I'll attempt to show that my divine love theory is a better explanation for objective morality than Wielenberg's godless normative realism. Since Wielenberg and I both affirm objective morality, its existence will not be argued for but assumed. Thus the apologetic task will involve challenging Wielenberg's proposal that objective morality can exist even if God does not and responding to his critiques of theistic moral theories.

If my divine love theory is true, or even close to true, then it would suggest that God is necessary for the existence of objective morality. Conversely, it would also suggest that if God doesn't exist, then there would be no ultimate foundation for morality, and thus we should conclude that morality doesn't exist objectively. Hence this apologetic part of the book, where my theory is compared and contrasted with Wielenberg's, could be crafted as an argument for the existence of God as follows:

1.   There are objective moral truths.
2.   A trinitarian God provides the best explanation for objective moral truths.
3.   Therefore, a trinitarian God exists.[11]

---

8.   Though I certainly affirm doing so is possible and important, it's beyond the scope of this book to argue for these assumptions. The interested reader can find such arguments in Swinburne, *Existence of God*, and Barr, *Modern Physics and Ancient Faith*.

9.   Hare, *God's Command*, v.

10. Whitfield, conclusion to *Trinitarian Theology*, 178.

11. This is the basic argument Adams presents, without the trinitarian aspect, in Adams, "Moral Arguments," 116–17.

As a theist, I believe that if God did not exist, then nothing else would either. Because God is a necessary being and thus exists in all possible worlds, I ultimately reject the notion of a possible world where humans exist and God does not. Mark Murphy explains well this theistic position:

> Here is a very crude picture of how to think about counterfactual thinking. You start with the way the actual world is, and then you ask what would be the case if the world were as close as possible to how it actually is, but differs in just a certain respect. But what you think about such counterfactual questions will of course differ based on what you think is actual. If you are an atheist, and you ask "what value would creatures have without God?," the "nearest" world is the one we live in. So just ask: what value do they have? If you are a theist, by contrast, the "nearest" world in which there is no God is outrageously remote. It is an impossible world, a deeply, deeply impossible world. It is of the essence of every possible creaturely substance that it is a creature. It is of the essence of God that all things distinct from God depend on God. When I try to take this thought experiment, as a theist, seriously, I go blank. And I think theists should go blank on this.[12]

In other words, theists believe that if God did not exist, then not only would objective morality not exist, but nothing else would either. However, when interacting with atheists, it's useful, for the sake of argument, to discuss a situation where humans exist and God does not, and then to argue that in such a scenario, though technically impossible, there would be no objective moral truth.

At one level this book has to do with a debate between theism and atheism—answering, Which is the better explanation for objective morality? Craig has often framed the theist's side of this debate as follows: "I. If theism is true, we have a sound foundation for morality. II. If theism is false, we do not have a sound foundation for morality."[13] A comprehensive case for these contentions would involve evaluating and debunking all the atheistic explanations for how objective morality could exist without God. Since such a task would take much more than one book, my task at hand is more narrow: it is to support these contentions by developing a divine love theory to show how trinitarian theism provides a superior explanation for morality compared to a leading atheistic explanation.

---

12. Murphy, "No Creaturely Intrinsic Value," 354.
13. Craig, *Goodness without God*, 30.

Therefore, yes, at one level this book is about a debate between theism and atheism, but at another level it is specifically between a particular theistic model and a particular atheistic model, both of which are trying to describe reality, how things really are. My divine love theory is unique but similar to Craig's, Adams's, and Hare's theories, much like Wielenberg's godless normative realism is unique but similar to Enoch's, Shafer-Landau's, and Huemer's theories. The point is that even if I'm successful here, I'll rule out only Wielenberg's atheistic explanation for objective morality, not necessarily all atheistic models. Similarly, if my divine love theory is inaccurate or has substantial failings, it doesn't necessarily mean theism is not the best explanation of morality, but only that my particular theistic model is wrong. If such is the case, then there may be a better theistic model that does successfully explain how God functions as the source, foundation, and ground of objective morality.

In my research for this book, I focused on primary works and secondary research in several fields, both historical and contemporary, including but not limited to metaethics, trinitarian theology, divine command theory, natural law theory, the moral argument for God, abstract objects, supervenience, Evolutionary Debunking Arguments, eternal functional subordination, the Euthyphro dilemma, moral epistemology, Platonism, and divine attributes. My research task required a comprehensive survey of the main views within each of these topics while focusing on particular writers who address the issues covered in this book. I especially engaged work by John Duns Scotus, Robert Adams, John Hare, William Lane Craig, and of course Erik Wielenberg.

PART 2

DIVINE LOVE THEORY

CHAPTER 4

THE TRINITY AS THE SOURCE AND FOUNDATION OF MORALITY

In this chapter I'll propose a divine love theory as the best explanation for objective morality. As I mentioned previously, I'll assume here without argument, since such a task is outside the scope of this book, that God exists and the Bible is from him. The moral theory that I'm proposing here wasn't built from scratch but on the insights of others who have thought deeply on these matters. In particular, I've utilized several aspects of Robert Adams's moral theory in constructing my theory.

The two most common theistic moral theories are divine command theory and natural law theory. These two theories share much in common, but there are definite differences between them. Though I've incorporated some elements from natural law theory, my divine love theory shares more in common with divine command theory. Divine command theories have been around a long time, but lately they've enjoyed a remarkable resurgence of sorts. Susan Peppers-Bates notes that the "debate swirling around divine command ethics, which engrossed many medieval and early modern thinkers, revived again in the 1980s and continues to the present day."[1] Though my divine love theory shares more in common with divine command theory than natural law theory, it is best not to classify it as a divine command theory for at least two reasons. First, as noted above, in my theory I incorporate insights that are affirmed by both divine command theory and natural law theory. Second, and more importantly, my theory maintains that God's triune nature is the most important aspect of God when it comes to how he serves as the source and foundation of morality. Since my theory claims that God's triunity, not his commands or the human nature he created, is the cornerstone of morality, it's best not to label my theory as a divine command theory or a natural law theory.

Let me provide a handy road map for part 2. Here in chapter 4, I'll begin by explaining the importance of God's triune nature as a first step toward understanding how the Trinity provides the foundation for morality. Then I will describe key aspects of Robert Adams's moral theory, modifying them and incorporating them into my divine love theory. In chapter 5, I'll consider various objections to my theory, some of which will prompt adjustments and refinements. In chapter 6, I'll show how my theory is a better explanation for objective morality than Wielenberg's godless normative realism.

The Importance of the Trinity

Ancient Greek philosophers spent a considerable amount of time speculating about what constitutes ultimate reality, often framing their theories as a search for the elemental "stuff" of which everything else is made. However, if Christianity is true, when the final curtain of reality is pulled back, what will be found is not fire, earth, air, or water but loving personal relationships between three divine persons. Alan Torrance goes so far as to say that there's no reason why we should "not conceive of the intra-divine communion of the Trinity as the ground of all that is."[2] Similarly, William Hasker affirms that "the doctrine of the Trinity is an integral part of the metaphysically necessary ultimate structure of reality."[3] In the context of explaining the loving relationships within the Trinity, Millard Erickson describes this love as "the attractive force of unselfish concern for another person" and thus the "most powerful binding force in the universe."[4] This is more than mere sentiment; if God is the ultimate reality, and if he exists

1.   Peppers-Bates, "Divine Simplicity," 361.
2.   A. Torrance, *Persons in Communion*, 293.
3.   Hasker, *Metaphysics*, 174.
4.   Erickson, *God in Three Persons*, 221.

as three divine persons in loving relationships with each other, then love is the basic fabric of reality.

Unfortunately, as Keith Whitfield remarks, Christians "have not always embraced the Trinity's central role in theologizing. The Trinity has been treated as one doctrine of many. But this doctrine is not just one article of faith among many other articles. It is the central article in which every other Christian doctrine is grounded and from which every other Christian doctrine is shaped. . . . We have assumed the trinitarian formulation for generations, but we have not always thought deeply about what it means to proclaim that God is triune and how that informs everything else."[5] One of my goals in this chapter is to describe how God's triune nature provides the foundation for morality and to explain how this important truth helps shed light on a host of moral issues. W. Norris Clarke says it well:

> The highest instance of being is a unity that is not solitary, like Plotinus's One, but *Communion*. Here we see in the most striking way how a specifically *Christian* philosophy can fruitfully shed light on a philosophical problem itself, by drawing on Revelation. The light from Revelation does not operate strictly as the premise for a philosophical argument, properly speaking, but operates as opening up for reflection a new possibility in the nature and meaning of being that we might never have thought of ourselves from our limited human experience, but which, once opened up, is so illuminating that it now shines on its own as an insight into the nature of being and persons that makes many things suddenly fall into place whose depths we could not fathom before. More and more in recent years I have come to realize that the doctrine of the Trinity is a uniquely powerful source of illumination in both the philosophy of being and the philosophy of the person.[6]

I'll attempt to show here how the doctrine of the Trinity is also a powerful source of illumination in the realm of moral theory.

It may be best to begin with a brief overview of Christianity that highlights the importance of the Trinity as told through the common motifs of creation, fall, redemption, and restoration. However, it's important to note that even *before* creation, God existed as three divine persons in loving relationships with each other. Carl F. H. Henry writes, "The doctrine of the Trinity exhibits in the eternal

---

5. Whitfield, introduction to *Trinitarian Theology*, 14–15.
6. Clarke, *Person and Being*, 87.

nature of God a life of intimate love, communion and self-giving that in principle cancels the complaint that a timeless deity must be loveless and introvert."[7]

Understanding God's eternal trinitarian nature is helpful in illuminating the realm of morality for several reasons. For instance, because morality is inextricably tied to personal relationships, it makes more sense to talk about love and morality in the context of multiple divine persons than in a context of a single person existing in eternal isolation. It's difficult to even conceive of love, kindness, respect, and so on where there's only one divine person. Erickson's description of these eternal divine relationships is worth quoting at length:

> Love exists within the Godhead as a binding relationship of each of the persons to each of the others. Indeed, the attribute of love is more than just another attribute. The statement "God is love" in 1 John is a very basic characterization of God, which cannot be understood simply as a definition or an equation, but is more than merely, "God is loving." . . . In a sense, God being love virtually requires that he be more than one person. Love, to be love, must have both a subject and an object. Thus, if there were not multiplicity in the persons of the Godhead, God could not really be love prior to this creation of other subjects.[8]

Richard Swinburne even proclaims, "There is something profoundly imperfect and therefore inadequately divine in a solitary divine individual."[9] God had no need to create other persons in order to be loving, moral, and relational because, being three persons in fellowship, he has always been these things. Hasker explains, "Wholly apart from creation, love and relationship abound within God, in the eternal loving mutuality of the persons of the Trinity."[10]

If God existed before creation as a loving fellowship of divine persons, it may seem puzzling as to why he decided to create other persons at all. Though he didn't necessarily have to, he chose to create other persons, human beings in his image, to expand this fellowship of love. Thomas McCall argues, "There is no obvious incoherence in maintaining that the triune God who enjoys perfection in the intra-trinitarian life may desire to share that life while not needing to do so to reach fulfillment or perfection."[11] William Lane Craig explains that existing

7. Henry, *God, Revelation, and Authority*, 52.
8. Erickson, *God in Three Persons*, 221.
9. Swinburne, *Christian God*, 190.
10. Hasker, "Adequate God," 228.
11. McCall, *Which Trinity? Whose Monotheism?*, 210.

"alone in the self-sufficiency of His own being, enjoying the timeless fullness of the intra-trinitarian love relationships, God had no need for the creation of finite persons. . . . He did this, not out of any deficit in Himself or His mode of existence, but in order that finite temporal creatures might come to share in the joy and blessedness of the inner life of God."[12] In other words, God created us for loving relationships, to love him and to love each other. We were created to join him in the loving fellowship of the Trinity; the love we were created for is the same love that's found within the life of the triune God.

Understanding God's intent in creating human beings gives us insight concerning the meaning and purpose of our lives. Clarke explains, "The very inner life of God himself, the supreme fullness of what it means to be, is by its very nature *self-communicative Love*, which then subsequently flows over freely in the finite self-communication that is creation."[13] "To be an actualized human person, then, is to be a *lover*, to live a life of inter-personal self-giving and receiving."[14] Clarke argues, therefore, that "no one can reach mature development as a person without the experience of opening oneself, giving oneself to another in self-forgetting love of some kind. To be a true self, one must somehow go out of oneself, forget oneself. This apparent paradox is an ancient one and has been noted over and over in the various attempts to work out philosophies of love and friendship down the ages."[15]

This purpose and design in God's creation of humans can be seen in the very first human relationship God initiated between Adam and Eve. Created in God's image to reflect the Trinity, they were individual persons who were to come together in loving communion and become united as one (Gen. 2:24). Dietrich Bonhoeffer explains that in their union, they expressed "the two complementary sides of the matter: that of being an individual and that of being one with the other."[16]

One of the ways Adam and Eve were to freely express their love for God was through their obedience to him. The Bible explains that loving God and obeying God are closely connected. For example, Jesus says, "He who has My commandments and keeps them is the one who loves Me; and he who loves Me will be loved by My Father, and I will love him and will disclose Myself to him. . . . If anyone loves Me, he will keep My word; and My Father will love him, and We will come to him and make Our abode with him" (John 14:21–23).

---

12. Craig, *Time and Eternity*, 241.
13. Clarke, *Person and Being*, 12.
14. Clarke, *Person and Being*, 76.
15. Clarke, *Person and Being*, 96.
16. Bonhoeffer, *Creation and Fall*, 99–100.

Unfortunately, Adam and Eve made a terrible choice to disobey God's command and eat the fruit God forbade. If obeying God is the way to love God, then this disobedience was akin to not loving God, thus ruining their loving communion with him. Concerning this event, John Hare explains, "The basic command is not about the fruit, but is the command to love God that comes out of the experience of being loved by God. Refraining from the fruit is merely a symbol of that response."[17]

Thankfully, God continued to love us in spite of our disobedience and orchestrated a way to restore our loving communion with him. One of the divine persons, the Son, became incarnate as a human being and lived the perfect life of loving obedience to God the Father that we've all failed to live. In addition, by dying on the cross he paid the penalty that we deserved for our disobedience—death and eternal relational separation from God. God has promised that anyone who chooses to trust in Christ and what he did for us will be forgiven and reconciled back to a loving relationship with him. Though God desires everyone to experience this restored fellowship (1 Tim. 2:4), he doesn't force this decision on anyone but instead calls, woos, and draws people to himself through the work of the Holy Spirit in our lives. Those who decide not to trust in Christ will continue to be relationally separated from God for all eternity (2 Thess. 1:6–10). The primary suffering of people in hell is that they'll no longer be able to love but instead will be cut off forever from having a loving relationship with God and loving relationships with others; they won't be able to fulfill the purpose they were created for.

Many have remarked on how God's trinitarian nature first instigates and then beautifully permeates his plan for our salvation. While commenting on Scott Swain's view of the Trinity, Malcolm Yarnell notes, "Swain stands in a long line of orthodox writers when he considers communion with God and God's redemption of humanity as an essential outworking of the doctrine of God the Trinity."[18] For example, Hare, explaining Duns Scotus's theology, writes that the "journey we are on is a journey towards our final good, which Scotus takes to be that we become 'co-lovers' of God (*condiligentes*), entering into the love that the three persons of the Trinity have for each other."[19] For a more contemporary example, consider Thomas Torrance's summary of salvation: "The Love that flows between the Father, the Son, and the Spirit freely flows in an outward

17. Hare, *God's Command*, 302.
18. Yarnell, "From God to Humanity," 84.
19. Hare, *God and Morality*, 254.

movement of loving activity toward us with whom God creates a communion of love corresponding to the Communion of Love which he ever is in himself. . . . It is as this infinite, unlimited, transcendent self-giving Love that God is, that God the Father, the Son and the Holy Spirit, three Persons, one Being, seeks and creates fellowship with us in order to reconcile us with himself and to share with us his own eternal Life and Love."[20]

John 17, where Jesus prays to his Father concerning his desire to restore fallen humanity back to a right relationship with the Trinity, is one of the clearest windows into the trinitarian nature of our salvation. In this chapter Jesus explains the eternal love within the Trinity as follows: "You, Father, are in Me and I in You. . . . You loved me before the foundation of the world" (17:21, 24). He expresses his desire for his disciples to join this fellowship when he prays "that they also may be in Us" (17:21). In response to this verse, Vern Poythress clarifies, "We who are human do not become divine ourselves, but the fellowship that we have with the Father and the Son is analogous to that exalted and perfect fellowship that the Father and the Son have with each other."[21]

Jesus continues in his prayer by explaining that "the glory which You have given Me I have given to them, that they may be one, just as We are one; I in them and You in Me, that they may be perfected in unity, so that the world may know that You sent Me, and loved them, even as You have loved Me" (John 17:22–23). Royce Gruenler notes, "Jesus' prayer reveals that the goal of the divine family is to bring the separated and fallen into a redeemed and unified family that reflects the relationship of the divine persons in their ultimate oneness."[22] Salvation, then, is ultimately a restoration of our relationship to the loving communion of the Trinity that we were initially created for. Jesus, while praying to the Father, explains, "I have made Your name known to them . . . so that the love with which You loved Me may be in them, and I in them" (17:26). Whitfield notes, "Jesus, as the beloved Son of the Father, came to allow us to participate in the love that he has with his Father by the power of the Spirit."[23] To participate in this mutual indwelling is to know God, which is eternal life (17:3).

With this summary of trinitarian Christianity in mind, it's time to consider the importance of these inner-trinitarian relationships when it comes to God being the source and foundation of both objective moral value and moral obligation.

---

20. T. Torrance, *Christian Doctrine of God*, 166.
21. Poythress, *Knowing and the Trinity*, 52.
22. Gruenler, *Trinity in the Gospel of John*, 129.
23. Whitfield, conclusion to *Trinitarian Theology*, 176.

Moral Value in the Divine Love Theory

My divine love theory borrows key ideas from Robert Adams's moral theory, an important contemporary example of grounding morality in God. He describes his theory as a modified version of divine command theory.[24] However, the name "divine command theory" can cause confusion because it implies that God's commands are the key feature of his model. In actuality, within Adams's model it is God's nature that provides the ultimate foundation for morality (what's good and evil), and his commands merely generate our moral duties—that is, our moral obligations (what's right and wrong). This is evident in Adams's proposal as he distinguishes the first part of his model as a theory of moral value from the second part, dependent on the first, as a theory of moral duties. Thus, it might be slightly inaccurate to call his model a divine command theory because technically only the second part has to do with divine commands, the part that deals with moral obligation. It may be more appropriate to call the first part of his model, the part that deals with moral value, a divine nature theory, though Adams doesn't use that term.

As far as God being the foundation of morality in his model, Adams explains, "The part played by God in my account of the nature of the good is similar to that of the Form of the Beautiful or the Good in Plato's *Symposium* and *Republic*. God is the supreme Good, and the goodness of other things consists in a sort of resemblance to God."[25] Thus his view is Platonic in the sense that the "role that belongs to the Form of the Good in Plato's thought is assigned to God, and the goodness of other things is understood in terms of their standing in some relation, usually conceived as a sort of resemblance, to God."[26] Therefore, according to Adams, humans are morally good when they resemble God in a morally pertinent way.

Several questions arise as to what it means for a human to "resemble" God morally. Since my divine love theory borrows key ideas from Adams's model, it leans on and affirms his discussion on how these questions about "divine resemblance" are to be answered.[27] According to Adams, though resembling God is what it means to be morally good, not just any resemblance to God is sufficient. Rather, the resemblance must be in terms of important properties and involve a faithful portrait of God, not a distorting caricature of him. Additionally, since "most of the excellences that are most important to us, and of whose value we

---

24. Adams, *Finite and Infinite Goods*, 3.
25. Adams, *Finite and Infinite Goods*, 7.
26. Adams, *Finite and Infinite Goods*, 14.
27. Adams, *Finite and Infinite Goods*, 21–42.

are most confident, are excellences of persons or of qualities or actions or works or lives or stories of persons,"[28] then the pertinent resemblance will pertain to properties distinctive to persons, particularly their personal qualities, actions, and works.

Adams isn't alone in proposing that God is the ultimate good and that humans are good inasmuch as they resemble him. First, several ancient Greek philosophers expressed similar ideas—Socrates said that we should "become like God, so far as this is possible; and to become like God is to become righteous and holy and wise. . . . God is in no wise and in no manner unrighteous, but utterly and perfectly righteous, and there is nothing so like him as that one of us who in turn becomes most nearly perfect in righteousness."[29] Plato assured a prosperous life to "anyone whose desire is to become just and to be like God, as far as man can attain the divine likeness, by the pursuit of virtue."[30] Aristotle wrote, "God's self-dependent actuality is life most good and eternal. We say therefore that God is a living being, eternal, most good, so that life and duration continuous and eternal belong to God; for this *is* God."[31] This quote from Aristotle is found in *Metaphysics* 12; Hare summarizes this particular chapter by Aristotle as follows: "Aristotle says that God moves by being loved, drawing us to be as like God as we are capable of being."[32]

Second, the Bible also explains numerous moral principles (especially the greatest ones—love God and love others) in terms of imaging, resembling, or reflecting what God is like. For example, Christ says to "be perfect, therefore, as your heavenly Father is perfect" (Matt. 5:48). Paul exhorted people to "be imitators of God, as beloved children; and walk in love, just as Christ also loved you and gave Himself up for us, an offering and a sacrifice to God as a fragrant aroma" (Eph. 5:1–2). In addition, if Jesus is God, and I believe he is, then it's appropriate to note that the New Testament is replete with exhortations to be like Jesus in the way we live and act. For example, speaking of Jesus, John writes, "The one who says he abides in Him ought himself to walk in the same manner as He walked" (1 John 2:6). Through the Spirit we can be transformed more and more into the image of God: "But we all, with unveiled face, beholding as in a mirror the glory of the Lord, are being transformed into the same image from glory to glory, just as from the Lord, the Spirit" (2 Cor. 3:18).

---

28. Adams, *Finite and Infinite Goods*, 42.
29. Plato, *Theaetetus* 176b–c (Fowler).
30. Plato, *Republic*, in *Six Great Dialogues*, 453.
31. Aristotle, *Basic Works of Aristotle*, 880.
32. Hare, *God and Morality*, 60.

Third, Christian theologians throughout history have also affirmed that God is the supreme good and that humans are morally good when they resemble him. Augustine poetically wrote, "Consider this good and that good, abstract from the 'this' and the 'that,' and consider, if you can, simply the good itself, and thus you will see God, who is not good by reason of some other good but is the goodness of all that is good."[33] In the first chapter of his *Monologion*, Anselm argued that there must be one thing through which all good things are good, and that it alone is supremely good.[34] Thomas Aquinas provided a more detailed account when he explained that "each good thing that is not its goodness is called good by participation. But that which is named by participation has something prior to it from which it receives the character of goodness. This cannot proceed to infinity. . . . We must therefore reach some first good, that is not by participation good . . . but is good through its own essence. This is God."[35] In addition, Aquinas wrote that nothing created "will be called good except in so far as it has a certain likeness of the divine goodness."[36] Lastly, John Calvin, in considering God's commands, remarked, "It will not now be difficult to ascertain the general end contemplated by the whole Law, i.e., the fulfillment of righteousness, that man may form his life on the *model of the divine purity*. For therein God has so delineated his own character, that anyone exhibiting in action what is commanded, would in some measure exhibit a *living image of God*."[37]

Fourth, in addition to Adams, there are many other contemporary philosophers who also affirm that God is the ultimate good and that other things are good when they resemble him. William Alston suggests, "We can think of God Himself, the individual being, as the supreme standard of goodness. . . . Of course, we can have general principles, e.g., 'lovingkindness is good.' But this principle is not ultimate; it or the general fact that makes it true does not enjoy some Platonic ontological status; rather, it is true just because the property it specifies as sufficient for goodness is a property of God."[38] Similarly, Mark Murphy writes, "God is Goodness, God has no choice about whether God is the ultimate end of all things; God's nature sets, of necessity, the measure for goodness."[39]

As for objective moral value, I agree with Adams that the ultimate good is God and that humans are morally good if they resemble God in a morally

33. Augustine, *On the Holy Trinity*, 8.3.5.
34. Anselm, *Monologion*, in *Major Works*, 5–82.
35. Aquinas, *Summa Contra Gentiles Book One*, I-38.4.
36. Aquinas, *Summa Contra Gentiles Book One*, I-40.3.
37. Calvin, *Institutes*, 2.8.51 (emphasis added).
38. Alston, "Some Suggestions," 319.
39. Murphy, *God and Moral Law*, 176.

pertinent way. However, my divine love theory goes one step further by proposing that the specific thing being resembled is God's trinitarian nature as found in, and expressed among, the loving relationships between the persons of the Trinity. Therefore, I propose that God's inner-trinitarian relationships provide the ultimate foundation for objective morality and that humans are good when they resemble these loving divine relationships in a morally pertinent sense.

Most theistic moral theories focus only on God's nature, claiming that it's simply his moral nature that provides the foundation for objective morality. Little attention has been given to God's triunity in this context. Adams's model is no exception; he writes, "I assume that the character and commands of God satisfy certain conditions. More precisely, I assume that they are consistent with the *divine nature* having properties that make God an ideal candidate, and the salient candidate, for the semantically indicated role of the supreme and definitive Good."[40] Instead, my theory goes further and proposes that the ultimate Good is specifically God's triunity, which includes the loving relationships between the persons of the Trinity.

Adams mentions the Trinity only once in his major work on moral theory, *Finite and Infinite Goods*, and that in a short footnote. This footnote appears in a section where he is discussing how some theists have argued that God is a person in the following way: because persons are the most excellent things we know of, the supremely excellent Being must also be a person. Adams goes on to provide what he describes as a more cautious line of reasoning: begin with the premise "that most of the excellences that are most important to us, and of whose value we are most confident, are excellences of persons. . . . So if excellence consists in resembling or imaging a being that is the Good itself, nothing is more important to the role of the Good itself than that persons and their properties should be able to resemble or image it. That is obviously likelier to be possible if the Good itself is a person or importantly like a person."[41] After that last sentence he includes the following footnote:

> A similar but doubtless shakier line of argument might be used to support the conclusion that the Good itself is also importantly like a *society* of persons, as claimed by the Christian doctrine of the Trinity. For we confidently ascribe excellences to social systems and to interpersonal relationships, and we value those excellences highly. So if we think excellence consists in resembling or

---

40. Adams, *Finite and Infinite Goods*, 250 (emphasis added).
41. Adams, *Finite and Infinite Goods*, 42.

imaging the Good itself, we seem to be committed to the belief that societies and social relationships can resemble or image the Good itself. And that is likelier to be possible if the Good itself is importantly like a society.[42]

By "shakier line of argument" he presumably means that it's shakier to argue that "God is a society of persons" than it is to argue that God is a person. It's easier to see what argument he's referring to if we take his original argument quoted above, that God is a person, and replace "person" with "society of persons" as follows: Begin with the premise "that most of the excellences that are most important to us, and of whose value we are most confident, are excellences of [societies of persons]. . . . So if excellence consists in resembling or imaging a being that is the Good itself, nothing is more important to the role of the Good itself than that [societies of persons] and their properties should be able to resemble or image it. That is obviously likelier to be possible if the Good itself is a [society of persons] or importantly like a [society of persons]."

In response to Adams's comment about this shakier line of argument, I should note that in this book I'm not arguing that God is importantly like a person, or importantly like a society of persons. However, I am assuming that there are loving relationships between the persons of the Trinity because that's what seems to be revealed in the New Testament, and, on the basis of good reasons and evidence, I've come to believe the New Testament is from God. However, knowing this truth about ultimate reality helps us better understand the larger picture of the metaphysics of objective moral values and duties. If one accepts the New Testament as revelation from God and believes it teaches that there are loving relationships between the persons of the Trinity, then it's a viable approach to utilize this information and show how exploring God's trinitarian nature provides a fuller explanation of how he is the ultimate foundation for objective morality.

In this section I'm arguing that God, as the Good, includes loving relationships between the persons of the Trinity and that humans are morally good when they image this love. I'll give three reasons for the importance of including God's inner-trinitarian relationships when it comes to understanding morality and how God serves as the foundation of moral value.

First, because the loving inner-trinitarian relationships are a key aspect of God, at a minimum it should be expected that they would aid us in understanding how God serves as the foundation of morality. To say only that morality is based on his nature doesn't include the entire picture of all that God is, because,

---

42. Adams, *Finite and Infinite Goods*, 42.

by leaving out the loving inner-trinitarian relationships, it ignores the important relational aspect of God that's helpful in plumbing the depths of love and morality. Including these divine relationships in a moral theory provides a more complete picture of how God is the source of morality, and helps resolve various philosophical problems and puzzles. Thus my divine love theory brings in important truths regarding God's triunity and shows how loving relationships exist at the highest level of ultimate reality—that is, within God.

Thomas McCall has strongly advocated for seeing God's inner-trinitarian relationships as essential to the very being of God. He testifies, "I am convinced that divine love *is* essential to God. I believe that holy love is of the essence of God. But I think this is accounted for and grounded in the Trinity."[43] He affirms the following statement by John Zizioulas: "Love is not an emanation or 'property' of the substance of God . . . but is constitutive of his substance, i.e., it is that which makes God what He is, the one God. Thus love ceases to be a qualifying—i.e., secondary—property of being and becomes the *supreme ontological predicate*."[44] Thomas Torrance is also a strong proponent of elevating the metaphysical importance of divine loving relationships. He writes that the three persons of the Trinity "who indwell One Another in the Love that God is constitute the Communion of Love or the movement of reciprocal Loving which is identical with the One Being of God."[45]

Many others have recognized the importance of emphasizing God's personal inner-trinitarian relationships alongside our metaphysical categories of substance and essence. Eleonore Stump insists that "since, on the doctrine of the Trinity, the persons of the Trinity are not reducible to something else in the Godhead, then, persons are an irreducible part of the ultimate foundation of reality."[46] According to Clarke, Josef Ratzinger, before he became Pope Benedict XVI, dared even to reproach "St. Thomas himself for this [i.e., for not emphasizing enough God's relational aspects], and calls for a new, explicitly relational conception of the very nature of the person as such, wherein relationality would become an equally primordial aspect of the person as substantiality."[47] Ratzinger proclaimed that within the theology of the Trinity "lies concealed a revolution in man's view of the world: the undivided sway of thinking in terms of substance is ended; relation is discovered as an equally valid primordial mode of reality."[48]

43. McCall, *Which Trinity? Whose Monotheism?*, 172.
44. Zizioulas, *Being as Communion*, 46.
45. T. Torrance, *Christian Doctrine of God*, 165.
46. Stump, "Francis and Dominic," 1.
47. Clarke, *Person and Being*, 2.
48. Ratzinger, *Introduction to Christianity*, 132, 137.

In light of Ratzinger's emphatic proclamation, a qualifying comment may be pertinent here. While it's important not to ignore the inner-trinitarian relationships, it's also incorrect to say that morality is grounded solely in these loving relationships, because, though they're essential to God, they are only one essential aspect of him. It would be inaccurate to separate off this particular aspect of God and claim that all of morality is based only on this one aspect.

In other words, it doesn't make sense to ask what's more metaphysically ultimate, these inner-trinitarian relationships or God's nature, because it's God himself who is ultimate and nothing within God is more ultimate than something else within God. That's why at the beginning of this book I stated my main idea as follows: I'll argue that the ultimate ground of objective morality is God's trinitarian nature as found in, and expressed among, the loving relationships between the persons of the Trinity. Thus, I'm merely drawing out the implications of God's trinitarian nature and showing how it's a critical aspect of God in terms of how he functions as the source and foundation of morality. The role these inner-trinitarian relationships play in God being the ultimate good illuminates our understanding of the metaphysics of morality. Clarke sums this issue up well:

> To be a person is to *be with* . . . to be a sharer, a receiver, a lover. Ultimately the reason why all this is so is that this is the very nature of the Supreme Being, the Source of all being, as revealed to us in the Christian doctrine of God as three Persons within the unity of one being, so that the very being of God is to be self-communicative love. This dynamism is then echoed in all of us, his creatures, and in a preeminent way in created persons. Thus the Christian revelation of the Trinity is not some abstruse doctrine for theologians alone but has a unique illuminating power as to the meaning of being itself which carries metaphysical vision beyond what was accessible to it unaided. This is Christian philosophy at its most fruitful.[49]

When it comes to resembling God, it's true that human beings were made in God's image and thus are "good" in the sense that human nature images, or resembles, God's nature, regardless of whether people make good or evil choices. This first aspect of imaging God involves certain attributes and abilities essential to the nature of human beings—the ability to make choices, reason, will, love, be in relationships, and so on. While human beings resemble God in this static sense via their human nature, they also have the potential to further image God

---

49. Clarke, *Person and Being*, 112.

(or not) in a more dynamic sense through the various moral choices they make. Humans dynamically resemble the loving relationships between the persons of the Trinity when they choose to love God and love others. Hence humans are morally "good" when they image the ultimate Good—that is, the loving relationships between the persons of the Trinity.

Second, without the inner-trinitarian relationships, it's not clear that love, the cornerstone of morality, is a necessary aspect of ultimate reality. If love isn't an aspect of ultimate reality (i.e., God), then it's difficult to see how God could be the foundation of morality. However, if the inner-trinitarian relationships are affirmed and included in the account, then it's more clearly the case that love is part of the bedrock of reality. Because loving relationships are a primordial aspect of God, we can more easily affirm that love is necessarily good. In light of this, consider the following syllogism:

A. God is the Good, as affirmed in Adams's model above.
B. God is necessarily a communion of three divine persons in loving relationship with each other, and thus God is love.
C. Whatever God necessarily is, is part of what constitutes the goodness of God.
D. Therefore, loving relationships, and thus love in general, are necessarily good.

According to B, God is essentially relational and loving. These are not contingent properties of God that began only when he created humans to love but are part of his essential attributes. Consider the following explanation from McCall:

> If the loving relationships that exist between and among the divine persons are essential to God, the triune God just is essentially loving. . . . If God is Trinity, then God's own internal life consists in the loving communion shared between and among the three divine persons, and God is not contingently relational at all but is necessarily so. . . . The love and relationality of God toward the creation are merely contingent. . . . But wholly apart from creation, love and relationship abound within God, in the eternal loving mutuality of the persons of the Trinity, the Father, the Son, and the Holy Spirit.[50]

---

50. McCall, *Which Trinity? Whose Monotheism?*, 247.

If these loving inner-trinitarian relationships were not an essential aspect of God, if love didn't exist until creation, then love would be contingent, not necessary. In such a scenario, love, which is the fabric of morality, would be contingent and thus, in a sense, arbitrary because God could have created differently such that there was no love. Something that could be otherwise does not seem metaphysically "stable" enough to serve as the foundation of morality. Instead, since God is triune, love is not something new and contingent that came about through creation but is eternally necessary. In this way God's inner-trinitarian relationships allow us to affirm that loving God and others, the bedrock of morality, is necessarily good.

Third, God's inner-trinitarian relationships explain what we know from our human experience—that love is one of the highest goods, and the meaning of life is inextricably tied to loving relationships. We all understand that the most important part of our lives is our loving relationships. Our purpose and the very meaning of our lives are intimately connected with our loving relationships. Of course, these relationships change throughout the years; when we're younger, our most cherished relationships are usually with our parents; later in life our friends are the primary focus, followed by (for some) a spouse and then our children and grandchildren. Regardless, on our deathbed we all realize that the most important part of our lives is our loving relationships—that they are a, if not *the*, key part of our very purpose.

While describing the relationships within the Trinity, Clarke powerfully explains why this is the case:

> The dynamism of self-communication is part of the very nature of being and so of the person. But the metaphysician would like to probe further, if he can, into *why* all this should be the case. I think we now have the answer: the reason why all being, and all persons preeminently, are such is precisely because that is the way the Supreme Being, the Source of all being, actually is, and, since all creatures—and in a special way persons—are participants and hence images of their divine Source, then it follows that all created beings, and more intensely persons, will mirror in some characteristic way the divine mode of being.[51]

Our lives are a reflection of the inner-trinitarian life of God. We were created to image him by loving people, and we do this by selflessly putting others first and

---

51. Clarke, *Person and Being*, 88.

focusing on them instead of ourselves. Clarke further explains how this knowledge of God as Trinity should inform the direction, meaning, and purpose of our lives:

> Another, and more dynamic, aspect of the solution, stemming from our perfection rather than our imperfection, is that as images of God we too must imitate in our own way the ecstatic, outgoing self-sharing of God as infinite Good. Personal development in a created person is to become more and more like God. And since the self-diffusiveness of the Good in a supremely personal being like God is nothing else than love, then God is Love, the infinite Lover, and we too, as his images must be lovers. So the ultimate mystery of being turns out to be that to be is to be a lover.[52]

Not only our individual lives but the entire universe, being infused with meaning through God's loving intentions for it, is purposefully heading toward the culmination of meaningful love and purpose. Thus, God's triunity helps explain the very meaning of life and existence. Clarke sums it up well:

> Since all finite goods are good only by participation in the Infinite Good, every finite being tends, as far as its nature allows, towards imitating, becoming a likeness of, the Divine Goodness. In personal beings, endowed with intelligence and will, this universal dynamism towards the Good turns into an innate implicit longing for personal union with the Infinite Good, "the natural desire for the Beatific Vision," as Aquinas puts it. The whole universe, then, for him, turns into an immense implicit aspiration towards the Divine.[53]

The doctrine of the Trinity is a key that unlocks conceptual doors for us to better understand the meaning and purpose of life.

Moral Obligation in the Divine Love Theory

As I noted above, my divine love theory shares much in common with Robert Adams's theory; I built mine on its framework and then added to it important truths concerning God's triunity. Thus, it's important to keep in mind the distinction between the two parts of Adams's model. To summarize briefly, in

---

52. Clarke, *Person and Being*, 97.
53. Clarke, *Person and Being*, 24.

the first part, his theory of moral value, Adams posits God as the supreme Good and argues that the goodness of other things consists in a sort of resemblance to him. He writes, "All other good things are good by virtue of their relation to one supremely good thing, the central relation being a sort of resemblance or imaging."[54] Thus a human, or an action performed by a human, is morally *good* if it images God in a morally pertinent sense.

The second part of Adams's model is a theory of moral duties, which is sometimes referred to as moral obligation. Moral duties have to do with what we should or ought to do. In moral theory it's important to distinguish between moral value, what's good and bad, and moral duty, what's right and wrong, because in some situations only one or the other applies. For example, there are actions that would be morally good for me to do, such as building an orphanage or developing a cure for cancer, but it's not necessarily my moral duty to do such actions. Moral value and moral duty are closely connected, but because there are important distinctions between them, moral theorists often attempt to provide separate explanations for them.

As for Adams's theory, he argues that our moral duties are generated by God's commands, which God gives us because of his essential goodness. Adams goes so far as to insist that God's commands constitute our moral duties such that without commands from God, we'd have no moral obligations.[55] It's important to note that Adams claims this second part of his model is grounded in the first. He repeatedly stresses how important the first part, his theory of moral value, is to the second part, that God's commands constitute our moral obligations. He explains that "anything we can plausibly regard as moral obligation must be grounded in a relation to something of real value. . . . The goodness of finite things consists in fragmentary and multidimensional resemblance to a supreme Good [i.e., God]."[56] As we'll see below, it's vital to remember the proper order of these two parts of his model. Adams stresses that the "order of presentation is significant here. . . . A theory of the good for which God is the constitutive standard of excellence need not presuppose moral obligation, but my theory of moral obligation does presuppose my theory of the good."[57] This second part of his model is the portion that can rightly be called a version of divine command theory.

---

54. Adams, *Finite and Infinite Goods*, 40.
55. Adams, *Finite and Infinite Goods*, 262.
56. Adams, *Finite and Infinite Goods*, 232–33.
57. Adams, *Finite and Infinite Goods*, 255.

Divine command theory has a long and rich history within Christianity because of the importance placed on God's commands throughout the Bible. For example, Joshua admonishes the Israelites to "be very careful to observe the commandment and the law which Moses the servant of the LORD commanded you, to love the LORD your God and walk in all His ways and keep His commandments and hold fast to Him and serve Him with all your heart and with all your soul" (Josh. 22:5). The psalmist sings, "The precepts of the LORD are right, rejoicing the heart; the commandment of the LORD is pure, enlightening the eyes" (Ps. 19:8). Jesus tells his disciples, "This is My commandment, that you love one another, just as I have loved you" (John 15:12).

There was a time when divine command theory had fallen out of favor among moral theorists, most likely because of Immanuel Kant's supposed critical assessment of the theory. However, Hare has provided a thorough argument, filled with evidence from Kant's own work, that this is a misinterpretation of Kant.[58] Regardless, as noted above, divine command theory has made a tremendous comeback over the past few decades. There's disagreement among this new crop of divine command theorists as to whether our obligations are simply identical to God's commands, brought about or caused to exist by God's commands, constituted by God's commands, or supervene on God's commands. For example, Philip Quinn maintains a causal relationship, whereas Adams argues that God's commands constitute our obligations.[59] C. Stephen Evans sums up the debate well when he argues, "We might know that moral obligations are grounded in God's commands, even if we did not know exactly how the two were related, indeed, even if we found the relation mysterious. . . . It might well be possible to know that God's commands or decrees generate moral obligations even if we could not decide if the relation between God's commands and our moral obligations should be understood as a causal one or as identity, or in some other way."[60]

One final aspect of Adams's moral theory should be noted: obligation arises from social relationships. He begins his explanation of this aspect by affirming a social theory of the nature of obligation, affirmed by many ethicists, which says that our obligations arise in the context of personal relationships. He then argues, "A system of human social requirements can go some distance toward meeting this requirement although, in the end, I believe the moral pressure not to make

---

58. Hare, *God's Call*, 87–119.
59. Quinn, "Divine Command Theory," 54–55; Adams, *Finite and Infinite Goods*, 250.
60. Evans, *God and Moral Obligation*, 108.

an idol of any human society pushes us toward a transcendent source of the moral demand."[61] He claims, "Human social requirements fail to cover the whole territory of moral obligation" and gives several reasons for thinking that "actual human social requirements are simply not good enough to constitute the basis of moral obligation."[62] A "divine command theory of the nature of moral obligation can be seen as an idealized version of the social requirement theory . . . [because] our relationship with God is in a broad sense an interpersonal and hence a social relationship."[63] Therefore, "a theory according to which moral obligation is constituted by divine commands remains tenable, and is the best theory on the subject for theists, inheriting most of the advantages, and escaping the salient defects, of a social theory of the nature of moral obligation."[64]

Now that Adams's theory of obligation has been explained, it's time to develop my divine love theory by adding in important truths concerning the Trinity. Below I'll give four reasons for the benefits and importance of including God's inner-trinitarian relationships when it comes to understanding how God serves as the foundation of moral obligation.

First, understanding the trinitarian context of ultimate reality helps us see how and why obligation arises from social relationships, as Adams has argued. Since God exists as divine persons in loving relationships with each other, there's a sense in which ultimate reality itself is relational and thus all of reality takes place in a social context. Social relationships were not something new that came about when God created other beings sometime in the finite past but are a necessary part of ultimate reality. This tells us that relationships are part of the fabric of being itself, and thus we shouldn't be surprised that personal relationships play such a large role in moral obligation. The obligations that arise in our social relationship with God are but an image of, and flow out of, the social relationships within God. It makes sense that creation would reflect important aspects of the Creator.

Second, according to Duns Scotus, God's commands are instructions he's given us for the path that best achieves our ultimate purpose—becoming a co-lover with the persons of the Trinity by joining their divine fellowship.[65] Understanding that this is the purpose of God's commands takes the teeth out of the most common complaints against divine command theory—namely,

---

61. Adams, *Finite and Infinite Goods*, 244.
62. Adams, *Finite and Infinite Goods*, 248.
63. Adams, *Finite and Infinite Goods*, 249.
64. Adams, *Finite and Infinite Goods*, 249–50.
65. Duns Scotus, *Will and Morality*, 20.

that his commands are arbitrary or that divine command theories are overly authoritarian. While it's true that God has authority over us, his creation, his commands flow not from a despotic desire to control us but from a desire that we would enjoy the greatest thing possible—loving relationships with him and with others.

Hare is a strong proponent of Duns Scotus's idea that God's commands serve the purpose of directing us toward our end of joining the loving communion of the Trinity and excelling in that love. He explains that in the "Jewish and Christian scriptures, the central notion is that of God commanding us. . . . It is true, I think, that the notion of obligation makes most sense against the background of command. . . . [However,] the Judeo-Christian account adds God's love to the notion of God's commands, so that the commands are embedded in a covenant by which God blesses us and we are given a route towards our highest good, which is union with God."[66] God's commands provide directions for the best path on our journey toward fellowship with God, as Clarke describes so beautifully: "To be a person is to be a dynamic act of existence on the move, towards self-conscious, free sharing and receiving, becoming a lover, and finally a lover totally centered on Infinite Being and Goodness itself, the final goal of our journey as embodied spirits towards being-as-communion—the very nature of the Source of all being, and hence of all beings created in its image."[67]

Third, the inner-trinitarian relationships illumine Jesus's proclamation that the greatest commandments are to love God and to love others and his explanation that all of God's other commands rest on this foundation (Matt. 22:36–40). The other commands rest on this foundation because the two greatest commands instruct us to be like God—that is, like the persons of the Trinity who, from all eternity past, both love God (the other persons of the Trinity) and love others (the other persons of the Trinity). Love is the basis of morality, and it originates from within God's inner life of three divine persons in perfect loving fellowship with each other. Humans are good when they resemble God, but specifically when they image his love by reflecting the loving communion in the Trinity. Erickson argues that, since the relationships of Father and Son and Spirit are "bound by *agape*, self-sacrificial, giving love . . . the type of relationship that should characterize human persons, particularly believing Christians who have accepted the structure of intratrinitarian relationships as the pattern for their own relationships to others, would be one of unselfish love and submission

---

66. Hare, *God and Morality*, 81.
67. Clarke, *Person and Being*, 112–13.

to the other, seeking the welfare of the other over one's own. Humility, then, in the best senses of the word, will be one of the prized virtues."[68] Understanding God's trinitarian nature sheds light on how God's commands generate our moral obligations.

Fourth, understanding God's trinitarian nature and his purpose in creating us (to join the fellowship of these inner-trinitarian loving relationships) helps solve a problem that has dogged divine command theories for centuries—namely, the question of what obligates us to obey God's commands in the first place. Evans calls this problem "the prior obligations objection" to divine command theory and gives a brief history of its development as well as various responses that have been proposed.[69] His summary of the objection is worth quoting at length:

> A full-fledged [divine command theory] holds that all moral obligations are divine commands. (Or, on some versions, that they stem from divine commands.) The prior obligations objection argues that there must be some moral obligations that are not grounded in divine commands because they hold antecedently to or independently of divine commands. Specifically, the claim is that humans have a moral obligation to obey God. This obligation is not itself grounded in God's commands. Rather, it is precisely because there is a prior obligation to obey God that God's commands can create new obligations. There must therefore be some moral obligations other than those that are created by God's commands.[70]

In other words, it seems there's one obligation that doesn't come from God's commands—namely, the obligation to obey God's commands. Critics of divine command theory argue that it's circular, or results in an infinite regress, if one claims this obligation also comes from God's command.

Drawing on Duns Scotus's moral theology, Hare has provided the best answer to the question "Why are we obligated to obey God's commands?"

> It is necessarily true, Scotus holds, that God is to be loved. We know this just by knowing the terms "God" and "to be loved." This is because we know that, if God exists, God is supremely good, and we know that what is supremely good is to be loved. It is also true that we know that to love God

---

68. Erickson, *God in Three Persons*, 333.
69. Evans, *God and Moral Obligation*, 64–66, 98–101.
70. Evans, *God and Moral Obligation*, 99.

is at least to obey God. . . . Loving God is not simply to repeat God's will in our will, because there are things God wills that God does not will for us to will. So what we are to repeat in our wills is God's will for our willing. But willing what God wills for our willing is obedience. So it is necessarily true not just that God is to be loved, but that God is to be obeyed. If I justify the claim that the moral demand is a proper demand upon me by saying that God's command makes things obligatory, I am not terminating the justification in something that *itself* requires justification, except in as far as I have to justify the claim that God exists. This means that divine commands do not generate *all* our obligations, because there is one important exception, namely the obligation to obey divine commands. But this is not a troubling exception once one accepts the necessary truths (if God exists) that God is to be loved and that God is to be obeyed.[71]

If Hare is correct, and I believe he is, then our obligation to obey God's commands comes from the necessary truth that God should be loved. If God should be loved, and obeying God's commands is one of the primary ways we can love him, then we should obey his commands in order to love him. The fact "God should be loved" generates our moral obligation to obey God's commands because obeying God's commands is how we express our love for God.

This is another reason why I call my theory "divine love theory" instead of "divine command theory"; there's a sense in which ultimately our obligations come not from God's commands, but from the necessary truth that God should be loved. It is this necessary truth that comes first and stands before God's commands, that obligates us to obey his commands, because obeying his commands is how we love him. In turn, his commands generate all our other obligations. Thus, the ultimate source of our moral obligations isn't God's commands per se but the truth that God should be loved. I'll discuss this topic further in chapter 13 when I respond to Wielenberg's accusation that all theistic theories contain ungrounded ethical facts because, in that context, the question arises: What grounds the truth that God should be loved?

---

71. Hare, *God's Command*, 17–18.

CHAPTER 5

OBJECTIONS TO THE DIVINE LOVE THEORY

In this chapter I'll address five objections to my divine love theory. First, some Christians may be concerned that my theory posits loving relationships between the persons of the Trinity, but I'll argue that nearly all Christian positions on the Trinity should be able to support my theory. Second, divine will theorists may object to my theory because it leans more toward divine command theory instead of divine will theory, but I'll show how my theory incorporates important insights from divine will theory, which in turn should alleviate their objections. Third, natural law theorists may object to my theory because it leans more toward divine command theory instead of natural law theory, but I'll argue that natural law theories are inadequate in several respects. Fourth, some may be concerned that my theory makes morality arbitrary by basing it on God's will, but I'll explain that this is a misunderstanding of my theory. Fifth, some may be concerned that my theory is too Platonic and thus susceptible to some of the same criticism aimed at Wielenberg's Platonic model, but I'll explain that my theory is Platonic in a different sense than Wielenberg's model.

Objection 1: Concerns with Loving Relationships Within the Trinity

Some Christian theologians may have concerns about my divine love theory because it claims there are loving relationships between the persons of the Trinity. Theologians most likely to be concerned about this claim are those who hold to what is often referred to as classical trinitarianism. Many classical trinitarians affirm there are loving relationships between the persons of the Trinity, but some vehemently reject this notion. In this section I'll address arguments against such relationships that come mostly, but not exclusively, from classical trinitarians.

Classical trinitarianism is often compared and contrasted with social trinitarianism. Keith Whitfield explains that in "recent years, debates over trinitarian doctrine have emerged within evangelicalism. . . . One of those points of discussion relates to whether the classical (or Latin) and social (or Eastern) conceptions of the Trinity are both appropriate biblical models for conceptualizing the Trinity."[1] Social trinitarianism became popular during the latter part of the twentieth century, though adherents claim there is continuity between their position and those of various older Christian traditions, a claim that hasn't gone unchallenged.

While there are many varieties of social trinitarianism, all of them affirm inner-trinitarian loving relationships. Because some classical trinitarians also affirm loving relationships between the persons of the Trinity, this aspect of the Trinity is not what distinguishes social trinitarians from classical trinitarians. Instead, what most distinguishes social trinitarians from classical trinitarians is that the former claim that each divine person of the Trinity is a distinct center of consciousness, whereas the latter claim there's only one center of consciousness shared by the three divine persons. Cornelius Plantinga notes that the number-one condition for a theory to be considered a social trinitarian theory is that "Father, Son, and Spirit would be viewed as distinct centers of consciousness."[2] William Hasker, a social trinitarian, agrees that this distinguishing condition "is clearly the most important."[3] Classical trinitarians argue that when the early church theologians used the term *person* to describe the three persons of the Trinity, they didn't mean that they're distinct individual centers of consciousness. Classical trinitarians claim that this conception of personhood, a distinct center of consciousness, is a modern development and should not be anachronistically applied to the term *person* as used by the early church theologians.

---

1. Whitfield, introduction to *Trinitarian Theology*, 2.
2. C. Plantinga, "Social Trinity and Tritheism," 22.
3. Hasker, *Metaphysics*, 22.

In this section I'm not attempting to defend social trinitarianism or argue against classical trinitarianism. My only goal here is to defend the idea that there are loving relationships between the persons of the Trinity. As long as they accept this idea, both classical and social trinitarians can support my divine love theory. My response to arguments against the existence of loving relationships between the persons of the Trinity will mostly follow this pattern: though some who hold that there are loving relationships in the Trinity affirm X, holding that there are loving relationships in the Trinity does not require affirming X. One of the reasons I'm following this pattern of argumentation is to explain that while I, like all social trinitarians and most classical trinitarians, affirm there are loving relationships between the persons of the Trinity, I reject various ideas often associated with Social Trinitarianism which I discuss below.

First, some may reject that there are inner-trinitarian loving relationships because they believe this entails three centers of consciousness, or three wills, among the persons of the Trinity. However, though some who hold that there are loving relationships in the Trinity claim there are three centers of consciousness, or wills, among the persons of the Trinity, holding that there are loving relationships in the Trinity does not require affirming this claim.

For at least three reasons there must be *some sort of distinction* between the persons of the Trinity, regardless of the term we use to signify this distinction. First, there has to be some sort of distinction between the persons of the Trinity in order to avoid patripassianism, the idea that because the Son knows what it's like to suffer and die on a cross, the Father must know this as well. William Lane Craig explains that the "Father knows, for example, that the Son dies on the cross, but He does not know and cannot know that He Himself dies on the cross—indeed, the view that He so knows even has the status of heresy: patripassianism."[4] Second, there must be some sort of distinction between the persons of the Trinity because the Son decided to empty himself, take the form of a bond servant, and be made in the likeness of humanity (Phil. 2:6–7). Thomas McCall points out that since this decision was made before the incarnation, this distinctiveness in decision-making could not have been part of the Son's taking on human nature.[5] Third, there must be some sort of distinction between the persons of the Trinity because Jesus said that the Father "loved Me before the foundation of the world" (John 17:24). This description is also about Jesus's preincarnate state, so the distinction it implies cannot be limited to his

---

4. Craig, "Problem of Material Constitution," 83.
5. McCall, *Which Trinity? Whose Monotheism?*, 71.

incarnation. Whatever we decide to call the distinction between the persons of the Trinity, on the basis of this verse from John 17 we can be certain it is *enough of a distinction* for them to be in loving relationships with each other. McCall argues, "If the divine persons love one another, they must be capable of doing so. That is, they must be relationally *distinct* enough to do so."[6]

Some who affirm that there are loving relationships in the Trinity claim this distinction involves distinct centers of consciousness or distinct wills. But one doesn't have to take the distinction that far in order to affirm there are loving relationships in the Trinity. Alternatively, some understand this distinction merely as three modes of subsistence. For example, classical trinitarians Matthew Emerson and Luke Stamps maintain that

> while there is only one divine will, there are three modes of subsistence (or existence) in that one will. . . . The will is identical, but the three persons subsist in it according to their distinct personal modes. . . . Defenders of the classical Reformed doctrine of the *pactum salutis*, or covenant of redemption, have appealed to this distinction between one will and three modes of subsistence in order to demonstrate how there can be an eternal "agreement" between persons who share the same will. . . . So God's will is singular, but this singularity does not erase the real distinctions that exist between the three modes of subsistence in the one divine will.[7]

Bruce Ware explains how seeing the distinction between the persons of the Trinity as three modes of subsistence is enough of a distinction such that it allows one to affirm loving relationships within the Trinity. He begins his explanation with the question, "Can there be a unity of the one divine will while also affirming a distinction in just how that one will is expressed?"[8] He replies to his own question as follows: "My answer is yes. . . . We should affirm what the church fathers did, that . . . each of the three persons possesses the identically same will, just as each of them possesses the identically same power, and knowledge, and holiness, and love."[9] After noting his belief that there is only one will in God, he explains that

> each can also make use of that volitional capacity in distinct yet unified ways, according to his distinct hypostatic identities and modes of subsistence.

---

6. McCall, "Relational Trinity," 126.
7. Emerson and Stamps, "On Trinitarian Theological Method," 123–24.
8. Ware, "Unity and Distinction," 47.
9. Ware, "Unity and Distinction," 47.

. . . [This displays] the particular ways each divine person activates that common will from his particular personhood in distinct yet undivided personal action. This way of understanding the will of God . . . is akin to how we should understand, for example, the intratrinitarian love of God. . . . The Father's expression of love for the Son is distinctly paternal, as the Son's expression of love for the Father is distinctly filial, and the Holy Spirit's expression of love for Father and Son is distinctly his own—one common attribute of love with three expressions or inflections of that capacity of love through each of the three trinitarian persons.[10]

Thus, Emerson, Stamps, and Ware have shown that one doesn't have to maintain that the distinction between the divine persons entails distinct centers of consciousness, or wills, in order to affirm there are loving relationships in the Trinity.

There has always been disagreement among theologians over how to understand and describe the exact distinctions between the persons of the Trinity. Even though we may not be able to delineate the precise distinctions, there must be, in light of Jesus's statement in John 17:24, some sort of a distinction that is sufficient enough such that they can be in loving relationships with each other.

Second, some may reject the idea that there are inner-trinitarian loving relationships because they believe this idea entails making the persons of the Trinity too humanlike. For example, Emerson and Stamps fear that those who emphasize relationships in the Trinity often project on God facts that are true merely of humans.[11] While some who hold that there are loving relationships in the Trinity make the persons of the Trinity too humanlike, holding that there are loving relationships in the Trinity does not require making the persons of the Trinity too humanlike.

There are in fact similarities between God and humans because God created us in his image. The Bible often refers to these similarities, and sometimes quite explicitly, as in 1 Corinthians 2:10–11, where Paul explains that the spirit of a man is in the man and knows the thoughts of the man just like the Spirit of God is in God and knows his thoughts. However, to avoid the danger of making God too humanlike, these similarities between God and humans should be understood analogously. Concerning these verses from 1 Corinthians, Vern Poythress writes that the "text uses an analogy between the spirit of a human being and the Spirit of God. . . . The expression 'so also' that begins the last sentence in

---

10. Ware, "Unity and Distinction," 47–48.
11. Emerson and Stamps, "On Trinitarian Theological Method," 112.

1 Corinthians 2:11 indicates that there is an analogy between a human person and God."[12]

Elsewhere Poythress warns against the danger on both sides of this issue, explaining that if "we treat the analogy like an identity, it is univocism. We fall into non-Christian immanence, and we pretend that we can bring God down to our level and capture perfectly the nature of God. . . . On the other hand, if we treat the analogy as though God were completely different . . . in every respect, we have equivocism. We fall into non-Christian transcendence, according to which God is unknowable."[13] Classical trinitarians Emerson and Stamps express their agreement with this analogous approach when they write, "Even in Scripture, God uses analogical language accommodated to our finitude. As creatures, we cannot describe the essence of God exactly as God knows himself (univocal language). But because he has revealed himself to us, we are not left in a situation where our language always misses the mark in describing him (equivocal language). Rather, our God-talk is always analogous; creaturely words are analogical pointers to the reality of God in himself."[14] Poythress sums up well the proper ontological order that should be kept in mind when we consider similarities between God's inner-trinitarian love and human love: "No analogy with created things can capture the uniqueness of who God is. . . . There remains the distinction between the Creator and the creature. God's love is the love of the infinite Creator. It is analogous to human love; human love imitates divine love. God is the original pattern or archetype for love. Human beings love *on the level of the creature*; they have love in a derivative form."[15]

Some who affirm loving inner-trinitarian relationships make God too humanlike by using their trinitarian model to advocate for various human social arrangements, such as the relationships between men and women, church order, forms of governments, or economic systems. Classical trinitarians have rightly pointed out concerns with this practice.[16] Unfortunately, this is such a common practice among those who advocate for loving relationships between the persons of the Trinity that it's easy to associate these two ideas. However, not all those who affirm inner-trinitarian relationships make such applications from their understanding of the Trinity. In fact, Hasker, who holds to loving relationships between the persons of the Trinity, warns against this practice:

12. Poythress, *Knowing and the Trinity*, 58.
13. Poythress, *Knowing and the Trinity*, 104.
14. Emerson and Stamps, "On Trinitarian Theological Method," 104–5.
15. Poythress, *Knowing and the Trinity*, 47–48.
16. Kilby, "Perichoresis and Projection," 442.

I feel the need to underscore even more strongly . . . the difficulty inherent in deriving general prescriptions for human society from the doctrine of the Trinity. . . . If . . . we persist in finding social, political, and economic prescriptions in the Trinity, we are likely to be indulging in a process of circular reasoning. We take our own social-political convictions, derived from whatever source, read them back, in a suitably disguised form, into the doctrine of the Trinity, and then "discover" in that doctrine the blueprint for a just society. There is, furthermore the very real danger that in the process we will distort the trinitarian doctrine by molding it in the direction of our preferred social program.[17]

McCall, who also argues there are loving relationships in the Trinity, similarly notes that "there is, alas, a real danger here [in using a particular trinitarian model to advocate for various human social arrangements], and we should heed the warnings sounded by critics of this exercise."[18] Therefore, just because some who emphasize the loving relationships between the Trinity use this strategy, which involves making God too humanlike, this strategy is not necessarily a part of affirming there are loving relationships in the Trinity.

Third, some may reject inner-trinitarian loving relationships because they believe affirming these relationships entails denying that God has a nature. Though some who hold that there are loving relationships in the Trinity do deny that God has a nature, holding that there are loving relationships in the Trinity does not require denying that God has a nature.

Affirming God's nature (here the term *nature* will be used interchangeably with *essence*, *substance*, and *ousia*) is important because this is what grounds his unity and maintains his unchangeableness. Whitfield explains, "The classical model prioritizes the unity of the persons, because they share the divine essence and divine operations."[19] For example, Emerson and Stamps write that "the *ousia* connotes what the three divine persons share in common: the simple, ineffable divine essence, which creatures signify in terms of the divine attributes, the divine mind, and the divine will. This *ousia* is not some fourth thing in addition to the three persons, but is instead the being that each person is—the divine nature they share in common from all eternity. As the Nicene Creed famously affirms, the Son is consubstantial (Greek, *homoousia*, of the 'same substance')

17. Hasker, *Metaphysics*, 212–13.
18. McCall, *Which Trinity? Whose Monotheism?*, 226.
19. Whitfield, introduction to *Trinitarian Theology*, 3.

with the Father."[20] We want to avoid denying God's nature because such a move can lead not only to a denial of God's unity but also to the changeable God of process theology.

Some theologians who are well known for affirming loving relationships between the persons of the Trinity have challenged the idea that God has a nature. For example, John Zizioulas and Robert Jenson argue that such a notion is drawn more from Greek philosophy than from the Christian Scriptures, though ironically they don't seem to be bothered by the fact that they themselves admittedly draw notions from Hegelian and existentialist philosophy.[21] In addition, Jürgen Moltmann claims that positing that God has a fixed nature makes him out to be too static, more like Aristotle's statue-like unmoved mover than the dynamic, interactive, relational God of the Bible.[22] Such theologians disdain the practice of describing God as a static essence instead of as a communion of dynamic loving relationships because, they argue, God cannot be the loving relational God portrayed in the Bible if he exists as a fixed immutable and impassible nature.[23] Many of these theologians who reject God's nature claim God's unity is instead grounded in the divine *perichoresis*—that is, the loving communion of fellowship between the persons of the Trinity.[24]

However, even though some who believe there are loving relationships in the Trinity have denied that God has a nature, many who hold to inner-trinitarian loving relationships affirm God's nature. Three such theologians will be noted here. First, in his critique of Moltmann's theology, Hasker argues that the "doctrine of *perichoresis*, while still important, does not have to carry by itself the whole burden of the unity of God—a task for which it is arguably insufficient."[25] Since humans are invited to join this *perichoresis*, and we certainly do not want to conclude that they become united with God in the same way that the divine persons are united, God's unity must be grounded in something beyond the *perichoresis*. Hasker concludes that the "union and communion of the persons does not . . . say everything that needs to be said about the divine unity. The doctrine of the Trinity affirms that the three persons are together a single concrete being—that they share between them a single trope of deity, a

---

20. Emerson and Stamps, "On Trinitarian Theological Method," 111.
21. Zizioulas, *Being as Communion*, 29, 70–71, 100–103; Jenson, *Systematic Theology*, 1:9; Jenson, "Holy Spirit," 169.
22. For example, see Moltmann, *Trinity and the Kingdom*, 43–45.
23. Moltmann, *Trinity and the Kingdom*, 21–60.
24. Moltmann, *Trinity and the Kingdom*, 95, 150.
25. Hasker, *Metaphysics*, 101.

single concrete instance of the divine nature."[26] Second, McCall similarly affirms both that "the divine persons are three . . . fully divine entities who know and love one another" and that "the divine persons share the divine essence; they are *homoousios*."[27] Lastly, Clarke also affirms both God's nature and the importance of recognizing the loving relationships between the persons of the Trinity. He even claims this recognition is found in Aquinas's work in that the "innate dynamism of being as overflowing into self-manifesting, self-communicating action is clear and explicit in St. Thomas. . . . Not as explicit, however, though necessarily implied, it seems to me, is the corollary that *relationality* is a primordial dimension of every real being."[28] Clarke was dismayed that so many theologians, in emphasizing the relationships in the Trinity, tended to eschew the importance of God's nature. He notes that these "analyses have almost without exception been suspicious of, or even positively hostile towards the notion of person as substance, which was so heavily stressed in the classical tradition."[29] Clarke argues that without God's nature providing the ontological grounding, there would be no enduring foundation to support such relationships. He writes, "Even though we have been stressing the relational aspect of being so far in this discussion, since it was underdeveloped in the Aristotelian-Thomistic tradition, it should not be forgotten that the aspect of substantiality, already well developed in this tradition, is indispensable, as the necessary grounding for relationality itself. . . . This is the ontological role of substance in a being: to provide the abiding unifying center for all the being's relations and other attributes."[30] Instead of pitting relationality and nature against each other, he claims that "substantiality and relationality are here equally primordial and necessary dimensions of being itself at its highest intensity. And the ultimate reason why all lower beings manifest this relationality as well as substantiality is that they are all in some way images of God, their ultimate Source, the supreme synthesis of both."[31]

Some reject the inner-trinitarian relationships because they believe affirming them involves denying God's nature. However, these three theologians— Hasker, McCall, and Clarke—make it clear that one doesn't have to deny God's nature in order to maintain that there are loving relationships in the Trinity.

---

26. Hasker, *Metaphysics*, 257.
27. McCall, "Relational Trinity," 129.
28. Clarke, *Person and Being*, 13–14.
29. Clarke, *Person and Being*, 4.
30. Clarke, *Person and Being*, 16.
31. Clarke, *Person and Being*, 15.

Fourth, some may reject that there are inner-trinitarian loving relationships because they believe this requires disagreeing with the early church theologians. While some who hold that there are loving relationships in the Trinity blatantly disagree with the early church theologians on certain matters, to hold that there are loving relationships in the Trinity does not require disagreeing with these theologians. Below it will be shown that several early church theologians affirmed inner-trinitarian loving relationships. (Note that I'm not arguing here that the early church theologians affirmed social trinitarianism—that is, that there are three centers of consciousness in the Trinity—but only that they affirmed there are loving relationships between the persons of the Trinity.)

Khaled Anatolios has shown how Athanasius drew "on the Johannine motif of the mutual love of Father and Son in interpreting the characterization of Wisdom in the Old Testament" and depicted "the oneness of trinitarian being as a oneness of mutual love."[32] Further, Augustine is well known for his description of the Trinity as lover, beloved, and love itself. Lewis Ayres states that Augustine "consistently founds the unity of God in the Father's eternal act of giving rise to a communion in which the mutual love of the three constitutes their unity of substance."[33] In addition, Richard of St. Victor argued that "perfection of charity requires a Trinity of persons."[34] Also, though Karl Barth obviously was not an early church theologian, he's regarded by many as a stalwart of classical trinitarianism. He wrote that "as and before God seeks and creates fellowship with us, He wills and completes this fellowship in Himself. In Himself He is Father, Son and Holy Spirit and therefore alive in His unique being with and for and in another. . . . He does not exist in solitude but in fellowship."[35] Lastly, even Aquinas, whom many consider to be the epitome of classical trinitarianism, wrote that the "Father and the Son love each other and love us by the Holy Spirit."[36]

After providing a similar survey of early church theologians who affirmed loving relationships between the persons of the Trinity, McCall writes, "It should be clear . . . that a deeply relational account of divine personhood is far from antithetical to orthodox trinitarian theology. On the contrary, such a relational view is consistent with orthodoxy. Does anyone in the tradition of orthodox Christian theology deny that the divine persons love one another?"[37] Thus we

---

32. Anatolios, *Retrieving Nicaea*, 153.
33. Ayres, *Augustine and the Trinity*, 319.
34. Richard of St. Victor, *Book Three of the Trinity*, 385.
35. Barth, *Church Dogmatics* II/2, 275.
36. Aquinas, *Summa Theologica* 1:37a2.
37. McCall, "Relational Trinity," 125.

can conclude that one doesn't have to disagree with the early church theologians in order to maintain that there are inner-trinitarian relationships of mutual love.

In this section I've explained that classical trinitarians might be a bit leery of my divine love theory at first because they may think it entails erroneous aspects of social trinitarianism. However, I've argued that classical trinitarians can support my theory if they affirm that there are loving relationships between the persons of the Trinity, which is the cornerstone of my theory. Though social trinitarians are better known for discussing the loving relationships between the persons of the Trinity, I've shown that classical trinitarians can, and many do, also affirm these inner-trinitarian relationships even though they reject, as do I, the notions discussed above that are often associated with social trinitarianism.

Objection 2: Concerns from Divine Will Theorists

As I noted above, my theory should be referred to as a divine love theory, not a divine command theory, because in my theory God's triune nature, not his commands, plays the central role. However, my theory affirms what many divine command theories do—namely, that God's commands generate our moral obligations. Therefore, objections often made against this aspect of divine command theories will also apply against my divine love theory. In this section I'll cover objections made by those who argue that the foundation of our obligations is not God's commands but his will.

While there are several scholars, Mark Murphy being just one example,[38] who have argued that obligation is dependent on God's willing, not his commanding, there are other theories similar to, but distinct from, divine will theory that also argue against the idea that divine commands are the foundation of our moral obligations. For example, Thomas Carson claims our obligations rest on God's preferences rather than God's commands,[39] and Linda Zagzebski has proposed a distinct divine motivation theory.[40] There are also divine desire theories, divine intention theories, and so on. Though there are important and interesting differences between these theories, they all maintain that the ultimate foundation of our moral obligations is not divine commands but something else found "inside" God, such as his will, preferences, motivations, desires, or intentions. For the sake of responding to their similar objections to divine command theory, I'll refer generally to these various theories as divine will theories.

---

38. Murphy, "Divine Command."
39. Carson, *Value and the Good Life.*
40. Zagzebski, *Divine Motivation Theory.*

Divine will theorists argue that God's commands don't make something oblig-atory, but that God's will does, and that commands merely convey this obligation to us. Thus, they claim God's will, not divine commands, is the ground of our obli-gations. For example, Zagzebski points out that one "could maintain either that a command is simply God's way of revealing His will, where His will is the actual ground of obligation, or that a command is itself the ground."[41] Philip Quinn seems to embrace the former option when he writes, "It is at the deepest level God's will, and not his commands, which merely express his will, that determines the deontological status of actions."[42] William Mann illustrates well the distinction between these two theories when he explains that differences "emerge when we consider cases in which the two theories might part ways. Might there be cases in which God commands something that he does not will? Conversely, might there be cases in which God wills something that he does not command? In either case, which creates the obligation, the command or the will?"[43]

One problem with the idea that God's will makes our obligations come about is that it seems to eliminate the possibility of supererogatory acts, of going above and beyond what is commanded, by collapsing such acts into the category of obligatory acts. According to this model, whatever God wills for us to do is obligatory, and certainly God wills for us to go above and beyond in our moral lives. Divine command theory doesn't encounter this problem because, accord-ing to this theory, only what God commands us to do is obligatory, and when someone goes above and beyond this requirement, it is supererogatory. In this model God wills for us to do supererogatory acts, but since he doesn't command them, they're not obligatory.

In response to this issue, Mann points out that divine will theory runs into the problem of eliminating supererogatory acts only if it maintains that God's will for us *always* creates moral obligations.[44] Thus, according to Mann, divine will theory could make room for supererogatory acts by claiming a distinction between God's intentions, which are obligatory for us, and his desires, which don't ground our obligations but merely our supererogatory acts. Beyond being a bit ad hoc, this solution runs into the difficulty of us having to split apart God's intentions and desires. Even if we can separate these things conceptually, how would we know in practice what God intends versus what he desires?

41. Zagzebski, *Divine Motivation Theory*, 258–59.
42. Quinn, "Argument for Divine Command Ethics," 293.
43. Mann, *God, Modality, and Morality*, 234.
44. Mann, *God, Modality, and Morality*, 234.

A better solution would be to affirm that divine will theorists are making a good point when they argue that our obligations *originate* in God's will for us, but still to maintain with divine command theorists that the obligations only become *effective* for us when he makes us aware of them somehow. In other words, grounding moral obligations involves both a metaphysical component (divine will) and an epistemological component (divine commands), and these components are not at odds with each other. In addition, according to my divine love theory, our obligations originate specifically in God's ultimate intention, or telos, for us, which is that we would enter into the loving communion that exists between the persons of the Trinity. Thus, his commands are primarily about giving us the best path for this ultimate goal.

Alvin Plantinga agrees that God's will is the fount of our obligations: "God's will is more basic, more fundamental, and explanatorily prior to obligation; obligation depends upon God's will in a way in which God's will does not depend upon obligation."[45] However, it's important to maintain that God's will doesn't *generate* moral obligations for us until he somehow makes us aware of his will. Others have come to similar conclusions; for example, Susan Peppers-Bates writes, "While God's commands *simpliciter* are not the foundation of morality or the source of moral obligation, we can still say that . . . knowledge of divine commands remains essential epistemologically."[46] Thus I affirm that God's will is the ground, or foundation, of our obligations but that technically it's God's commands that *make* our obligations obligatory for us.

There are at least two good reasons to think that our obligations, though they originate in God's will, are not applicable to us unless God makes us aware of them somehow. First, it seems implausible that someone could have moral obligations if they were unaware of them. C. Stephen Evans argues this point as follows: "Suppose one says that moral obligations are established by God's will alone, rather than God's commands. A morally right act is one that conforms to God's will and a morally wrong act is one that does not so conform. The difficulty with such a view is that it seems to make morality impossible unless God's will is somehow expressed in such a way that it can be known. If God's will constitutes our moral obligations, and God's will is a closely guarded secret, then the best humans could do would be to guess about their moral obligations."[47] In addition, while explaining his concerns with divine will theories, Robert Adams

45. A. Plantinga, "Naturalism," 271.
46. Peppers-Bates, "Divine Simplicity," 369.
47. Evans, *God and Moral Obligation*, 37.

notes that the idea that God's will could impose obligations without being revealed to us "yields an unattractive picture of divine-human relations, one in which the wish of God's heart imposes binding obligations without even being communicated. . . . Games in which one party incurs guilt for failing to guess the unexpressed wishes of the other party are not nice games."[48]

Second, Paul's argument in Romans 2 seems to indicate that no one will be able to avoid God's judgment by using the excuse that they were unaware of what was right and wrong. Even those who never had God's law in the form of direct verbal instructions will have no excuse because when those "who do not have the Law do instinctively the things of the Law, these, not having the Law, are a law to themselves, in that they show the work of the Law written in their hearts, their conscience bearing witness and their thoughts alternatively accusing or else defending them" (Rom. 2:14–15). By arguing that no one will be excused from judgment because everyone is aware of what is right or wrong, Paul seems to imply the alternative—that is, *if* someone was somehow unaware of what was right or wrong, then they would be excused (i.e., have no obligations). Thus, we can conclude from this that, though our obligations originate in God's will, they are only effective for us if God makes us aware of them somehow.

Two important points stem from this second argument. First, as Romans 2 indicates, God can make his will for us known in many ways. Unfortunately, the term *command* in the name "divine command theory" has led some to mistakenly think that advocates of this theory believe people have obligations only if God gives them direct verbal instructions. Because of this confusion, it's necessary to clarify that many divine command theorists, including Adams, don't use the term *command* in this context to mean only direct verbal instructions. They maintain that God has communicated his will to us in many ways, including but not limited to direct verbal commands, moral intuition, and our consciences. For example, Evans explains that "when I speak of 'divine commands' I will use the term 'command' in an extended sense to refer to what God wills humans to do insofar as his will has been communicated to humans."[49] Thus the term *command* is used within most divine command theories, as well as my divine love theory, as a general term to encapsulate *all* of the ways that God makes us aware of his will for us, not merely direct verbal commands. Evans suggests several possible ways God can make us aware of his will for us apart from direct

48. Adams, *Finite and Infinite Goods*, 261.
49. Evans, *God and Moral Obligation*, 38.

verbal instructions, such as through our consciences and our moral intuition.[50]
Similarly, John Hare describes our conscience as "the human capacity that serves
as the vehicle for general revelation about obligation."[51]

Second, someone can have obligations even if they don't understand that
these obligations actually come from God. This is an important point because it
addresses one of Wielenberg's concerns—namely, that if divine command theory
is true, then those who don't believe in God wouldn't have moral obligations.
He summarizes his concern as follows: "[Adams's theory] implies that reasonable non-believers have no moral obligations at all, since they do not recognize
any command as having been issued by God. . . . The Adams/Evans-style divine
command theory is unable to account for the moral obligations of reasonable
non-believers not in the sense that the theory implies that non-believers have
moral obligations but are unaware of them (an epistemological worry), but
rather in the sense that the theory implies that non-believers lack moral obligations altogether (a metaphysical worry)."[52] In response to this concern, I affirm
that someone can be morally obligated so long as she is aware of what's right and
wrong and that she should do the right; it doesn't matter whether she's aware of
the metaphysical details concerning how these obligations are generated. Thus,
God must make someone aware of the obligations, even if she is unaware that
the obligations come from God. In other words, God can make the *content* of
his will, what's right and wrong and that we should do what's right, known to us
without making us aware of the fact that the *source* of these things are his will.

Further, understanding what's right and wrong, and knowing we should do
what's right, is enough to generate obligations for us, even if we don't understand
that these things originate in God's will. For example, an atheist who knows
what's right and wrong, and knows she should do what's right, is obligated to
do so even if she doesn't understand that these-things-being-God's-will is part of
what makes them obligatory. For us to have moral obligations, God only has to
make us aware of the *content* of his will—that is, what's right and wrong and that
we should do the right; he doesn't have to make us aware that these things *are*
his will nor that these-things-being-his-will is part of what makes them obligatory. Hare explains well the important distinction "between our knowledge of
moral goodness or obligation and our knowledge of what makes them good or
obligatory. It is possible that what makes something good or obligatory is some

---

50. Evans, *God and Moral Obligation*, 39–42.
51. Hare, *God and Morality*, 270.
52. Wielenberg, *Robust Ethics*, 78–79.

relation to God (different in the two cases), but that we can know by right reason that the thing is good or obligatory without knowing this relation. On some versions of the doctrine of general revelation, God can reveal that some route to our end is required of us without our knowing that it is God who requires it."[53] In other words, people don't have to understand *how* or *why* they have moral obligations in order to have them and know *that* they have them. Certainly Wielenberg would agree; he wouldn't claim that people have to understand his metaphysical explanation for *how* and *why* moral obligations are instantiated in order for them to have them and know *that* they have them.

To summarize, my divine love theory affirms that God's will and his commands are both necessary for us to have moral obligations. Our obligations *originate* in God's will for us but are only *generated*, or go into effect for us, when he makes us aware of the content of his will in some way. There's a sense in which God's will is more foundational—that is, more primordial—than his commands, but this doesn't take away from the importance of divine commands because we must be aware of God's will in order for the obligations to become effective for us. In this way God's will and his commands are both important aspects of the overall story of our moral obligations.

Objection 3: Concerns from Natural Law Theorists

Of the two most common moral theories among Christians, divine command theory and natural law theory, my divine love theory shares more in common with the former. Therefore, in defending my theory against possible objections, it's necessary to consider objections that natural law theorists often make against divine command theory. Since there are many different natural law theories, it's important to keep in mind that not every natural law theorist would affirm these objections or agree with how I'm describing natural law here. Thus, these objections from, and descriptions of, certain natural law theories apply only to some, not all, versions of natural law.

The first objection that some natural law theorists have against divine command theory stems from their belief that this theory claims humans are unable to know moral truth unless God specifically reveals it to them via direct verbal instructions, such as what's often found in the Bible. They raise this objection because natural law theorists strongly maintain that people can know moral truth via reason and intuition apart from special revelation from God. For example, Craig Boyd and Raymond VanArragon claim that "any properly

---

53. Hare, *God's Command*, 75.

functioning person will know in his heart, and can determine by reason, that such actions [i.e., immoral actions such as adultery and murder] do not contribute to true happiness and that they are immoral."[54] In addition, David Haines and Andrew Fulford argue that "there is an order or rule of human conduct which is . . . knowable by all men, through human intuition and reasoning (beginning from his observations of creation, in general; and human nature, in particular) alone, independent of any particular divine revelation provided through a divine spokesperson."[55]

One reason this rift often arises between natural law and divine command theory is that, in general, natural law theorists are more comfortable with, and place more emphasis on, natural theology and general revelation—that is, truths that humans can know apart from Scripture. For theological reasons, some divine command theorists view fallen human reason as completely untrustworthy and therefore are doubtful that humans can know much, if anything, apart from God's special revelation. These types of divine command theorists thus place more emphasis and importance on the direct verbal commands God gave us in Scripture.

While some divine command theorists hold that humans are unable to know moral truth unless God reveals it to them via direct verbal instruction, many of them affirm that God reveals moral truth to humans in numerous ways, including through reason, moral intuition, and our consciences. As explained above, the term *command* in the name "divine command theory" is used by many divine command theorists, and in my own divine love theory, as a general term encompassing all the ways God makes moral truth known to us, including but not limited to direct verbal commands. Thus, while this first objection might apply to some divine command theories, it doesn't apply to all of them, and it doesn't apply to my theory.

In response to those divine command theorists who feel that, by affirming these things, my divine love theory elevates fallen human reason too highly, it should be noted that what I'm affirming here isn't the ability of autonomous human reason to discover moral truth on its own, which would overestimate the ability of human reason, but that God reveals these truths to us through human reason and intuition as a form of general revelation (Rom. 2:14–15). Understanding natural theology this way, as general revelation, prevents us from

---

54. Boyd and VanArragon, "Ethics," 308–9.
55. Haines and Fulford, *Natural Law*, 46.

elevating human reason too highly by keeping the emphasis on God's activity of revealing instead of on our ability to discover things on our own.

The second objection that some natural law theorists may have has to do with Adams's claim, also affirmed by my divine love theory, that what makes something morally good is that it images, or resembles, God in a morally pertinent way. Those natural law theorists who may object to this claim would do so because they believe instead that what makes something morally good is based on human nature—that is, if it leads to human flourishing. Though Evans is a divine command theorist, he explains that "natural law theorists characteristically offer an account of goods that are universally and naturally good, and most have done so by offering an Aristotelian-inspired account of the good for humans in terms of what completes or perfects human nature, or that enables human flourishing. . . . The vast majority of natural law theorists have explained the good for humans in terms of human nature, and I shall take this as a defining characteristic of natural law theory."[56]

For example, natural law proponents Boyd and VanArragon, who claim their version "leans heavily on the natural law tradition that originated with Aquinas,"[57] affirm that natural law theory "grounds morality in the human nature that God has created."[58] Elsewhere they explain, "According to the version of [natural law morality] that we are defending, human beings share a common nature. Moral rules and principles are grounded in this nature."[59] As I noted above, because there are many different natural law theories, it's important to remember that not every natural law theorist would agree with how natural law is being described here or affirm Boyd and VanArragon's interpretation of Aquinas. In response to the numerous interpretations of Aquinas, Hare writes, "I have made a lifetime habit of not attributing views to Aquinas, because I have found that Aquinas scholars have such different views and hate each other so much that any attribution is likely to occasion deep animosity."[60] Regardless, Boyd and VanArragon's understanding of natural law is not uncommon; Haines and Fulford also explain that by "natural law, then, we mean that order or rule of human conduct which is . . . based upon human nature as created by God."[61] Incidentally, one of the reasons that human reason often plays a larger role in

---

56. Evans, *God and Moral Obligation*, 59–60.
57. Boyd and VanArragon, "Ethics," 303.
58. Boyd and VanArragon, "Ethics," 310.
59. Boyd and VanArragon, "Ethics," 305.
60. Hare, *God's Command*, 21.
61. Haines and Fulford, *Natural Law*, 5.

knowing moral truth in natural law theories than in divine command theories is that many natural law theorists maintain that through human reason we can ascertain moral truth by evaluating human nature to see what causes humans to flourish or not.

My first response to this objection is that the proposal of basing what's morally good on human nature makes it possible, though not necessary, to leave God completely out of the picture. Hare explains that the "danger of some kinds of natural law theory is that God disappears into creation, in the sense that . . . we think we can get morality from our nature."[62] This concern is even raised by Mark Murphy, in spite of the fact that he has often been sympathetic to natural law theory. He argues that, because a truly theistic explanation of morality should include God as the immediate ground of morality, basing what is morally good on human nature "is on its face unacceptable as a theistic explanation of moral law" because "one explains moral law in an entirely Godless way if one explains moral law as the natural law theorist explains it."[63]

Some natural law theorists, especially those that strongly embrace theism, have pushed back against this concern by pointing out the important role that God, as the one who created human nature, plays in their respective theories. For example, Haines and Fulford maintain that "as the creator of everything, nothing was brought into existence which was not caused by God; thus, God is the creator of man, and has established a moral standard over man."[64] However, it's still concerning to many that some natural law theories don't give God a more immediate and prominent role when it comes to defining moral good. Evans affirms that "to give a satisfying account of morality as a whole . . . we need God to play a more central role than simply as the creator of natural kinds that determine the good."[65]

My second response to this objection is that human nature is insufficient as the core foundation for morality because, since human nature isn't necessary but contingent, basing morality on human nature results in a relative morality. At least as far back as Plato, it has seemed to many thinkers that, in order for morality to be objective and absolute, it must have a necessary foundation that isn't contingent or relative in any way. Human nature fails to provide such a foundation because, since human nature itself is contingent, grounding morality in it ultimately results in a morality that is contingent and, at least in one sense,

---

62. Hare, *God's Command*, 313.
63. Murphy, *God and Moral Law*, 70, 74.
64. Haines and Fulford, *Natural Law*, 21–22.
65. Evans, *God and Moral Obligation*, 58.

relative—that is, relative to human nature. Evans expresses this concern when he writes that, according to some versions of natural law theory, moral good is "in some way determined by our nature, such that if human nature were fundamentally different, what would be good for humans would be fundamentally different as well."[66] In order for morality to be objective and absolute, it must be grounded in something sturdier and necessary—that is, less contingent—than human nature.

Human nature can't be the absolute foundation of morality because God could have created us with different natures. If God had created us with different natures, it's reasonable to think our moral principles would have been different. For instance, he could have created us to be asexual like angels, and then our moral principles concerning sexuality would have been quite different. Morality that's based on our human nature is thus relative in the sense that it's relative to our contingent nature. For this reason, our human nature is insufficient to serve as the absolute core foundation of human morality; all of human morality can't be encompassed under the umbrella of our human nature. My divine love theory delves deeper, beyond human nature, and locates the absolute core foundation of morality in God's trinitarian nature, something that can't be relative or contingent in any sense. Only by grounding morality in something necessary like this can we avoid every sense of relative morality.

Even if we grant that some aspects of morality stem from human nature, it's still God, not human nature, who provides the ultimate foundation for morality. This result follows because it's God who chose to create human beings such that they have the natures they do. Hugo Grotius, considered by many as the father of modern natural law theory, admitted as much when he explained that "even that Natural Law of which we have spoken . . . although it do [sic] proceed from the internal principles of man, may yet be rightly ascribed to God; because it was by His will that such principles came to exist in us."[67] Further, it seems that there are certain things about our human nature that God necessarily had to make a certain way, for if he had not, it would have violated his own trinitarian nature. Though there are many aspects of human nature that God could have created differently without violating his trinitarian nature, certainly there are some aspects of our human nature that God created the way he did necessarily because of his trinitarian nature. For example, it seems reasonable to think that, because of God's trinitarian nature, he could not have created humans such that it would be morally

---

66. Evans, *God and Moral Obligation*, 61.
67. Grotius, *Rights of War and Peace*, xxvi.

good for us to be unloving toward God or toward others. Hence, even if we grant that some aspects of morality stem from human nature, the ultimate foundation would still be God's trinitarian nature, not our human nature.

My third response to this objection from natural law theorists is that grounding moral good in human nature ignores God's role as moral exemplar. Since I made the case in chapter 4 that God is the ultimate moral exemplar and that everything else is morally good if it resembles him, I won't repeat those arguments here. It should be noted that the belief of some natural law theorists, that morality is based on certain properties of human nature, is not altogether unlike Wielenberg's proposal that certain natural properties of human beings, such as their cognitive faculties, cause moral properties to be instantiated. Of course, the difference is, at least with theistic natural law theories, that God is still the source of morality in that he is the one who chose to and then did create human nature the way it is. In my third response here I'm arguing that natural law theorists, and Wielenberg in a sense as well, have highlighted an important aspect of morality—human nature—but have erred by focusing solely on this one aspect while ignoring God's role as moral exemplar, thus painting overall an incomplete picture.

Mark Murphy has suggested a way to complete the picture. Murphy affirms Adams's notion, which I also affirm in my divine love theory, that God is the Good and that humans are morally good when they resemble him. He writes that Adams's account's "central distinctive feature—the goodness of creaturely goods consists in their resemblance to God—should be preserved within any theistic account of the good and provides a basis for an adequate theistic explanation of moral law."[68] However, he argues that this too is an incomplete picture because it doesn't specify in what sense humans are to resemble God. For example, Zagzebski, who also agrees that valuable moral properties of persons get their value from their similarity to the properties of God,[69] points out that it's not always good to be like God. She explains, "In eating of the tree of the knowledge of good and evil, Adam and Eve did acquire that knowledge . . . [but] it is a knowledge we are better off without. In trying to be like God, not only have we been cut off from God, we have also succeeded in acquiring the mind of a judge."[70] In other words, it's not good for humans to try to be like God in determining or deciding for ourselves what's good and evil, because that's something

---

68. Murphy, *God and Moral Law*, 150.
69. Zagzebski, *Divine Motivation Theory*, 341.
70. Zagzebski, *Divine Motivation Theory*, 243.

only God should do. Therefore, according to Murphy, what's missing in Adams's account is the specific ways that God intends humans to resemble him.

Murphy claims that these divine intentions for how humans are to resemble God are built into and reflected in human nature. Thus, his proposed addition to Adams's model is that humans are good when they resemble God in a specific way—that is, the way God intended them to resemble him. The good for each kind of thing, humanity being one kind of thing, is resembling God in the way that kind is supposed to, according to his intended purpose for that kind. Murphy concludes, therefore, that "facts about God and facts about the creaturely nature cooperate in fixing the character of creaturely goodness."[71] According to Murphy, then, his revision of Adams's model brings two incomplete pictures (natural law's account that the good is based on human nature and Adams's account that the good is based on resembling God) together to provide the complete picture.

It may be the case that Adams's model, either explicitly or implicitly, already included these points that Murphy has made, and thus his self-proclaimed revision of Adams's model should instead be understood merely as a clarification of it.[72] Regardless, Murphy's proposal seems correct; it incorporates the natural law theorist's insight concerning the important role human nature plays in determining moral goodness while not ignoring the important role God plays as the ultimate moral exemplar. My divine love theory adds to this proposal that God's ultimate intention is for humans to specifically resemble God's inner-trinitarian relationships by joining this fellowship of love—that is, by loving him and loving others.

Some may question how human actions could possibly resemble the trinitarian relationships, considering how different human persons are from divine persons. To understand this resemblance, consider two examples: first, a human being protecting an innocent person from a murderer, and second, a human being murdering an innocent person. It may seem puzzling how these actions could resemble the trinitarian relationships, or fail to resemble them in the second example, because the divine persons can't die. The reason protecting an innocent person from a murderer reflects the trinitarian relationships is that, because of the way God created humans—that is, human nature—such an act is a loving thing to do, and doing something that is loving resembles the loving relationships between the persons of the Trinity; thus it's morally good.

---

71. Murphy, *God and Moral Law*, 149.
72. Adams, *Finite and Infinite Goods*, 28–49.

Conversely, because of the way God created humans, the act of murdering an innocent person is not a loving thing to do, and thus it doesn't resemble the loving relationships between the persons of the Trinity; thus it's morally bad.

In other words, it's not the protecting of the innocent (or the murdering of the innocent) but the loving (or unloving) aspect of that action that resembles (or doesn't resemble) the relationships among the persons of the Trinity. Thus, hypothetically, if God had made beings that felt great pleasure at being murdered and then came back to life shortly after, murder would be a loving thing to do and thus morally good. In this way, then, facts about the human nature God created and facts about the relationships between the persons of the Trinity work together to determine what's morally good and bad.

The reason Jesus's incarnation—that is, his taking on human nature—is so important for us in terms of learning what's morally good, and why the New Testament often encourages us to imitate him, is that he gives us a perfect example of what it looks like to love others (which reflects the trinitarian relationships) within the specific context of human nature. He gives us an example to follow of how a human should love other humans, given human nature is the way it is, and thereby how humans in particular can resemble the loving relationships between the persons of the Trinity.

My fourth response to this objection is that natural law theory, compared to my divine love theory, doesn't provide an adequate explanation for why communion with God is good. According to some versions of natural law theory, something is good for a particular kind—that is, something with a particular nature— if it leads to, or accomplishes, the purpose that kind was created for according to God's intention for it. For example, natural law theorist J. Budziszewski writes, "Nature may be conceived as an ensemble of things with particular natures, and a thing's nature may be thought of as the design imparted to it by the Creator— in traditional language, as a purpose implanted in it by the divine art, that it be moved to a determinate end."[73]

In the case of human beings, some natural law theorists, as seen above, argue that God intended humanity to flourish and therefore whatever accomplishes this divine intention is what is morally good. In addition, some natural law theorists claim, much like I do in my divine love theory, that the ultimate human flourishing—that is, the ultimate purpose, or telos, God has for humans—is that they would be in loving communion with him. Thus, according to these versions of natural law theory, this communion with God is the ultimate moral

---

73. Budziszewski, *Line through the Heart*, 10–11.

good for humanity. For example, Haines and Fulford write, "There is also an end which is natural to humans as humans—the ultimate end or final cause of human nature, God—who is the ultimate telos of all human action, regardless of whether or not individual human beings are aware of it. Indeed, as many theologians have remarked, man was made to be united with God. . . . For man's ultimate good, and thus only source of ultimate and eternal happiness, is union with God."[74]

Thus, there's a deep similarity here between these versions of natural law theory and my divine love theory, which holds that God's ultimate intention for humans is that they would join the loving fellowship that already exists between the persons of the Trinity. However, these natural law theorists don't have an adequate explanation for why communion with God is good. This highlights once again the following important difference between some versions of natural law theory and my theory: according to the former, something is good if it accomplishes God's intention for it, whereas according to the latter, something is good if it resembles God. With the former, the story ends with God's intentions—something is good if it accomplishes what God intended it to. Hypothetically, then, if God intended humans to *not* be in communion with him, then that result would be good for them. My theory provides a fuller explanation for why communion with God is good; it's good because it resembles God's inner-trinitarian communion of loving relationships. My theory is a more adequate and satisfying explanation because it goes deeper than God's intentions and explains *why* that intention itself, for humanity to commune with God, is necessarily good and thus could not be otherwise.

My fifth response to this objection is that some natural law theories, because they maintain that moral good is based on human nature, promote the unnecessary misunderstanding that therefore it's improper to characterize God as a moral being. For example, Brian Davies argues that it's inappropriate to call God either morally good or a moral agent.[75] Such natural law theorists arrive at this conclusion because they mistakenly define moral good as that which leads a being to flourish or achieve its telos, and since God is already a perfect and maximally great being, there's nothing he can do to flourish more or to further achieve his telos. Natural law theorist Richard Howe explains that, assuming this definition of moral good, it "follows that God is not a moral being. This is so

---

74. Haines and Fulford, *Natural Law*, 35–36. To make their point, they provided quotes from Augustine, Aquinas, and Calvin that affirm that union with God is the chief purpose, or telos, of humanity.

75. Davies, *Reality of God*, 84–111.

because God does not choose a course of action to perfect Himself as He aims at a *telos*. God does not have a *telos* and cannot be perfected because He already is infinite being itself."[76]

It should be noted that *if* we define what's morally good as that which leads a being to flourish or achieve its telos, then certainly God isn't morally good or a moral being at all. But the pertinent question is whether this is the correct definition of what's morally good. In response to this issue, David Baggett and Jerry Walls write that

> much of Davies's analysis of Aquinas is consistent with the best work in theistic ethics over the last several decades, but this further denial of God's goodness is exactly where Davies is most vulnerable to criticism, in our estimation. The way he defines his terms, he's not exactly wrong, for we would admit that God is neither morally good nor a moral agent in the way that Davies casts such notions; but the sober fact is that his definition of moral goodness in particular is overly narrow and lacks sufficient motivation. So, by our lights, it betrays a failure of conversational cooperation.[77]

They continue by arguing that Davies's position, which they call a "Copernican paradigm shift to deny God's moral goodness," seems to "strain credulity, and smacks of a game of semantics—this trotting out of the category of God as 'perfectly complete' and castigating of the category of moral goodness, a much less obscure idea."[78]

Baggett and Walls clarify that "Davies is not saying that God is evil, but that the characterization of him as morally good is somehow inappropriate, smacking of anthropomorphism."[79] Brian Huffling affirms this line of thinking and thus also concludes that "God is not a moral being." He goes on to attempt to explain away the Bible's various descriptions of God as morally good by arguing that these descriptions are merely anthropomorphisms: "The Bible often uses various figures of speech and metaphor to talk about God. In fact the Bible more often than not uses physical terms to describe God. However, orthodox Christians do not think that God is physical, even though there are probably more descriptions of God that seem to indicate him having a material body than being merely a spirit. . . . These descriptions of God are anthropomorphic,

---

76. Howe, "Does Morality Need God," 8–9.
77. Baggett and Walls, *Good God*, 56.
78. Baggett and Walls, *Good God*, 56.
79. Baggett and Walls, *Good God*, 55.

meaning that they are just ways of describing God in human language without really being literal."[80] Christians have historically taken the physical descriptions of God in the Bible as anthropomorphisms because the Bible also says God is nonphysical—that is, spiritual. But nowhere in the Bible does it say that God isn't a moral being or that moral concepts don't apply to God. The idea that God isn't a moral being is a conclusion that these natural law theorists come to through their philosophical reasoning. There's nothing wrong with philosophical reasoning per se, but when it leads you to the conclusion that much of the Bible should be dismissed as mere figures of speech and metaphor, that's a good sign that something has gone awry in your philosophical reasoning.

Some natural law theorists are drawn to the conclusion that God is not a moral being because, similar to some classical trinitarians, they want to avoid making God too humanlike. However, Baggett and Walls insightfully point out that, while it is true that moral

> language as applied to God functions in an importantly different respect from when it applies to us . . . the new contribution by Davies here is the further inference that, owing to such distance between God and us, and to his unique status as Creator and as an ontologically complete being, God is not properly understood as morally good at all. We think that this claim is wrongly predicated on an overly narrow view of what moral goodness means. It's far from clear that Davies's inference is warranted in any way by the category of the "completely actual"—a Thomistic notion that in truth is not nearly as transparent or pertinent as the more straightforward category of moral perfection. . . . God's goodness may be more than moral, but it's not less.[81]

Certainly we don't want to think of God as more humanlike than he really is, but we should be careful, in protecting against this error, that we don't go too far in the other direction and conclude there are no similarities between God and the human beings he created in his image.

The natural law theorists who affirm that God is not a moral being and that moral concepts don't apply to him do so primarily because they have made the initial mistake of defining moral good as that which accomplishes the flourishing, or telos, of a being. Baggett and Walls sum up their evaluation of this issue: "We are left with the nagging suspicion that, having invoked this metaphysical

---

80. Huffling, "God Is Not a Moral Being."
81. Baggett and Walls, *Good God*, 57.

category of perfect completeness, Davies then, through a subtle semantic maneuver, ends up denying rational ascriptions of moral goodness to God in a way that invites unnecessary misunderstanding and leaves the door open to things that should never be admitted."[82] Alternatively, my divine love theory, since it maintains that something is morally good if it images, or resembles, God, doesn't result in this unnecessary misunderstanding.

The third objection that some natural law theorists may have against my divine love theory has to do with moral obligation. As a reminder, my theory affirms, along with most divine command theories, that our moral obligations are generated by God's commands. In the previous sections I made two important qualifications concerning this proposal: (1) our obligations originate in God's will but only become effective for us when he makes us aware of his will somehow, and (2) the term *command* here is being used as a general term to encompass all the ways God makes us aware of his will, which include direct verbal commands but also our reason, moral intuition, and conscience.

Many natural law theorists reject this theory of moral obligation because they maintain, similar to their position on moral good, that our moral obligations are generated by facts about human nature, not divine commands. For example, natural law theorists Boyd and VanArragon explain that "those who subscribe to divine command morality . . . hold that the rightness of actions is determined solely by the commands of God. . . . By contrast, those who subscribe to a natural law morality . . . hold that God commands actions because they are right. They claim, further, that the rightness of actions is determined by various features of human nature rather than by God's commands."[83] Later they assert that "*what makes an act right or wrong is whether it does or does not contribute to human flourishing.* God *knows* what acts are right and wrong, and God commands and forbids accordingly."[84]

In spite of this difference, it should be noted that my divine love theory and natural law theory are similar in that both claim our obligations originate in God's will—that is, in his intentions for us. But the former claims they only become effective when God makes us aware of his will somehow, whereas the latter claims these intentions are built into, and reflected in, human nature such that they are effective because of the way God created human nature. In other words, according to some natural law theories, human nature ultimately determines

---

82. Baggett and Walls, *Good God*, 58.
83. Boyd and VanArragon, "Ethics," 300.
84. Boyd and VanArragon, "Ethics," 305.

what our moral obligations are, rather than God's commands determining our moral obligations. The two theories could be brought even closer together if one considers God's creation of human nature as a form of command—that is, a form of making humans aware of his will for them. However, natural law theorists do not usually see it that way but instead maintain that human nature itself, being the way it is such that certain things cause it to flourish and other things do not, ontologically instantiates our moral obligations.

Murphy has been an adamant proponent of this facet of natural law theory and hence a sharp critic of divine command theory. He affirms Aquinas's position on natural law and explains that on "Aquinas's account, the binding power of moral norms—their obligatoriness—is to be understood by reference not to divine commands but to the human good, promotion, protection, and respect for which is dictated by those norms."[85] Murphy even calls divine command theory "perverse," "paradoxical," and "bizarre" because it claims that nondivine facts about human nature can of themselves morally necessitate God's action (the giving of certain commands) but cannot of themselves morally necessitate human action (generate moral obligations for humans). He laments that this "is a perverse result. The notion that while created nature can of itself morally necessitate *God's* action, it cannot of itself morally necessitate *human* action is exceedingly paradoxical—that created nature has the power to bind God to action but lacks the power to bind us to action is a bizarre combination."[86]

My first response to this third objection regards Murphy's complaint that divine command theory is perverse. Hare has already pushed back against this complaint by arguing that divine command theory doesn't entail that God's action is necessitated, or obligated, by nondivine facts about human nature but is merely constrained by them. He also argues that we shouldn't find it odd that God is constrained by these facts, yet we are not obligated by them, because, to put it simply, we are different from God. His response to Murphy's lament is worth quoting at length:

> God is constrained though not determined by facts about our nature. . . . [Murphy] proposed that it is odd to say that *we* are not obligated by the maximal set of non-moral, non-divine facts (where these include facts about our nature), but *God* is so constrained. The response is that this is not odd at all. We and God are different. Both God and we are constrained by the non-

---

85. Murphy, *God and Moral Law*, 77.
86. Murphy, *God and Moral Law*, 124.

moral and non-divine facts, and neither God nor we are obligated by those facts. But we are obligated by God's commands. God does not require an obligator at all, but *is* the obligator. Even in those cases of moral law (if there are any) in which God's command is constrained by the non-moral, non-divine facts, we are obligated not by those facts but by God's command.[87]

Hare points out that Murphy was mistaken when he claimed that divine command theorists think God is *obligated* by facts about human nature in the same sense that humans are *obligated* (either by God's commands, according to divine command theorists, or by facts about human nature, according to natural law theorists). As Hare helpfully clarifies, divine command theorists don't think God is obligated in this sense by these facts about human nature, but only constrained by them.

My second response to this objection is that, as I argued in chapter 4, moral obligation is inherently personal and social. It's personal because we're obligated only to persons, not facts, principles, or natures. Moral obligation is also social, as Adams argued, in that obligations arise in the context of social relationships between persons. The claim of some natural law theories that obligations are generated by facts about human nature does not satisfy these two important aspects of moral obligation. Hare summarizes the inadequacy of this component of natural law theory well: "Moral obligation requires not just a presumption against doing something but an obligator, and that deducibility from human nature and non-divine facts alone therefore has to be denied."[88] Alternatively, my divine love theory includes these two critical components of moral obligation, the personal and the social, in that it maintains we're ultimately obligated to a personal being—that is, God—and that our obligations arise in the context of our social relationship with him.

My third response to this objection is that moral obligation cannot be determined by facts about what causes human nature to flourish and reach its end, or telos, because there are multiple ways humans can do this. As a reminder, some natural law theorists maintain that our moral obligations are determined and generated by facts about human nature, and specifically by facts about what leads human nature to flourish, with the ultimate flourishing being our telos—union with God. According to them, God then commands certain things because of these facts, but it's these facts that determine and generate our obligations, not

---

87. Hare, *God's Command*, 112.
88. Hare, *God's Command*, 112.

the commands themselves. For example, Boyd and VanArragon present the following central tenets of the natural law theory they defend:

1. All human beings have a specific nature, with a specific end, in common.
2. Moral precepts are grounded in that human nature.
3. The basic moral precepts cannot change unless human nature changes.
4. These precepts are teleological in character—they direct human beings to their end.
5. All properly functioning human beings know what the basic moral precepts are.[89]

They explain that a divine command theory that would be most similar to their theory is one that agrees that God chooses the commands he does because they lead to human flourishing. However, they explain the main difference would still be "that we believe that an act's contributing to creaturely flourishing makes it morally right, while [this hypothetical divine command theory they're considering] claims that though God commands in accordance with what enable creatures to flourish, it is God's commanding that makes an act morally right."[90]

My third response mostly comes from the work of Duns Scotus and his contemporary advocate John Hare. The key underlying assumption behind this response is that there are multiple paths that lead to human flourishing and eventually to union with God, our ultimate end. Hare, drawing on Duns Scotus's work, makes a compelling case that this is a reasonable and plausible assumption.[91] Insofar as this assumption is correct, there "are innumerable ways God could have ordered us towards union [with God], even given the nature with which we were created. The route God has in fact chosen is binding upon us because God has chosen it."[92] In other words, God chose one of these possible paths and gave us commands that lead us along this particular route.

The commands God has given us *do* lead to human flourishing and to union with him, but there are other paths that would accomplish this too that God hasn't commanded. The flourishing of human nature does influence what God commands in that certainly he wouldn't command us down a path that didn't lead to flourishing and union with him, but human flourishing alone doesn't necessitate the particular commands he gives because there are multiple paths

89. Boyd and VanArragon, "Ethics," 303.
90. Boyd and VanArragon, "Ethics," 313.
91. Hare, *God's Command*, 99–141.
92. Hare, *God's Call*, 77.

to such flourishing. Hare explains that "contrary to some versions of natural law theory . . . [God's commands are] not deducible from our human nature [because] God could have chosen a different route for beings with our nature to reach our final end."[93] Regardless of why God chose the particular route for us that he did, since there were multiple routes he could have chosen from, it's more plausible that the commands to follow this particular route generate our obligations, not the fact that the route leads to our final end.

I affirm that there is a harmony between the commands God has given and human flourishing. Hare explains, "Since God has prescribed for us a route to our final end that is in perfect harmony with our nature, we can expect to see this harmony by means of our reason. We can see that when we tell the truth, respect each other's lives and property, honor our parents, and so on, we progress towards the life that we are made for, the life of being co-lovers with God. But Scotus insists that what we see is a harmony, or a beauty, or a fittingness, and not an entailment of the commands from our nature."[94] The mistake of some natural law theorists is that, when they see this harmony between God's commands and human flourishing, they incorrectly assume the flourishing is what generates the obligations for us and determines God to give us the commands he does. Hare clarifies that "God does indeed fit the commandments to our nature, so that we can flourish by keeping them. But this is not the justification of the obligation. We have the obligation just because they are commanded. The fittingness with our nature is not a justification but a partial explanation (in Aristotelian terms a 'cause,' which we can partially see retrospectively after being given the commandments) of God's giving them to us in the first place."[95] That the commands God gives lead to flourishing cannot be the determining reason God commanded them because there are multiple routes to human flourishing. Though his commands do accord with what leads to human flourishing, it's God's commands that make an act morally obligatory. Thus, we're not obligated by facts about what causes human nature to flourish but by the commands God has given us for the particular path of flourishing he has chosen for us.

Objection 4: Concerns with God's Will Being Arbitrary

Some have expressed concern with theories that claim our moral obligations are generated by God's commands because they believe this grounds morality on

---

93. Hare, *God's Call*, 115.
94. Hare, *God and Morality*, 103.
95. Hare, *God's Command*, 242.

God's will alone, which would make morality arbitrary. Since nearly all divine command theorists claim our obligations are generated by God's commands, this concern is most often directed toward divine command theory in general. However, this concern also applies to my divine love theory because it shares this feature with divine command theories.

This concern stems from a perceived implication of divine command theories—namely, that if morality is based on what God wills to command, and if God could have willed to command anything, then this means morality is arbitrary. For example, natural law theorists Boyd and VanArragon claim that divine command theorists "hold that the rightness of actions is determined solely by the commands of God. . . . God is not subject to some independent standard of moral rightness but is free to command whatever he wills."[96] As William Mann notes, this "can conjure up images of a God who might have approved of just any kind of action, including murder, and who might have disapproved of just any kind of action, including neighborly love."[97]

Though natural law theorists aren't the only ones who have raised this concern, historically their theory is the one that's often compared and contrasted with divine command theory. For example, in defending Duns Scotus against this criticism, William Frank explains that in the natural law theorist's

> Aristotelian framework . . . cosmic and ethical order finally comes to rest in ultimate ontological essences or natures. By contrast, where such forms are eliminated in the name of divine liberty and omnipotence, cosmology and morality lose their substantive, rational foundation. In the often told story of the history of ideas, the philosopher-theologians of the late medieval and early renaissance period opted for the nominalist, anarchical alternative [God's arbitrary will as the basis of morality]. . . . Most versions of this narrative portray Duns Scotus as a patriarch of later nominalistic theologians.[98]

This regularly given narrative frames the difference between natural law theory and divine command theory around the historic move from essentialism, which affirms the existence of essences, to nominalism, which in this context means rejecting the existence of essences. In presenting the narrative this way, some try to associate divine command theory with nominalism by claiming that

---

96. Boyd and VanArragon, "Ethics," 300.
97. Mann, *God, Modality, and Morality*, 273.
98. Frank, "Preface to This Edition," x.

premodern morality was based on human nature (I'm using the terms *nature* and *essence* interchangeably here) but that in the modern era, when natures were rejected, all that was left to base morality on was God's bare arbitrary will.

In other words, some claim that divine command theorists adopted their theory, which supposedly bases morality on God's will instead of human nature, in response to their rejection of essences, including human nature. It should be noted that just because some were motivated to adopt divine command theory because they embraced nominalism, this doesn't mean that all who affirm that obligations are generated by God's commands necessarily embrace nominalism and reject essentialism. As Frank goes on to argue, Duns Scotus didn't reject essentialism, and neither does my divine love theory.

However, it should be admitted that there are versions of divine command theory, most famously William of Ockham's, that do embrace nominalism and also ground morality sheerly in God's will, thus facing this problem of arbitrariness. Zagzebski describes these versions as "strong" divine command theories and explains they maintain that "God's will is logically or metaphysically prior to both good/bad and right/wrong. . . . God's will is the metaphysical ground of evaluative properties, at least the evaluative properties of acts and the ends of acts."[99] Elsewhere she describes "strong" divine command theories as those that make "the divine will the source of moral value"[100] and maintain that "God created morality by an act of his free will and imposed it upon us."[101]

Natural law theorists often press this issue against divine command theorists while arguing that their theory doesn't face this problem since, on natural law theory, morality isn't arbitrary because it's determined by human nature. It's debatable whether this alternative really solves the arbitrariness problem or just kicks it down the road a bit because God's choice to create human nature the way he did seems as though it could be just as arbitrary as his choice of what to command. If he had created human nature differently, and if morality is based on human nature, then morality would have been different too, and then we're back to the root of morality, in this case God's choice to create human nature the way he did, being arbitrary. Regardless, I covered several major problems with natural law theories above, and thus here I'll provide other responses to this concern of arbitrariness.

---

99. Zagzebski, *Divine Motivation Theory*, 279.
100. Zagzebski, *Divine Motivation Theory*, 258.
101. Zagzebski, *Divine Motivation Theory*, 185.

Is there something else, something that's not arbitrary in any way, that could constrain God's will from choosing nefarious commands? If this constraining factor existed outside God, then God wouldn't be the ultimate source of morality because this external factor would be what determined morality, not God. Therefore, many have come to the conclusion that this constraining factor is internal to God and have proposed this factor is his own moral nature. Peppers-Bates explains, "Internal constraints flowing from God's own perfect nature are not theologically worrisome as external constraints."[102] She helpfully contrasts the difference between this proposal and what Zagzebski calls "strong divine command theory" with these rhetorical questions: "Are God's commands grounded in His bare will, in total, radical, freedom with no criteria or constraint? Or does God's being (encompassing His will/wisdom/goodness, etc.) ground God's commands?"[103] I affirm God's being grounds His commands, as do most divine command theorists. For example, divine command theorists James Hanink and Gary Mar maintain, "God's creative will has given us a nature that cannot be perfected by such acts [cruel ones], nor could God do otherwise in the light of His nature. So God's legislative will could not mandate such norms. . . . Just as God's will is one with God's reason, so also is God's will one with the goodness—and the love—that God is. But such a will cannot bring into existence a human nature that would be perfected precisely in acting in a fashion that made it less like its creator."[104] Thus, we can say that God's nature guides his will to choose both what to create human nature to be like and what commands to give.

Most contemporary divine command theorists have embraced this solution, as do I in my divine love theory. Quinn writes that it "is the divine nature itself, and not divine commands or intentions, that constrains the antecedent intentions God can form [in choosing which commands to give]."[105] I also affirm that the ultimate ground of God's commands is not his will but his moral and trinitarian nature. As a reminder, my theory, like Adams's, bases only moral obligation, not moral value, on God's will. In addition, as I've explained in this section, though obligation is based on God's will in the sense that he chooses which commands to give us that then generate our obligations, his will is actually constrained in this context by his nature. Thus, God's trinitarian nature is ultimately the foundation for both moral value, in that other things are morally

102. Peppers-Bates, "Divine Simplicity," 367.
103. Peppers-Bates, "Divine Simplicity," 367.
104. Hanink and Mar, "Euthyphro," 251.
105. Quinn, "Divine Command Theory," 71.

good if they resemble him, and moral obligation, in that his trinitarian nature guides and constrains his will in choosing what obligations to generate for us via his commands. In chapter 9, in response to an objection from Wielenberg, I'll further explore the exact relationship between God's nature and his commands.

Objection 5: Concerns with Platonism

Some may be concerned that my divine love theory is too Platonic, thus incurring some of the same criticism Wielenberg's Platonic model incurs, because it affirms Adams's notion that God plays the role Plato assigned to the Good. While it's true that Adams's model is Platonic in this regard, it is Platonic in a different sense than Wielenberg's. Wielenberg affirms the existence of Plato's abstract objects, or something close to them, whereas Adams posits that God, as a concrete object, functionally serves in the role that Plato assigned to the ultimate abstract object, the Good. Adams explicitly explains, "If God is the Good itself, then the Good is not an abstract object but a concrete (though not a physical) individual."[106] Jay Richards similarly describes God as "the one necessarily existing, personal, concrete being and causal agent."[107]

My divine love theory rejects the existence of abstract objects insofar as abstract objects are understood to be uncreated, eternal, and separate from God, because affirming such objects would conflict with the traditional Christian doctrine of God's aseity. The term *aseity* comes from a Latin word that means "of itself." Christians have traditionally believed that God is a self-existent being that doesn't exist through, or in dependence on, anything else; he is the sole ultimate reality. If there were abstract objects that were, like God, uncreated and eternal, then God wouldn't be the sole ultimate reality.[108]

This denial of abstract objects, sometimes called concretism, may cause some people to be concerned if they think that such a position also entails the rejection of universals. William Lane Craig and J. P. Moreland explain that a "universal is an entity that can be in more than one place at the same time or in the same place at different, interrupted time intervals. Redness, justice, being even, humanness are examples of universals. If redness is a universal, then if one sees (the same shade of) redness on Monday and again on Tuesday, the redness seen on Tuesday is identical to, is the very same thing as the redness seen on Monday."[109] Unfortunately, the term *nominalist* has been used both to describe someone who

---

106. Adams, *Finite and Infinite Goods*, 42.
107. Richards, *Untamed God*, 95.
108. Craig, *God Over All*, 3.
109. Craig and Moreland, *Philosophical Foundations*, 147.

rejects abstract objects and to describe someone who rejects universals. While it's possible for someone to adopt both forms of nominalism, this is not necessarily the case. For instance, Gonzalo Rodriguez-Pereyra explains, using the Aristotelian realist as an example, that a person can deny abstract objects and still affirm universals.[110] To avoid this confusion, Craig prefers to call his position against abstract objects "anti-realist" instead of nominalist.[111]

How could one affirm universals while believing that only concrete objects exist? The category of concrete objects isn't limited to just physical objects, nor is it limited to just particulars—a concretist also views nonphysical objects such as angels, thoughts, and God as concrete objects. While describing concretism (though he uses a different term for it), Paul Gould writes that such a position "is not to be understood necessarily as the rejection of properties, relations, propositions, possible worlds, and so on, rather, what is required of those who believe in such entities is that they think of them as concrete objects."[112]

For an example of a position that rejects abstract objects but affirms universals, Craig describes a person who identifies universals as thoughts in someone's mind yet considers those thoughts to be concrete objects.[113] This is a common position among Christians, with the added proviso that the mind in question is God's—thus a concretist interpretation of divine conceptualism. Adams notes that divine conceptualism achieves two of our deeply held intuitions—that truth exists beyond our human minds and that truth seems to be something that can only exist in minds.[114] It should be noted that Craig himself rejects divine conceptualism, though he sees it as the "most promising concretist view" and admits it is his "fallback position."[115] Craig describes himself as an anti-realist, and what he means by that description is that he rejects the reality of abstract objects as well as the concretist version of divine conceptualism (which he classifies as another form of realism).[116]

Should God's thoughts be considered as abstract or concrete objects? Greg Welty, a proponent of divine conceptualism, notes, "If divine ideas are 'concrete objects,' then my position is that abstract objects functionally speaking are concrete objects ontologically speaking."[117] In other words, God's thoughts (as

---

110. Rodriguez-Pereyra, "Nominalism in Metaphysics," §1.
111. Craig, *God Over All*, 8.
112. Gould, "Introduction," 12.
113. Craig, *God Over All*, 8.
114. Adams, *Virtue of Faith*, 218.
115. Craig, *God Over All*, 206.
116. Craig, *God Over All*, 72.
117. Welty, "Theistic Conceptual Realism," 95.

concrete objects) can play the functional role people often assign to abstract objects. Welty describes this interpretation of divine conceptualism as follows:

> It would be a version of nominalism [toward abstract objects, that is] insofar as the divine concepts are (presumably) concrete entities, perhaps mental events (images, dispositions, or intentions). An advocate of this interpretation of TCR [theistic conceptual realism] could hold the traditional nominalist view that the only things which exist are concrete substances. But insofar as the thoughts of one concrete substance in particular (God) satisfy the functional concept of universals, this is a nominalism that concedes, interestingly enough, that universals really exist. And so this interpretation of TCR would still be a realism about universals, insofar as the divine concepts exist independently of any human cognitive activity, and would exist even if there were no human thinkers at all. Indeed, they would exist even if there were no concrete substances in existence (besides God, of course).[118]

As a reminder, one of the motivations for taking the position that God's thoughts are concrete objects rather than abstract objects is to protect God's aseity, as I discussed above.[119]

While I've shown that properties can be considered as concrete objects in the mind of God, this cannot be the case for all properties; for example, God's essential properties would have to be an exception. Therefore, some affirm that all other properties, besides God's essential properties, are ideas in the mind of God.[120] But why couldn't God's essential properties also be properties that merely exist in God's mind? The problem with such a position is that it runs into the bootstrapping objection.

The bootstrapping objection is most well known as a problem for absolute creationism, another position concerning God's relationship to abstract objects. This position was brought to prominence by Thomas Morris and Christopher Menzel, who maintain that God created all concrete objects and all abstract objects (including all properties).[121] Many have rejected absolute creationism because of its vicious circularity that comes into play when one recognizes that

---

118. Welty, "Truth as Divine Ideas," 59–60.
119. For a dialogue about whether Thomas Aquinas should be considered a concretist in this regard, see Bridges, "Moderate-Realist Perspective."
120. Craig, *God Over All*, 1.
121. See Morris and Menzel, "Absolute Creation"; Menzel, "Theism." For a fuller treatment, see Leftow, *God and Necessity*.

some properties must exist prior to God's creation of them—for instance, God's property of being able to create properties. As Craig and Moreland explain, "God cannot coherently be said to create his own properties, since in order to create them, he must already possess them."[122] Gould notes that "many (including myself) think this [bootstrapping] problem fatal for the absolute creationism of Morris and Menzel."[123]

The bootstrapping objection also presents a problem for the divine conceptualist who claims that *all* properties are ideas in God's mind. Divine conceptualism runs into the bootstrapping circularity as well because some properties must exist prior to God conceiving of them—for example, God's property of being able to conceive of properties.[124] Richards explains this problem for divine conceptualism as follows: "The bootstrapping problem rears its ugly head again . . . [for] this would entail, for example, that God is all-powerful just because, from eternity, God has reflected on the fact that he is all-powerful. But clearly for this to be possible, God would have had to have the Property P01 of being able to think his omnipotence into existence. But perhaps, one might retort, God also thought *that* property into existence from eternity. Well, then he would have had to have another property P02, and off, once again, goes an infinite regress."[125]

The bootstrapping objection doesn't have to be the death knell for concretism, however. A concretist can view some properties as ideas in God's mind and other properties as essential properties of God himself. The important notion for the concretist is that all properties are concrete, not that they are all ideas in God's mind. Though they note that such a distinction among properties might appear ad hoc, Craig and Moreland describe a similar position as follows: "Perhaps . . . [someone] might maintain that all the properties that God exemplifies as part of his nature—for example, *being loving, being powerful* and so on—do not exist . . . as do other properties. Rather, as a brute fact, God, along with his nature, simply exists *a se*. Other properties, such as *being red*, are sustained by God, either by his intellect, will or in some other way."[126]

To summarize, because my divine love theory rejects abstract objects, it doesn't incur the same criticisms that Wielenberg's model incurs for being

---

122. Craig and Moreland, *Philosophical Foundations*, 505.
123. Gould, "Introduction," 10.
124. Craig and Moreland, *Philosophical Foundations*, 506.
125. Richards, *Untamed God*, 245. In a footnote Richards thanks Greg Welty for helping him see this point clearly.
126. Craig and Moreland, *Philosophical Foundations*, 505.

Platonic. Further, in this section I've explained that just because someone rejects the existence of abstract objects, she doesn't have to reject the existence of universals. I described and briefly defended an example of such a position, a concretist version of divine conceptualism, which rejects abstracts objects but affirms the existence of universals.

CHAPTER 6

DIVINE LOVE THEORY VERSUS
WIELENBERG'S ATHEISTIC MORAL THEORY

We now transition from theology to apologetics. Thus far this book has been mostly theological in the sense that I have attempted to describe reality using information from special revelation (Scripture) and general revelation (reason, intuitions, experience, etc.). Starting here, and continuing through the final chapter, this book will mostly be apologetic in that I will argue that my divine love theory is a better explanation for objective morality than Wielenberg's theory.

As a reminder, both Wielenberg and I agree on the *explananda*—that there are objective moral values and duties. However, I'm proposing that my divine love theory is a superior *explanans* for objective morality compared to Wielenberg's godless normative realism. In this section I'll show how my theory contains elements that are required for morality to be objective and that Wielenberg's theory lacks these elements. There are four such elements my theory provides that Wielenberg's does not: an exemplar for moral value, a human telos for moral obligation, a social context for moral obligation, and a head at the chain of moral obligation. For each of these four elements, I'll follow this pattern of argumentation:

1. Element X is required for morality to be objective.
2. My divine love theory contains element X.
3. Wielenberg's godless normative realism does not contain element X.
4. Therefore, my divine love theory is superior to godless normative realism as an explanation for objective morality.

I acknowledge that the force of these four arguments is conditioned on the strength of the first premise in each argument. In order to defend the first premise in each of these four arguments, that each respective element is required for morality to be objective, I'll summarize arguments by various philosophers but not fully reproduce said arguments. Though Wielenberg may or may not agree that these four elements are required for morality to be objective, the burden is on him to refute the arguments I'll summarize below. Even if these arguments fail to support the case that these four elements *are required* for morality to be objective, at a minimum they show that a theory that has these four elements *is a more plausible explanation* of objective morality than a model that lacks them.

An Exemplar for Moral Value

The first element required for objective morality that my theory provides, and Wielenberg's model does not, is an ultimate standard of morality from which to judge whether other things are good. Linda Zagzebski summarizes well the vital role an exemplar plays in moral theory when she explain its function "is to fix the reference of the term 'good person' or 'practically wise person' without the use of any concepts, whether descriptive or nondescriptive. An exemplar therefore allows the series of conceptual definitions to get started. The circle of conceptual definitions of the most important concepts in a moral theory—*virtue, right act, duty, good outcome*, and so on—is broken by an indexical reference to a paradigmatically good person."[1] Later she notes that an exemplar serves "as a standard of perfection against which the rest of us are measured [and thus] what is good for us in that sense is to imitate the exemplar."[2] Without such a fixed absolute exemplar, there's no standard by which to measure whether something is good or bad. While discussing how important it is for the exemplar to be morally perfect,

---

1. Zagzebski, *Divine Motivation Theory*, 45–46.
2. Zagzebski, *Divine Motivation Theory*, 113.

Zagzebski argues that "perfection has the capacity to ground value in a way that nothing short of perfection can. Like the sun in Plato's allegory of good in the *Republic*, perfect goodness is essentially diffusive, the source of all lesser goods."[3]

Like Robert Adams, Zagzebski maintains that God is the best candidate for this exemplar: "I have argued that the world is good because God is good. Persons are good because God is good. Motives are good because God's motives are good. And if God is not only good, but perfectly good, His perfect goodness is the standard for, and the source of, all evaluative properties."[4] With a perfectly moral being as the exemplar, there's something by which we can measure the goodness of other things. Zagzebski concludes, "God is good in the same way that the standard meter stick is one meter long. God is the standard of goodness."[5] Therefore, God, as perfect goodness, is the moral measuring tool to determine how good other things are.

I affirm, along with Adams and Zagzebski, that God is the Good, but my theory extends this idea by emphasizing that it's specifically God's triune nature that provides the ultimate exemplar for morality. This has the advantage of including loving relationships within the exemplar itself, helping explain what we know from human experience—namely, that loving relationships play a key role, if not the key role, at the very root of morality. God exists as three loving persons in eternal loving relationships with each other, and thus it's these relationships that provide an essential and constitutive part of the absolute standard of moral goodness. These loving personal relationships among the persons of the Trinity function as part of the foundational exemplar on which all of morality rests and by which other things can be morally measured. In other words, something is morally good if it resembles, in a morally pertinent way, the loving relationships between the persons of the Trinity.

Wielenberg's model has no such concrete exemplar. It's difficult to think how abstract brute ethical facts could serve as an exemplar when they have no moral value in and of themselves. Further, what makes more sense out of our human experience of valuing, above all else, our loving relationships—a perfect fellowship of loving persons or abstract brute ethical facts? Given our understanding that loving relationships are so valuable, when we pull back the final curtain of reality, it's more plausible to expect we will find there, not abstract objects, but concrete relationships of love. Compared to Wielenberg's proposal of brute ethical facts, it's much more plausible that there are real, concrete relationships

3. Zagzebski, *Divine Motivation Theory*, 274.
4. Zagzebski, *Divine Motivation Theory*, 274.
5. Zagzebski, *Divine Motivation Theory*, 285.

between divine persons that function as the ultimate exemplar and source of love, morality, and meaning. A God who exists as three persons in loving relationships with each other provides a fitting exemplar for morality that godless normative realism just doesn't have. Therefore, because an exemplar for moral value is required for morality to be objective, and since my divine love theory contains this element while Wielenberg's model does not, my theory is a superior explanation for objective morality compared to Wielenberg's.

A Human Telos for Moral Obligation

The second element required for objective morality that my divine love theory provides, and Wielenberg's theory does not, is a telos—that is, a purpose—for human beings. Alasdair MacIntyre explains well the importance of a telos in a theory of objective morality when he writes, "Unless there is a *telos* which transcends the limited goods of practices by constituting the good of a whole human life . . . , it will both be the case that a certain subversive arbitrariness will invade the moral life and that we shall be unable to specify the context of certain virtues adequately."[6]

As I detailed above in chapter 1, MacIntyre gives a thorough historical account of how, after the teleology-laden classical tradition was discarded, several conceptual systems were proposed that attempted to provide a new account of morality that would maintain the status, authority, and justification of moral rules. There were several attempts to find or construct a new basis for morality such that morality would apply objectively to all and not be merely an appeal to individual desire or will. However, he argues that ever since belief in "teleology was discredited moral philosophers have attempted to provide some alternative rational secular account of the nature and status of morality, but . . . all these attempts, various and variously impressive as they have been, have in fact failed, a failure perceived most clearly by Nietzsche."[7] MacIntyre even argues that Kant "in the second book of the second *Critique* . . . does acknowledge that without a teleological framework the whole project of morality becomes unintelligible. . . . If my thesis is correct, Kant was right; morality did in the eighteenth century, as a matter of historical fact, presuppose something very like the teleological scheme of God, freedom and happiness as the final crown of virtue which Kant propounds. Detach morality from that framework and you will no longer have morality."[8]

---

6. MacIntyre, *After Virtue*, 203.
7. MacIntyre, *After Virtue*, 256.
8. MacIntyre, *After Virtue*, 56.

Similarly, Thomas Nagel, an atheist and a moral realist like Wielenberg, affirms the vital role teleology must play in a theory of objective morality. He argues that if reductive materialism is true, then there is no telos, and if there is no telos, then one would have to conclude that there are no objective moral truths, that our moral beliefs are merely an accidental side effect of natural selection.[9] However, he suggests that on "a teleological account the existence of value is not an accident."[10] While he rejects the existence of God, he posits a naturalistic teleological order that governs the world from within: "The teleological hypothesis is that these things may be determined not merely by value-free chemistry and physics but also by something else, namely a cosmic predisposition to the formation of life, consciousness, and the value that is inseparable from them."[11] Though I find implausible Nagel's idea that teleology could exist without an intentional agent (i.e., God) behind it, I wholeheartedly affirm his argument that objective morality requires a telos. In other words, since a telos is required to avoid the conclusion that our beliefs about moral value are merely accidental, moral theories with a telos are superior explanations of objective morality than theories without it.

My divine love theory, as opposed to Wielenberg's godless normative realism, contains a telos for human beings. As noted previously, I, along with Duns Scotus and John Hare, maintain that God's ultimate intention, or telos, for humans is that they join the communion of loving relationships among the persons of the Trinity.[12] Hare chronicles how throughout history "all sorts of figures [say] . . . that humans are made for some kind of union with God, and that this is the fundamental basis for the moral life."[13] C. Stephen Evans concurs with this point when he says, "A plausible [divine command theory] will see moral obligation as something that has as its *telos* the transformation of humans. The point of morality is to help humans acquire the virtues or excellences that will make it possible for them to become friends of God."[14]

As I explained above, this is an area of agreement among many divine command theories and natural law theories. For example, according to Aquinas, natural law is merely the part of eternal law that is known by humanity through general revelation, whereas the eternal law is God's overall plan, or purpose,

---

9. Nagel, *Mind and Cosmos*, 122.
10. Nagel, *Mind and Cosmos*, 122.
11. Nagel, *Mind and Cosmos*, 123.
12. Hare, *God and Morality*, 75–122.
13. Hare, *God and Morality*, 108.
14. Evans, *God and Moral Obligation*, 158.

for creation, including his intentions for humanity. Natural law theorists Craig Boyd and Raymond VanArragon explain that on "Aquinas's view, our *telos* as human beings is happiness. That is the goal to which we by nature strive . . . [but] the only sort of happiness that is truly satisfying for human beings is found in communion with God."[15]

In contrast, it seems difficult for Wielenberg's atheistic model to sustain objective morality when it has no intentional purpose for human life. This intentionality is a key difference between my divine love theory and Wielenberg's godless normative realism. With the former there is an intentionality at the root of reality that provides the *should* required for objective morality. Without it, the dreaded fact-value dichotomy raises its ugly head once again—how can you get a *should* from an *is*? Without divine intentionality behind the universe, it's unclear how anything can have objective purpose or meaning. Angus Menuge, while criticizing Wielenberg's model, sums up the situation well: "In a godless world, there is no underlying *telos* (such as a divine will) according to which some natural properties conform to the way the world is supposed to be, while others do not. In this world, an action which exhibits the natural property kindness is no more supposed to happen than one which exhibits the natural property of cruelty. In that context, it is arbitrary to assert that an act's being kind makes it right, or that an act's being cruel makes it wrong. . . . One needs some teleological principle that tells us how the world is supposed to go."[16]

Wielenberg begins his book *Robust Ethics* with an attempt to address this issue by explaining how life can have meaning even if there's no ultimate purpose in the universe.[17] He concludes that "by engaging in intrinsically valuable activities a person can make her life meaningful in one important sense: she can make her life *good for her*."[18] The problem with this is that this sort of meaning (meaningful *for her*) is subjective, not objective, and thus relative in that it could vary by person. It's hard to see how objective morality could be built on the foundation of subjective beliefs about purpose and meaning. An objective purpose to life, such as the telos provided by my divine love theory, seems a much more plausible and stable basis for objective morality. Therefore, because a human telos is required for morality to be objective, and since my theory contains this element while Wielenberg's theory does not, my theory is a superior explanation for objective morality compared to Wielenberg's.

---

15. Boyd and VanArragon, "Ethics," 304.
16. Menuge, "Vindicating the Dilemma," 8.
17. Wielenberg, *Robust Ethics*, 2–6.
18. Wielenberg, *Robust Ethics*, 5.

A Social Context for Moral Obligation

The third element required for objective morality that my divine love theory provides, and Wielenberg's theory does not, is a social context for moral obligation. As I detailed above in chapter 4, Adams has made a strong case that moral obligations arise from social systems of relationships. In chapter 10 of his book *Finite and Infinite Goods*, he writes that his "main project in this chapter is to argue that facts of obligation are constituted by broadly social requirements."[19] The argument has multiple steps, but he summarizes it as follows:

> The most important difference between the right, or obligation, and the good, in my opinion, is that right and wrong, as matters of obligation, must be understood in relation to a *social* context, broadly understood. . . . If I have an obligation . . . I believe it can only be in a personal relationship or in a social system of relationships. If an action is wrong, likewise, there must be a person or persons, distinct from the agent, who may appropriately have an adverse reaction to it. For the meaning of the obligation family of ethical terms is tied to such reactions to the wrong.[20]

Adams goes on to defend this argument, beginning with J. S. Mill on the semantics of obligation, continuing with points about guilt and social requirement, and closing with replies to multiple objections to his thesis. To summarize, because morality is inherently personal, it seems quite reasonable to think that, as persons, we're only morally obligated to other persons, not impersonal things, principles, circumstances, material objects, or moral properties.

Adams extends the social theory of obligation to our relationship with God and suggests that this is ultimately where our obligations come from. He argues that it's only by getting God into the picture that "a social theory of the nature of moral obligation" avoids the charge that "it is too subjectivist."[21] In other words, "a more powerful theistic adaptation of the social requirement theory is obviously available."[22] While affirming Adams's conclusion, Zagzebski argues, "The notion of obligation in the social context that holds between God and us is indirectly defended by its similarity to obligation that arises out of relationships among human beings. . . . If something like obligation arises in loving relationships between human persons, who make demands on each other that, if not

---

19. Adams, *Finite and Infinite Goods*, 233.
20. Adams, *Finite and Infinite Goods*, 233.
21. Adams, *Finite and Infinite Goods*, 247.
22. Adams, *Finite and Infinite Goods*, 248.

met, harm the relationship and make blame and guilt appropriate, then it is only a small step to the view that all obligation arises in a similar fashion."[23]

Adams and Zagzebski aren't alone in arguing that the relationship between God and humans provides the context from which our moral obligations are generated. Hare concurs and summarizes Adams's idea as follows: "Adams makes the argument that our notion of obligation or duty makes most sense against the background of a belief that we are under obligation to some person or persons, and argues that God is the most appropriate person for such a role, in regards to moral obligation."[24] Evans similarly concludes that moral obligations are universal because all "humans are God's creatures and thus all participate in the social relation that grounds moral obligations."[25]

I agree with Adams and these other authors that our moral obligations arise from our relationship with God. However, my theory also brings in important information regarding God's triune nature to show how loving relationships exist at the very deepest level of ultimate reality—that is, within God. This additional information helps explain how and why reality itself is inherently relational. Millard Erickson argues that if the Creator consists of three persons in loving relationships with each other, then "the fundamental characteristic of the universe is personal . . . [and] reality is primarily social."[26] Because relationships are a primordial part of reality, they enjoy the gravitas of a metaphysical necessity as opposed to merely a contingent reality that only came about when God created human beings.

It's not too much of a stretch to see an application for moral obligation from the following explanation by William Hasker, who, though not discussing morality in particular, notes how God's trinitarian nature reinforces the importance of personal relationships: "For those who find *personal relationships* to be central to what transpires between God and God's human creatures, a . . . doctrine of the Trinity provides a powerful reinforcement by finding such . . . relationships in the very being of God."[27] Erickson explains well some of the implications for human beings if in fact God exists as a communion of loving persons:

> To the extent that the individual reflects the image of the Triune God, that individual would not be solitary or independent, but would be related to

23. Zagzebski, *Divine Motivation Theory*, 263.
24. Hare, *God and Morality*, 262.
25. Evans, *God and Moral Obligation*, 32.
26. Erickson, *God in Three Persons*, 220–21.
27. Hasker, *Metaphysics*, 211.

other persons. . . . Note, too, the nature of such relationships, if they are to reflect the nature of the intratrinitarian relationships. . . . The type of relationship that should characterize human persons . . . would be one of unselfish love and submission to the other, seeking the welfare of the other over one's own. Humility, then, in the best senses of the word, will be one of the prized virtues.[28]

If in fact obligation is ultimately relational, God's triunity provides a fitting explanation for why there's a relational context to reality in the first place in which moral obligation can arise. God's trinitarian nature provides the overall relational context for reality in general and then his creation of human beings was merely an extension of that ultimate relational context. When God created us, it was a natural carryover from the ultimate reality of divine persons that we, as human persons created in his image, would be accountable to him via such a relationship.

That God exists as a fellowship of three persons in loving relationships with each other provides a foundation for the relational context of moral obligation that Wielenberg's theory does not have. While he could similarly affirm that obligation arises from our relationships with other humans, compared with my divine love theory, his theory lacks a good explanation as to how and why this is the case. If Wielenberg is correct, then personal social relationships only arose accidentally through a contingent evolutionary process when humans evolved to such a level. My theory provides a better explanation for the relational context of reality that is so vital for the existence of moral obligation. An essentially personal and relational source of morality (God as Trinity) fits the personal aspect of our experience of morality better than Wielenberg's proposed impersonal Platonic source. Therefore, because a social context is required for morality to be objective, and since my theory contains this element while Wielenberg's theory does not, my theory is a superior explanation for objective morality compared to Wielenberg's.

A Personal Authority at the Head of the Chain of Moral Obligation

The fourth element required for objective morality that my divine love theory provides, and Wielenberg's theory does not, is a personal authority at the head of the chain of moral obligation. If my argument in the previous section is correct, that objective moral obligations arise out of relationships, then there must be *someone* that humanity is in a relationship with to generate our obligations. This

---

28. Erickson, *God in Three Persons*, 332–33.

someone must be personal because we're obligated only to persons, not impersonal things such as objects or principles. In addition, this someone must also be an agent that we're accountable to such that, as our ultimate moral authority, this agent functions as the top of the hierarchy of our moral duties. A case can be made for both of these requirements from our moral experience and with reasoned arguments. Vern Poythress makes such an argument when he writes, "Moral absolutes imply personal responsibility. Persons are ultimately responsible only to persons. . . . The rule, to make a claim on us, must come from an authority. And authority is always personal. . . . If we doubt the personal character of authority, we can also observe that a rule must be specific, and this requires language like meaning and articulation, which belong only to persons. So moral authority is personal. And to have moral absolutes, the moral authority must be absolute. So we must have a personal absolute."[29]

The work of Immanuel Kant provides support for my line of reasoning here in that he too argued there must be an ultimate source of moral duty. This may come as a surprise to many because he's often portrayed as a critic of appealing to religion in general when it comes to morality and even a harsher critic of divine command theory in particular. However, Hare has made an extensive case that Kant was against only a specific type of divine command theory and that overall "Kant continued to believe and urged us to believe that a personal God exists, and that we should recognize our duties as God's commands."[30] Hare observes that the previously predominant secular interpretation of Kant has been "shifting somewhat in the last decade or so, and we are starting to see a new type of Kant scholarship that is much more faithful to his Christian background and continuing sympathies."[31] Hare admonishes Kant's secular followers by claiming that, "when we enter into his system from the inside, rather than reading into him our own preferences, we can see that the system depends on a large number of traditional theistic assumptions. If we abandon these assumptions, the system simply doesn't work."[32] It's beyond the scope of this book to wade through Kant's work in an attempt to ascertain his true intentions. However, even if Hare's interpretation of Kant is incorrect, such that the argument below is more Hare's than Kant's, it should be evaluated on its own merit, regardless of where it came from and whether Kant would agree with it.

---

29. Poythress, *Knowing and the Trinity*, 335–36.
30. Hare, *God's Call*, 87–88.
31. Hare, *God's Call*, 88. Hare gives several examples of such scholarship.
32. Hare, *God's Call*, 88.

To summarize Hare's case, it's best to begin with the following quote from the preface of Kant's *Religion within the Bounds of Bare Reason*, a quote often used by others to try to prove his disdain for thinking that religion is necessary for morality: "Morality, insofar as it is based on the concept of the human being as one who is free, but who precisely therefore also binds himself through his reason to unconditional laws, is in need neither of the idea of another being above him in order for him to cognize his duty, nor, in order for him to observe it, of an incentive other than the law itself. . . . Hence on its own behalf morality in no way needs religion. . . . Morality needs . . . no purpose, neither for cognizing what one's duty is, nor for impelling one to its performance."[33] However, just two paragraphs later Kant concluded his preface by claiming that "morality, therefore, leads inescapably to religion, through which it expands to the idea of a powerful moral legislator, outside the human being, in whose will the final purpose (of the world's creation) is that which at the same time can be, and ought to be, the final purpose of the human being."[34] Hare argues that these two statements can be reconciled when we understand that Kant was presenting a hypothetical conditional in the first section, as indicated by the following phrase from the first quote: "insofar as it is based on the concept of the human being as one who is free." He argues that Kant's point is that in fact "we are *not* merely free beings; we are also what he calls 'creatures of need.' If we were merely free, then we would not need the idea of a being over us, because we would be like God, who has no idea of a being over God. . . . Kant distinguished between ordinary members of the kingdom of ends and the head of the kingdom, who is also a member, but who (unlike the other members) is not subject to the will of any other."[35] In other words, God is the head of the kingdom of morality, the authority, if you will, to whom we are accountable.

Hare elaborates on Kant's position: "Kant distinguishes between the head of the moral kingdom to which we belong and the rest of the membership of this kingdom, and says that the head of the kingdom must be a completely independent being, without needs and with an unlimited power adequate to his will. There is no doubt that Kant is talking about God here, as head or king of the kingdom, and without such a king . . . there cannot be a kingdom at all."[36] According to Hare's interpretation of Kant, in order for us to have moral obligations, there must be a head at the chain of moral obligation who is completely

---

33. Kant, *Religion*, 1–2.
34. Kant, *Religion*, 4.
35. Hare, *God and Morality*, 163.
36. Hare, *God's Call*, 95.

independent, without needs, and unlimited in power. Kant was even more explicit about this in his *Critique of Practical Reason*, where he writes:

> The moral law leads through the concept of the highest good, as the object and final end of pure practical reason, *to religion, that is, to the recognition of all duties as divine commands, not as sanctions—that is, chosen and in themselves contingent ordinances of another's will*—but as essential *laws* of every free will in itself, which must nevertheless be regarded as commands of a supreme being because only from a will that is morally perfect (holy and beneficent) and at the same time all-powerful, and so through harmony with this will, can we hope to attain the highest good, which the moral law makes it our duty to take as the object of our endeavors.[37]

From this quote we can see that Kant added the following requirements for the head of the moral kingdom: he must be the supreme being, morally perfect, and all-powerful. According to Kant, then, for us to have real moral duties, there must be someone—a head, so to speak—at the end of the chain of moral obligation. Evans expresses his agreement with this interpretation of Kant when he writes that Kant "clearly holds that it is correct to understand moral obligations as divine commands, and also that God plays a significant role as the 'Head' of the Kingdom."[38]

My divine love theory fulfills this requirement in that it postulates God as the head of the chain of moral obligation. Of course, such an idea isn't unique to my theory, for nearly all divine command theories include this component. For example, Adams explains that obligations "that have full moral validity are aptly understood as constituted by divine commands, and thus by requirements arising in a social system in which God is the leading participant."[39] Though my theory shares this important element with other theistic theories, the point is that it satisfies this requirement for objective moral obligation, whereas Wielenberg's theory does not.

According to Wielenberg, the relationships between humans, and the circumstances that arise surrounding their relationships, are sufficient to generate moral obligations. For example, Wielenberg argues that if you encounter a horrible situation where an innocent child has accidently caught on fire, "the child's suffering,

---

37. Kant, *Critique of Practical Reason*, 107–8.
38. Evans, *God and Moral Obligation*, 142.
39. Adams, *Finite and Infinite Goods*, 233.

the presence of a bucket of water and so on give rise to your moral obligation to douse the flames. . . . My theory is that various features of the situation *cause* you to be obligated to help."[40] Certainly we *do* have objective moral obligations to fellow humans, but the key question is, *Would* we if there was no God—that is, no ultimate moral authority—that we were accountable to? If there's no God, we could possibly understand how the evolutionary process would have developed in us a strong subjective impulse to help the child, but it doesn't seem plausible to suppose that we have an objective obligation to do so that stems objectively from outside of us. Or, shall we say, it's more clearly the case that we do have objective obligations in such a scenario if there exists a God to whom we're accountable. Without an authority at the top of the moral hierarchy, it's unclear how there could be any ultimate objective moral accountability.

Hare similarly argues that our human-to-human relationships

> *do* sometimes make things morally obligatory. But we should see divine command theory as operating in answer to the normative question why we should hold ourselves under those obligations. Granted, for example, that, if I have promised to take my children out for lunch, and I have an obliga- tion to keep my promises, then I have an obligation to take them out for lunch. There is still the question why I should keep my promises. To draw the implication from my having said "I promise" to my obligation, I need to endorse the institution of promising, and the fact that God requires this faithfulness of me gives me a reason for this endorsement.[41]

Such an account doesn't deny the importance of the situational factors and the obligations we have to other humans, but both of those things are merely links in the chain, whereas God functions as the head of the chain pulling the whole thing along. The situation is similar to a truck that's pulling a trailer with a chain; the links in the chain are important, but without the pull of the truck the trailer goes nowhere. In an analogous way, God, because of his moral authority over us, generates the actual pulling force of objective obligations that we experi- ence coming from outside us. He is the ultimate source of the pull of our moral obligations, whereas the situational factors and the obligations we have to other humans are merely links in the chain.

---

40. Wielenberg, "Opening Speech," 40.
41. Hare, *God's Command*, 20.

Wielenberg's model is lacking because it's implausible to think that circumstances, natural events, situational factors, abstract objects, or even moral principles could, by themselves, apart from God, generate moral obligations. We're obligated not to impersonal things but to persons. In an impersonal universe with no personal authority at the head of the moral kingdom, there's no one we'd be guilty before and accountable to. Additionally, our human-to-human personal relationships alone, while important, are not sufficient enough to generate objective moral obligations because other humans don't have ultimate moral authority over us. Alternatively, an ultimate personal moral authority, such as a triune God, provides much greater warrant for thinking we really do have objective moral obligations. Therefore, because a personal authority at the head of the chain of moral obligation is required for morality to be objective, and since my divine love theory contains this element while Wielenberg's model does not, my theory is a superior explanation for objective morality compared to Wielenberg's.

CHAPTER 7

CONCLUSION TO PART TWO

In part 2 I proposed my divine love theory as an attempt to describe what objective morality is and where it comes from. It's trinitarian in that it maintains that God's triune nature is the source and foundation for all moral values and obligations.

I began in chapter 4 with an explanation as to why the loving relationships between the persons of the Trinity are so important to moral theory. Understanding the role that God's triune nature plays as the foundation of objective morality sheds light on a host of moral issues. To develop my theory, I used Robert Adams's model as a starting point. I affirmed Adams's theory of moral value—that is, that God is the ultimate good and other things are morally good if they resemble him in a morally pertinent sense. I also affirmed Adams's theory of moral obligation—that is, that our obligations are generated by God's commands. However, in both cases I showed how adding God's trinitarian nature elaborates and extends his model in significant and important ways.

In chapter 5 I addressed five objections to my divine love theory. First, I addressed objections concerning the loving relationships between the persons of the Trinity. Specifically, classical trinitarians may be concerned that positing inner-trinitarian relationships may entail erroneous aspects of social trinitarianism that should be rejected. I alleviated these concerns by explaining that one can, and many classical trinitarians do, affirm these divine relationships without accepting the aspects of social trinitarianism that most concern classical trinitarians.

Second, I addressed objections made by those who favor divine will theory over divine command theory. Though I raised problems with basing moral obligations on the divine will, I did affirm an important insight from divine will theorists—namely, that our moral obligations originate in God's will. However, I argued that these obligations apply to us only when God makes us aware of them somehow. In the midst of explaining how God can make us aware of our obligations in many ways, not just through direct verbal commands, I also addressed one of Wielenberg's objections. He argues that under divine command theory those who don't believe in God have no moral obligations. In response, I argued that for someone to have moral obligations, God must merely make the content of his will known to her somehow; he doesn't have to, in addition, make known to her that this content *is* his will in order for her to have moral obligations. God can make the content of his will known to us in many ways, including but not limited to our reason, conscience, and moral intuition.

Third, I discussed objections from natural law theorists because they've provided alternative explanations of how God serves as the foundation of moral value and moral obligation that conflict with my divine love theory. Specifically, some natural law theorists propose that human nature is the basis for moral value and that it also generates moral obligation. I argued that both of these proposals are riddled with problems, and thus my divine love theory is a superior explanation of how God functions as the source and foundation of objective morality.

Fourth, I addressed objections concerning the arbitrariness of God's will when it comes to moral theory. While some divine command theories ground morality solely in God's will, which would make morality arbitrary because then God could make anything morally right, most maintain that God's moral nature constrains his will, thus preventing morality from being arbitrary. Similarly, my divine love theory specifically maintains that God's will is constrained by his trinitarian nature.

Fifth, I addressed objections from those who may be concerned that my divine love theory is too Platonic. In response, I explained that my theory isn't Platonic in the sense that Wielenberg's model is Platonic. In brief, I explained that my theory rejects the existence of abstract objects and only affirms, like Adams, that God, as a concrete object, functions in the role Plato described for the ultimate abstract object, the Good.

In chapter 6 I began the apologetic task of showing how my divine love theory is a superior explanation for objective moral value and duties compared to Wielenberg's godless normative realism. First, my theory provides a more plausible moral exemplar, the triune God, compared to Wielenberg's proposed brute ethical facts. Second, my theory provides a purpose, or telos, for humanity, something quite vital to morality, whereas Wielenberg's model does not. Third, my theory provides a relational context for reality, an important aspect in explaining objective morality insofar as moral obligation is inherently relational, and Wielenberg's model lacks such a context. Fourth, building on the third way my theory is a superior explanation of objective morality compared to Wielenberg's model, I explained how God serves as the head of the chain of moral obligation. Wielenberg's theory, because it doesn't have an ultimate moral authority that we're accountable to, is a less plausible explanation for why we have objective moral obligations.

PART 3

THE BLOATED MODEL OBJECTION

CHAPTER 8

BLOATED ASPECTS OF
WIELENBERG'S THEORY

In this section I'll focus on critiquing Wielenberg's moral theory for its extravagant ontological claims. Such criticism will not come as a surprise to Wielenberg, for he admits that "by positing both *sui generis* normative properties and the making relation, my view is, as I would put it, ontologically well-endowed."[1] As he notes, there are primarily two aspects of his model that make it so well-endowed—*sui generis* normative properties, which he also calls brute ethical facts and sometimes describes as Platonic abstract objects, and his proposed making relation—namely, that certain natural properties robustly cause, or make, moral properties to be instantiated. His proposed brute ethical facts led William Lane Craig to write that Wielenberg's "Platonism is a metaphysical view which is so extravagant that it makes theism—which itself involves substantial metaphysical commitments!—look modest by comparison."[2] Craig notes, "The implausibility

---

1. Wielenberg, *Robust Ethics*, 35.
2. Craig, "Metaphysics of Morals," 335.

of Wielenberg's view is compounded by his account of the relation between the physical realm and these abstract moral objects."[3]

In this section I will not merely press the implausibility of Wielenberg's metaphysical claims but go further and evaluate ways he has tried to defend his model's bloated ontology. In chapter 8, I'll begin by showing how the ontological extravagance of his theory distances it from many of his fellow atheists. Then I'll consider metaphysical problems with his proposed brute ethical facts. Next, I'll consider metaphysical problems with his proposed making relation. In chapter 9, I'll address Wielenberg's accusation that theistic moral theories face similar objections by bringing in my divine love theory to consider important truths concerning God's triunity.

The Problem of Bloated Ontology

Atheists like Wielenberg who argue for objective morality find themselves battling on two fronts. To understand these two fronts, consider the two contentions that William Lane Craig often defends when it comes to morality and theism: "I. If theism is true, we have a sound foundation for morality. II. If theism is false, we do not have a sound foundation for morality."[4] Many atheists agree with these two contentions. Of the two, the second is heard more often from atheists than the first. For example, Richard Dawkins writes, "In a universe of blind physical forces and genetic replication, some people are going to get hurt, and other people are going to get lucky; and you won't find any rhyme or reason to it, nor any justice. The universe we observe has precisely the properties we should expect if there is at the bottom, no design, no purpose, no evil and no good; nothing but blind pitiless indifference. . . . DNA neither knows nor cares. DNA just is, and we dance to its music."[5] However, some atheists also express agreement with Craig's first contention, that theism provides a better explanation for objective morality than atheism. J. L. Mackie writes, "We might well argue . . . that objective intrinsically prescriptive features, supervening upon natural ones, constitute so odd a cluster of qualities and relations that they are most unlikely to have arisen in the ordinary course of events, without an all-powerful God to create them. If, then, there are such intrinsically prescriptive objective values, they make the

---

3. Craig, "Metaphysics of Morals," 335–36.
4. Craig, *Goodness without God*, 30.
5. Dawkins, *River out of Eden*, 133. For a substantial list of those who argue that atheism has difficulty accommodating moral realism, see A. Plantinga, "Naturalism," 247.

existence of a god more probable than it would have been without them."[6] For the purpose of this discussion, atheists such as these who reject the idea that morality is objectively real will be referred to as moral nonrealists. As an atheist arguing for moral realism, Wielenberg finds himself in a difficult minority position having to argue against critiques from two sides—theists who are moral realists and his fellow atheists who are nonrealists.

Atheists who are nonrealists often agree with Craig's contentions because they recognize that objective morality fits better with the ontology of theism than the most common ontology associated with atheism—that is, naturalism. Though the terms *atheism* and *naturalism* are sometimes used interchangeably, it's important to note the distinction between these two positions. At least for this discussion, I'll use the term *atheism* to refer to the position that there is no God, whereas I'll use the term *naturalism* to refer to the position that nothing exists beyond the physical (i.e., natural) universe. Naturalism includes atheism, but atheism does not necessarily include naturalism.

Since many atheists, though not all, affirm naturalism, it's important to consider how such atheists have argued that objective morality doesn't seem to make sense in, or fit with, a naturalistic universe. For example, atheist Paul Draper has proposed that "the probability that moral agents exist given naturalism is extremely low, much lower than it is given theism. . . . [There] is the possibility that some 'historical outcomes' like the existence of embodied moral agents are much more probable on theism than on naturalism and hence significantly raise the ratio of the probability of theism to the probability of naturalism."[7] Similarly, Bertrand Russell writes, "Man is the product of causes which had no prevision of the end they were achieving; that his origin, his growth, his hopes and fears, his loves and his beliefs, are but the outcome of accidental collocations of atoms."[8]

C. Stephen Evans, while evaluating Wielenberg's model, notes, "A world with brute moral facts does not seem very much like a Russellian world. One would think that in a Russellian world the 'deep' facts about the world would be facts about the basic particles of physics."[9] Evans comments that the various combinations of these positions have caused some unusual alliances for theists and atheists "in defending the claim that such obligations are hard to make sense of in a naturalistic universe. At the very least the fact that some of the arguments for these

---

6. Mackie, *Miracle of Theism*, 115–16.
7. Draper, "Cosmic Fine-Tuning," 311.
8. Russell, "Free Man's Worship," 416.
9. Evans, *God and Moral Obligation*, 153.

claims are defended by naturalists helps alleviate the suspicion that the theistic arguments beg the question by assuming a theistic worldview at the outset."[10]

J. P. Moreland argues that naturalists, if they want to be consistent, should reject Wielenberg's model. He explains that "an intellectually responsible naturalist owes us a broad, fundamental account of how all entities came-to-be . . . and if an entity is unlocatable in that account due to its irrelevance, then the intellectually responsible naturalist should eschew it."[11] He claims that Wielenberg's model "violates the inner logic of naturalism and depletes its explanatory power by bloating his ontology with myriads of brute entities."[12]

Wielenberg is well aware of the objections that come from his fellow atheists. He begins his book *Robust Ethics* by explaining his purpose was, in large part, to respond to atheists who are nonrealists. He notes that Gilbert Harman, as an atheist, "suggested that we ought to take seriously the possible truth of nihilism," and "Mackie himself, although an atheist, suggested that theism might be able to answer his worries about the queerness of the alleged supervenience relation between moral and natural properties."[13] Undoubtedly referring to such nonrealists, Wielenberg admits concerning his model that "some have found this sort of view to be deeply puzzling if not wildly implausible."[14]

As shown above, many atheists have pointed out that Wielenberg's two main proposals, his brute ethical facts and the power of robust causal making, seem quite fantastical within the belief system of naturalism. To make matters even worse on this front, while explaining his proposals, Wielenberg uses several concepts he borrows from theism, thus giving atheists more good cause to reject his model. For example, while proposing and arguing for his making relationship, Wielenberg uses as an example a belief that theists have—namely, that God has the power to make moral properties be instantiated. He points out that Michael DePaul, in an attempt to explain his notion of supervenience as making, used an example from William Paley where Paley claimed God's commands make certain activities morally obligatory.[15] Wielenberg also writes that a "paradigmatic example of the sort of robust causation I have in mind is the causal relation that many theists take to hold between a state of affairs being divinely willed and the obtaining of that state of affairs."[16] As a side note, Craig

---

10. Evans, *God and Moral Obligation*, 8.
11. Moreland, "Wielenberg and Emergence," 105.
12. Moreland, "Wielenberg and Emergence," 108.
13. Wielenberg, *Robust Ethics*, viii.
14. Wielenberg, *Robust Ethics*, 16.
15. Wielenberg, *Robust Ethics*, 11.
16. Wielenberg, *Robust Ethics*, 18.

has pushed back against Wielenberg's use of this theistic analogy by arguing it "fails, precisely because neither God nor the universe is an abstract object. God and the universe are concrete objects endowed with causal powers and dispositions, which can therefore be causally related to each other. But how physical objects can be causally connected to abstract objects is wholly obscure."[17]

Wielenberg has borrowed other concepts from theism as well; for example, he makes the following suggestion: "It may be helpful to consider the doctrine of divine conservation. . . . On at least some versions of this doctrine, there is a robust causal relation between divine willing and every contingent thing at each moment of its existence. One way of construing my proposal . . . is as a doctrine of *non-moral conservation*: whatever moral properties are instantiated are conserved or sustained by various underlying non-moral properties via a robust causal relation that holds between the relevant non-moral and moral properties."[18] After making this analogy with theism, Wielenberg even felt it necessary to warn his readers that this analogy "should of course not be understood as ascribing *agency* to non-moral properties."[19] Once again, Craig argues that this analogy "fails, for God is a personal agent who freely chooses to sustain in being certain contingent things. . . . Without agency how can these physical situations correctly select the right moral states of affairs to instantiate?"[20]

Wielenberg's numerous appeals to theistic concepts may be part of his strategy to preempt criticism from theists. In other words, it may be more difficult for theists to criticize these concepts within his model because they're also found within their own theistic models too. That this is part of his strategy is evidenced by his admission that "I highlighted some important common ground between my version of robust normative realism and traditional theism. I will argue . . . that the existence of this common ground short-circuits some common theistic objections to my brand of robust normative realism."[21] While it's debatable that his attempt at highlighting this common ground does in fact short-circuit theistic objections to his model, such a strategy certainly does further distance his position from atheists who are nonrealists. If someone rejects theism, it would seem that, to be consistent, she should also question the plausibility of Wielenberg's model because it includes many concepts borrowed from theism.

---

17. Craig, "Metaphysics of Morals," 336.
18. Wielenberg, *Robust Ethics*, 20.
19. Wielenberg, *Robust Ethics*, 20.
20. Craig, "Metaphysics of Morals," 337.
21. Wielenberg, *Robust Ethics*, 36.

By using numerous theistic concepts to build and explain his model, Wielenberg actually illustrates that objective morality is more plausible given theism as opposed to atheism. He touches on this point after he explains that his model "has an ontological commitment shared by many theists" in that it includes the existence of metaphysically necessary brute ethical facts.[22] In a footnote, he responds to Evans's observation that many atheists find such facts odd: "Evans questions the existence of basic ethical facts as characterized here as follows: 'The fact that so many naturalists, including philosophers such as Mackie and Nietzsche, find the idea of non-natural moral facts odd or queer, shows that they are indeed the kind of thing one would like to have an explanation for.' In light of the fact that the very same naturalists have similar doubts about the existence of God, it's hard to see how traditional theists can consistently press this sort of objection against a view like mine."[23] By pointing out that many atheists doubt the existence of brute ethical facts, Evans isn't agreeing with the reason (in this particular case, that the existence of brute ethical facts seem to have no explanation) atheists give for this doubt per se. If Evans was agreeing with their reason, then Wielenberg would be correct—Evans would be affirming a reason atheists often give for doubting the existence of God as well (that the existence of God seems to have no explanation). Instead, Evans is making the point that doubting the existence of God is similar to, as well as related to, doubting the existence of Wielenberg's brute ethical facts. If an atheist doubts God because there is no explanation for his existence, then, if consistent, she should also doubt the existence of brute ethical facts because, as Wielenberg admits, they too have no explanation. Theists might not be able to press this particular reason against Wielenberg's view, but atheists who are nonrealists certainly can—and that's what Evans is pointing out. In other words, Wielenberg's two key concepts, brute ethical facts and the power of robust causal making, seem ontologically out of place within the belief system of atheism.

This section has mostly drawn attention to the fact that many atheists find models like Wielenberg's to be implausible because of their bloated ontologies. If nothing else, this concern should give one pause as to the viability of Wielenberg's atheistic project. However, Wielenberg has a simple but effective reply to those who point out his model doesn't fit well with the popular type of atheism that affirms strict naturalism—he simply rejects such naturalism. He differs from naturalistic atheists in that he believes in the existence of objective moral

---

22. Wielenberg, *Robust Ethics*, 38.
23. Wielenberg, *Robust Ethics*, 38.

facts and properties that "are *sui generis*, a fundamental type of property not reducible to or fully constituted by some other type of property. Contra the Thaleans, all is not water, or physical, or natural."[24] That is why we must go beyond simply making the point that his model does not fit well with naturalism—for he acknowledges that himself—and press on to evaluate his specific nonnaturalistic ontological claims. In the following two sections I'll first evaluate his proposed brute ethical facts and then his proposed making relationship.

Wielenberg's Brute Ethical Facts

A Lack of Evidence for Brute Ethical Facts

I've shown above that many theists and atheists find the excessive ontology of models like Wielenberg's quite peculiar within the framework of atheism. However, the fact is that reality is often peculiar; therefore, Wielenberg's proposal can't simply be dismissed because many find it odd. Instead, we should ask, Are there good reasons and evidence to believe these brute ethical facts really exist? There's a sense in which it's difficult to argue against Wielenberg's assertion that these brute ethical facts exist because he provides no evidence or argument for them. Evans notes, "If the claim that such moral facts are brute in nature is simply put forward as a bald assertion, then there is no argument given that one could refute."[25]

The closest Wielenberg has come to making an argument for his brute ethical facts is when he maintains that his approach is analogous to a popular argument for God. While responding to Craig's critique of his model, he writes, "I get the impression that Craig's view is that in order for me to make my view plausible, I must *first* prove the existence of . . . [brute ethical facts] via some argument that has nothing to do with ethics."[26] He explains how he takes a different approach by first assuming the truth of his brute ethical facts and then making the case that they provide a better explanation for objective morality than other theories. He concludes that this "kind of argument parallels a familiar type of moral argument for God's existence. For example, it's similar to the approach taken by Robert Adams in *Finite and Infinite Goods*."[27] Most moral arguments for God have the following structure, as outlined by Adams:

---

24. Wielenberg, *Robust Ethics*, 14.
25. Evans, *God and Moral Obligation*, 153.
26. Wielenberg, "Reply," 368.
27. Wielenberg, "Reply," 368.

1.   Morality is objective: "certain things are morally right and others are morally wrong."[28]
2.   Objective morality is best explained by theism: "the most adequate answer is provided by a theory that entails the existence of God."[29]
3.   Therefore, there is good reason to think theism is true, and so "my metaethical views provide me with a reason of some weight for believing in the existence of God."[30]

In the beginning of his book, Adams states that he will not start by trying to prove the existence of God, but by showing the advantages of a theistic theory of ethics, he would thereby provide good reasons for accepting theism.[31] Wielenberg claims that he similarly aims to give good reasons for accepting brute ethical facts by showing the advantages of his model relative to other theories. He explains, "My attitude toward my own theory is similar to Churchill's purported attitude toward democracy: it's the worst theory of objective morality—except for all the other theories that have been tried."[32] In other words, Wielenberg recognizes his model is ontologically bloated, but he posits these entities because he thinks they are necessary for, or at least part of the best explanation for, the existence of objective morality. One of my purposes in writing this book is to challenge this claim and, using the process of abductive reasoning, to show that trinitarian theism provides a better explanation for objective morality than Wielenberg's model. Thus, to be consistent, theists who make moral arguments for God, such as Adams and Craig, must at least admit that Wielenberg's abductive reasoning approach is viable.

Certainly it may be the case that the belief theists have, that God exists, is incorrect. Presumably Wielenberg would also admit that his belief about the existence of brute ethical facts could be incorrect. Then the pertinent question becomes: Which belief has more substantial arguments and evidence, the theist's or Wielenberg's? If all theists had was the moral argument, their overall case for God's existence would be fairly weak. But that's not the case; the moral argument for God is merely one among many arguments that theists have provided for God's existence. Theists from various cultures throughout the ages have developed several lines of evidence and arguments for their belief in God—

---

28.   Adams, "Moral Arguments," 116.
29.   Adams, "Moral Arguments," 117.
30.   Adams, "Moral Arguments," 117.
31.   Adams, *Finite and Infinite Goods*, 5–7.
32.   Wielenberg, "Reply," 368.

cosmological arguments, teleological arguments, contingency arguments, and ontological arguments, just to name a few. All else being equal, theists have much more evidence and arguments for God than Wielenberg has for his brute ethical facts. It should be noted that Wielenberg has said he doesn't believe in the existence of God because of the problem of evil,[33] whereas many reject his brute ethical facts for the various reasons discussed in this chapter.

Brute Ethical Facts as an Unsatisfying Ontological Ultimate

Wielenberg has claimed, ontologically speaking, that there's ultimately no explanation for the existence of the brute ethical facts he has posited. Thus the discussion in this section differs from the previous one in that there's a distinction between having few good reasons to believe such entities exist, which is an epistemological issue (discussed in the previous section), and claiming there's no explanation, source, or cause of their existence, which is an ontological issue (discussed in this section).

Wielenberg defends his model against the criticism that his brute ethical facts have no ontological explanation by claiming theists also posit ultimate brute facts about God—for example, that he exists—that they claim have no further explanation. While discussing his brute ethical facts, he writes, "Such facts are the foundation of (the rest of) objective morality and rest on no foundation themselves. To ask of such facts, 'where do they come from?' or 'on what foundation do they rest?' is misguided in much the way that, according to many theists, it is misguided to ask of God, 'where does He come from?' or 'on what foundation does He rest?' The answer is the same in both cases: they come from nowhere, and nothing external to themselves grounds their existence; rather, they are fundamental features of the universe that ground other truths."[34] Presumably Wielenberg would also point out that my divine love theory also posits facts for which no further explanation has been offered, such as the existence of loving relationships among the persons of the Trinity. I affirm, in agreement with Wielenberg, that there must be an ultimate ontological stopping point, if for no other reason than to avoid an infinite regress. Thus, it boils down to the following question: What is a more plausible ontological ultimate—God or brute ethical facts that are akin to Platonic abstract objects?

Consider Platonic abstract objects as a potential ontological ultimate. While discussing Wielenberg's model, Evans argues that it "is far from

---

33. Wielenberg, "Questions and Answers," 87.
34. Wielenberg, *Robust Ethics*, 38.

obviously true" that ethical facts are brute in the sense of being without explanation because the "fact that so many naturalists, including philosophers such
as Mackie and Nietzsche, find the idea of non-natural moral facts odd or
queer, shows that they are indeed the kind of thing one would like to have
an explanation for."[35] Evans points out that it "seems almost irresistible for
a Platonist to ask what the fact that moral truths are deep truths about the
universe says about the nature of ultimate reality. Platonism itself in some
ways makes the world mysterious and posits features of the world that cry out
for explanation."[36] Even from the very beginning, when abstract objects were
first proposed by Plato, he himself posited the Good, which had strong theistic
overtones, as the explanation, or source, of his Forms.

Many throughout history have specifically posited God as the best explanation for the existence of abstract objects. Evans notes that "many theists in fact
have thought that Platonism itself makes far more sense in a theistic universe
than it does otherwise, since in a theistic world the Forms do not have to be seen
as independent realities but can be understood as Ideas in the divine mind."[37]
Thus, it "is no accident that there is a long tradition of theistic (and even Christian) Platonism."[38]

Some have even developed sophisticated arguments for God by starting
with the existence of abstract objects and showing that God is the best explanation for them.[39] The fact that these people have argued for the existence of God
in this way implies two things about their position: first, it implies that they
thought that abstract objects were not a satisfactory stopping point but that the
abstract objects themselves needed an explanation; and second, it implies that
they thought God is a satisfactory stopping point. God seems to fit the bill better
as the ultimate ontological stopping point that needs no explanation because he,
as commonly understood by theists, is an infinite, necessary, concrete, and, most
importantly, causal being. Since abstract objects are commonly understood, by
Wielenberg and others, to be noncausal entities, it's difficult to fathom how
they, as noncausal entities, could be the ultimate ontological stopping point that
caused everything else. It's more plausible to think that God is the ontological

35. Evans, *God and Moral Obligation*, 152.
36. Evans, *God and Moral Obligation*, 153–54.
37. Evans, *God and Moral Obligation*, 154.
38. Evans, *God and Moral Obligation*, 153.
39. Welty, "Theistic Conceptual Realism," 94. Though Welty's unpublished dissertation fully
    develops his argument for God from abstract objects, here he merely summarizes it by noting
    that Robert Adams's comments on this topic provide materials for a theistic argument.

ultimate because he, as a causal agent, could have caused everything else to come into existence.

While it is the case that theists believe there are certain necessary brute facts about God—that he exists, that he has a certain moral nature, that he is triune, and so on—these are facts about a concrete being that theists believe exists necessarily, whereas Wielenberg's brute ethical facts are supposed to be stand-alone abstract facts. There is a vast difference between positing facts about a proposed concrete being and mere facts that supposedly exist abstractly on their own. Wielenberg is free to posit the existence of such brute ethical facts of course, but it doesn't seem plausible to many theists or atheists that such facts could just exist on their own without any cause or explanation.

Wielenberg's Attempt to Drop His Platonism
In response to criticism by Craig concerning the implausibility of his proposed Platonic abstract objects (i.e., brute ethical facts), Wielenberg suggests that his model would still be viable without them. His suggestion is worth quoting at length:

> In *Robust Ethics* and elsewhere I committed myself to the existence of abstract entities . . . because I didn't see how, for example, people could have moral obligations without there being an abstract property like *being morally obligated*. But then I read Dr. Craig's book *God Over All*, in which he argues that concrete entities with various features can exist without there being abstract entities like propositions and properties. Suppose Craig is right about this. Great!—then I can dispense with such abstract entities. People can have moral obligations even if there's no such abstract entity as the property *being morally obligated* and particular things can be good and evil even if there are no such abstract entities as the property of *being good* or *being evil*. After all, the whole point of my metaphysics of morals is to account for the objective reality of particular, concrete entities possessing various moral features. If it turns out that the objective reality of such entities does not require the existence of abstract, Platonic entities, then I'm happy to give up belief in such entities. But perhaps Craig's argument . . . is flawed, and my view does require such abstract entities. In that case, we should believe in such entities because their existence is part of the most plausible theory about the nature of objective morality—namely, my theory.[40]

---

40. Wielenberg, "Reply," 367.

If Wielenberg is correct that his model works even without abstract objects, then he has effectively refuted all the criticism I've presented above in this chapter concerning his brute ethical facts.

Because I discussed Craig's nominalism concerning abstract objects in chapter 5, it will suffice here to simply summarize his position as concretism, the idea that only concrete objects exist. Wielenberg argued that if Craig's model can have objective moral truth without any abstract objects, then his model can too. Unfortunately, he seems to have missed Craig's point completely. According to Craig, absolutes like moral goodness are objectively true, not because they exist on their own as abstract objects or universals, but because God can be accurately described in such a way—that is, as morally good. Moral goodness then is simply an accurate description of what God, a concrete object, is like. God himself is objectively good; he is the Good. As Robert Adams writes, "if God is the Good itself, then the Good is not an abstract object but a concrete (though not a physical) individual."[41]

Moral goodness, as an essential attribute of God, doesn't exist on its own apart from concrete objects, but merely describes God, who exists as a concrete object. Thus, when we say Michael's caring for orphans is morally good, this statement has objective truth value—that is, it's objectively true in the sense that we're comparing Michael's action to what God, a concrete object, is like. This is similar to when people supposedly used to compare the length of things to a meter bar in Paris; one special concrete object was the objective absolute standard by which other concrete objects were measured. Thus, Craig is a moral realist in that he believes that God, as a concrete object, provides an objective paradigmatic moral standard by which we can morally measure other things. But Craig is an anti-realist when it comes to abstract objects and universals because he doesn't believe that the singular terms and quantified variables in these sentences carry ontological commitments.

If, as Craig argues, and I agree, only concrete objects exist, then there must be some concrete object that serves as an objective standard for morality, which, according to Craig, is God. But with Wielenberg's new proposed alternative model, there are no abstract objects and there's no God, so there's nothing to provide a standard or a foundation for objective morality. In other words, if Wielenberg removes abstract objects from his model, then, since he rejects the existence of God, he has no concrete standard for objective morality in his model like Craig does in his (i.e., God). If Wielenberg would respond

---

41. Adams, *Finite and Infinite Goods*, 43.

by insisting that, in his new proposed alternative model, these moral properties don't need a concrete object as a foundation, that they can just exist *sui generis* on their own, then that makes them abstract rather than concrete and we're back to his original Platonic model. Thus, Wielenberg cannot sustain objective morality with his model if he drops his Platonism because, unlike theists, he doesn't have a concrete exemplar like God to provide a perfect standard and therefore a foundation for objective morality.

Wielenberg's Making Relationship

As I noted at the beginning of this chapter, there are two aspects of Wielenberg's model that cause it to be, as he put it, ontologically well-endowed. The first, which I discussed in the previous section, is his proposed brute ethical facts, and the second, which I'll discuss in this section, is his proposed robust making relation. As a reminder, Wielenberg's proposal is that certain natural properties robustly cause, or make, moral properties to become instantiated. He suggests both that "instances of moral and non-moral properties are interwoven together and that the making relation is the cement that binds instances of these properties to each other."[42] Before discussing the ontological excessiveness of Wielenberg's making relationship, I'll first address another concern with this relationship.

Problems with Cognitive Faculties Instantiating Moral Properties

Wielenberg posits that human cognitive faculties *make* moral properties to be instantiated. He writes that "any being that can reason, suffer, experience happiness, tell the difference between right and wrong, choose between right and wrong, and set goals for itself has certain rights, including the rights to life, liberty, and the pursuit of happiness, and certain obligations. . . . Having such cognitive capacities *makes* one have such rights and duties. . . . Evolution has given us these moral properties by giving us the non-moral properties that make such moral properties be instantiated."[43] Critics have pointed out several problems with the idea that moral properties are instantiated by cognitive faculties. I'll discuss two of these problems below.

First, given atheism, why think that cognitive faculties are anything more than instrumental accidents of evolution that nature selected because they led to greater chances of survival or reproduction? Mark Linville argues that human

---

42. Wielenberg, *Robust Ethics*, 105.
43. Wielenberg, *Robust Ethics*, 56.

cognitive faculties are not a viable source of moral properties such as moral value, rights, or duties if they're merely instrumental abilities developed from a haphazard evolutionary process, much like opposable thumbs. He writes, "It is better for a human to have a pair of thumbs than not. But that is because having them allows people to open beer bottles and play the tuba. It does not follow (obviously), that thumbed creatures enjoy some special value not shared by their thumbless companions. To get anything like a real *rights view* up and running would seem to require more than appeal to such instrumentally valuable human characteristics."[44] Peter Singer famously claimed that our insistence of human moral rights is an unwarranted speciesist type of chauvinism on our part.[45] Given atheism, it's hard to see why he's wrong. If our cognitive faculties arose accidentally as helpful adaptions to our environment, then, as James Rachels points out, we "are not entitled . . . to regard our own adaptive behavior as 'better' or 'higher' than that of a cockroach, who, after all, is adapted equally well to life in its own environmental niche."[46]

The second problem with Wielenberg's idea that our cognitive faculties instantiate moral properties is that different human beings have different levels of cognitive abilities. Wielenberg's model would seem to indicate that we should attribute less moral rights and duties to those who have lesser cognitive faculties, such as infants or those with mental handicaps. This is a very precarious path that could be used to justify all sorts of horrendous practices such as eugenics, forced sterilizations, and involuntary euthanasia. Angus Menuge summarizes his concern with this part of Wielenberg's model as follows: "It is obvious that even amongst those who have the relevant cognitive faculties, there is wide variation in cognitive powers and capacities. Human rights are supposed to be equal, but it is implausible . . . to claim that all of these human beings would have the same human rights: if cognitive powers and capacities come in degrees, so would human rights."[47]

John Hare contrasts a notion like Wielenberg's to a common belief among theists concerning the moral value of all human beings: "It is unclear *why* we should give status to members of a species who do not themselves have the relevant capacities . . . for example, infants born with severe mental retardation, if it is the existence of just those capacities in some of its members that is supposed to make the species valuable in the particular way that moral status implies. I

44. Linville, "Darwin, Duties, and the Demiurge," 179–80.
45. Singer, *Animal Rights and Human Obligations*.
46. Rachels, *Created from Animals*, 70.
47. Menuge, "Vindicating the Dilemma," 11.

myself do not see how to overcome this difficulty. . . . [However,] within the Abrahamic faiths we do have a way to do this, starting from the premise that humans are created in the image of God."[48] While considering a similar notion, that we should ascribe value to human beings because they have the capacity for rational reflection, Evans makes the point that "many people believe that young infants and people suffering from dementia still have . . . intrinsic dignity, but in both cases there is no capacity for rational reflection."[49] In other words, Wielenberg's model seems to imply that if a particular human being doesn't have sufficient cognitive faculties, then they have less moral rights, or none at all. Surely Wielenberg himself doesn't believe that infants and people suffering from dementia have less moral rights, but the fact that his model seems to minimize, if not eradicate, such rights is an indication that his model is dangerously wrong.

Unexplained Necessary Connections Between Natural and Moral Properties
In this chapter I'm arguing that Wielenberg's moral theory should be rejected because it includes extravagant ontological claims. In this section I'll show just how extravagant his proposed making relationship is between natural and moral properties. Wielenberg has conceded that "the appeal to the making relation makes robust normative realism less attractive in some respects than at least some of its competitors. . . . It is plausible that, everything else being equal, a theory that posits more kinds of properties and relations is less attractive than a theory that posits fewer kinds of theories and relations."[50]

Platonists have historically struggled to explain how their proposed abstract objects are able to connect with concrete objects in the physical world. For example, how can the property redness, as an abstract object, be connected with a particular ball, a concrete object? Sometimes known as the problem of exemplification, this issue dates all the way back to Plato and his critics. It's fairly well agreed upon that abstract objects, if they exist, are noncausal entities, so much so that being noncausal is usually part of the definition of what an abstract object is. Therefore, the abstract objects themselves are unable to cause their connection with concrete objects. Many Platonists, including Plato himself, have suggested a theistic being as the agent that causes abstract objects to be exemplified in concrete objects.[51]

---

48. Hare, *God's Command*, 27.
49. Evans, "Moral Arguments," §5.
50. Wielenberg, *Robust Ethics*, 35.
51. Copleston, *Greece and Rome*, 1:214–17; 2:33, 38.

At least when it comes to understanding how moral properties can be connected to nonmoral properties, the idea that the former supervenes on the latter is currently the most popular explanation. However, some have criticized the idea of supervenience by claiming it's not an explanation at all but merely a filler word used to signify something for which we have no explanation.[52] In addition, as Wielenberg notes, some have "suggested that such supervenience is more at home in a theistic universe than in a non-theistic one."[53] He goes on to quote William Wainwright's comment that "the connection between the base property and the supervenient property can seem mysterious. For, in the absence of further explanation, the (necessary) connection between these radically different sorts of properties . . . is just an inexplicable brute fact."[54]

Wielenberg rejects the three explanations I discussed above for how moral properties connect with the physical world—that the moral properties themselves cause the connection, that a theistic being causes the connection, or that moral properties simply supervene upon natural properties. Instead, he has proposed that it's the concrete objects that cause this connection. Craig summarizes his position as follows: "Wielenberg recognizes that it would be implausible to say that this just happens, as if by magic. Rather he claims that the physical objects *cause* the abstract objects to supervene on physical situations."[55]

While Wielenberg sometimes uses the term *supervenience* to explain this phenomenon, his explanation of the process makes it clear he's proposing something much more elaborate than simple supervenience. He explains that his proposed making relationship is a form of robust causal D-supervenience, where the concrete natural properties (our cognitive faculties) actually cause the abstract moral properties to be instantiated. He coined the term *D-supervenience* as a way to refer to Michael DePaul's version of supervenience.[56] He explains that "given DePaul's understanding of dependency, if M depends on some base properties B, then M is not identical with, reducible to, or entirely constituted by B, but the instantiation of B explains the instantiation of M; it is B's instantiation that makes M be instantiated. . . . This making relation (as I shall henceforth refer to it) is distinct from supervenience."[57] His proposed D-supervenience, or making relationship, is distinct because supervenience, as it's normally understood, is

52. Mackie, *Ethics*, 41.
53. Wielenberg, "In Defense," 27.
54. Wainwright, *Religion and Morality*, 66.
55. Craig, "Metaphysics of Morals," 336.
56. DePaul, "Supervenience and Moral Dependence."
57. Wielenberg, *Robust Ethics*, 10–11.

merely a relationship of correlation, whereas making is actually explanatory and causal. He construes the making relationship involved in D-supervenience as a sort of robust causation, thus describing making as a type of causation.[58]

Craig has been one of the most vocal critics of Wielenberg's proposed making relationship between natural properties and moral properties; here I'll summarize some of Craig's critiques. First, since natural properties are not agents, how do they know which moral properties to instantiate? Craig rhetorically asks, "What if instead of picking out moral *goodness*, some physical situation might pick out moral *badness*? Indeed, what if it picks out some other abstract object like $\sqrt{2}$ to instantiate, so that two people's loving each other has the property of *being* $\sqrt{2}$ instead of *being good*?"[59] Second, and more problematic, and more related to the charge of ontological bloatedness, Craig points out that Wielenberg "imputes to physical objects causal powers that are mysterious and completely unknown to contemporary physics."[60]

In response, Wielenberg points out that in his model this "relation is a causal relation of a robust sort: the act's being a case of causing pain just for fun necessarily causes the act's wrongness. This causal relation holds between instances of properties—property-tokens—and so does not involve causation between concrete and abstract entities. This point is important because it means that Craig's objections to causation between concrete and abstract entities are directed against a doctrine that is not part of my view."[61] This seems to be a distinction without a difference that doesn't help his case at all. Wielenberg admits as much in a footnote to the above quote: "I should note, however, that some of Craig's concerns about my theory of robust causation are relevant to causation between property tokens. E.g., I offer no account of how such causation works nor do I offer an explanation of why certain nonmoral property tokens cause one moral property token rather than another. While I don't see these as serious weaknesses in my view, I want to make clear that I am not suggesting that Craig's misunderstanding of my account of robust causation renders all of his objections to such causation irrelevant."[62] In several places Wielenberg claims that this causal relationship is brute, unexplained, and necessary, and that he doesn't see this as a serious weakness of his model. He argues, "Explanation, as they say, must come to an end somewhere. Why does being an instance of torturing someone just

58. Wielenberg, *Robust Ethics*, 19.
59. Craig, "Metaphysics of Morals," 337.
60. Craig, "Metaphysics of Morals," 337.
61. Wielenberg, "Reply," 366.
62. Wielenberg, "Reply," 366.

for fun entail moral wrongness? Because being an instance of torturing someone just for fun *makes* an act wrong. . . . Eventually we hit bottom; no further
explanation is available. But I don't see why possessing this sort of explanatory
bottom is a problematic feature for a view to have."[63] Later he adds that this
causal relationship is necessary: "There is a necessary connection between the
cognitive faculties and moral rights."[64]

Wielenberg's insistence on these unexplained necessary connections between
nonmoral properties and moral properties has caused some to accuse his model
of being conveniently ad hoc. Consider the following quote by Shelly Kagan:

> An adequate justification for a set of principles requires an *explanation* of
> those principles—an explanation of why exactly these goals, restrictions,
> and so on, should be given weight, and not others. Short of this, the princi-
> ples will not be free of the taint of arbitrariness which led us to move beyond
> our . . . *ad hoc* shopping lists. . . . Unless we can offer a coherent explanation
> of our principles (or show that they need no further justification), we cannot
> consider them justified, and we may have reason to reject them. . . . This
> need for explanation in moral theory cannot be overemphasized.[65]

For instance, concerning models like Wielenberg's, Craig, reflecting Kagan's
concern above, writes, "If our approach to metaethical theory is to be serious
metaphysics rather than just a 'shopping list' approach, whereby one simply
helps oneself to the supervenient moral properties or principles needed to do
the job, then some sort of explanation is required for why moral properties
supervene on certain natural states or why such principles are true."[66] These
unexplained necessary connections within Wielenberg's theory don't prove it is
false, of course, but that they conveniently fit his theory such that it works out
just right does raise suspicions.

In this chapter I argued that Wielenberg's theory should be rejected because
it entails a bloated ontology. Both his proposed brute ethical facts and his
proposed making relationship entail ontological claims that many atheists and
theists find to be implausible.

---

63. Wielenberg, *Robust Ethics*, 24
64. Wielenberg, *Robust Ethics*, 145.
65. Kagan, *Limits of Morality*, 13.
66. Craig, *Goodness without God*, 180.

CHAPTER 9

A RESPONSE TO WIELENBERG'S
CRITIQUE OF GOD'S COMMANDS

Theistic Models and Unexplained Necessary Connections

A common defensive strategy of Wielenberg's is to accuse his opponent's model of having the same, or similar, weaknesses that his opponent has pointed out in Wielenberg's model.[1] Thus, it's not surprising that, in response to Craig's criticism that his model includes unexplained necessary connections (the making relationship between nonmoral and moral properties), Wielenberg argues that Craig's model also has unexplained necessary connections. In other words, he claims Craig's attack against models like his is actually detrimental to Craig's own theistic model, thus making Craig's overall position internally

---

1. Portions of this chapter were previously published in Adam Lloyd Johnson, "Fortifying the Petard: A Response to One of Erik Wielenberg's Criticisms of the Divine Command Theory," *Philosophia Christi* 20, no. 2 (2018): 357–64.

inconsistent. Because Craig's moral theory is similar in this regard to my divine love theory, it's worth addressing Wielenberg's criticism at length.

Wielenberg's defensive argument can be summarized as follows: Craig claims that it's unacceptable for a moral theory to include logically necessary connections without providing an explanation of why such connections hold. Wielenberg articulates Craig's point as follows, calling it P1: "Any approach to meta-ethics that posits logically necessary connections without adequately explaining why such connections hold is unacceptable."[2] Yet, according to Wielenberg, Craig himself posits certain logically necessary connections without providing an adequate explanation of them.[3]

It's worth noting that Wielenberg doesn't think that P1 itself is a valid concern and therefore doesn't consider it a threat to his model.[4] In other words, though Wielenberg disagrees with P1 himself, this is irrelevant when it comes to his attack against Craig in this context. The truth of P1 is incidental to his argument against Craig because his main contention is that it's self-referentially incoherent for Craig to use P1 to criticize models like his because Craig's model also violates P1.

What are the logically necessary connections that Craig supposedly posits without an adequate explanation? According to Wielenberg, the primary unexplained connection in Craig's model is between God's nature and his commands, that God's commands are necessary expressions of his nature and hence are logically necessary.[5] Wielenberg summarizes this notion as follows: "Craig's version of [divine command theory] . . . entails: P2: There are some divine commands C1 . . . Cn, such that the existence of the divine nature entails the issuing of C1 . . . Cn."[6] Wielenberg claims that Craig nowhere provides an adequate explanation for the existence of such necessary connections and thus Craig's model also violates P1.[7] He remarks, "What Craig seems not to notice is that . . . his brand of [divine command theory] . . . [posits] unexplained necessary connections, thereby running afoul of P1. In this way, Craig is hoisted by his own petard."[8]

---

2.   Wielenberg, *Robust Ethics*, 68.
3.   Wielenberg, "Inconsistency in Craig's Defence," 65.
4.   Wielenberg, *Robust Ethics*, 68.
5.   Wielenberg, "Inconsistency in Craig's Defence," 67. For example, Craig writes, "These commands flow necessarily from his moral nature." In Craig and Moreland, *Philosophical Foundations*, 491.
6.   Wielenberg, *Robust Ethics*, 69.
7.   Wielenberg, *Robust Ethics*, 70.
8.   Wielenberg, *Robust Ethics*, 71.

Hoisted by His Own Petard

It becomes evident that Wielenberg has misunderstood Craig's position when he tries to show that Craig's notion of a necessary relationship between God's nature and his commands is ambiguous. For example, Wielenberg quotes Craig's comment that "the theist can agree that God forbids rape because it is bad"[9] but then responds that this "fails to explain why God's nature *entails* that God forbids rape."[10] He continues by noting that "on Craig's view . . . the fact that an act is good does not entail that God commands it and the fact that an act is bad does not entail that God forbids it. Therefore, the fact that rape is bad cannot fully account for the alleged necessary connection between the divine nature and God's commands against rape."[11] Here Wielenberg leads the reader to wonder as follows: If God doesn't necessarily have to command an act because it's good, nor does he necessarily have to forbid something because it's bad, then what exactly is the necessary connection between God's nature and his commands? Wielenberg seems to imply by this that Craig's proposed necessary connection between God's nature and his commands is left hopelessly unclear and thus evidently unexplained.

Ironically, instead of showing Craig's model to be unclear, Wielenberg actually helps to clarify it. He's correct that the necessary relationship isn't always entailed by the act itself, whether it's a good or a bad act. In other words, that an act is good doesn't necessarily entail that God, because of his moral nature, must command it. There are numerous plausible explanations for this, one being that God doesn't command every possible good act because one person cannot do them all, as some are mutually exclusive.[12] In addition, just because an act is bad doesn't necessarily entail that God specifically forbids it. Again, there are numerous plausible explanations for this, one being that it would be ineffectual to specifically forbid all the innumerable bad actions that could be performed—such a list would be impractically long.[13] Thus, Wielenberg is correct that the necessary connection between God's moral nature and his commands isn't "if an

---

9. Craig, *Goodness without God*, 173.
10. Wielenberg, *Robust Ethics*, 69.
11. Wielenberg, *Robust Ethics*, 70.
12. For instance, God may call different people to do different good actions, one a doctor, another a social worker. Also, it's not proposed that God commands every possible supererogatory act, though all of them of course are, by definition, good.
13. Of course, according to most divine command theories, a command from God is required for there to be a moral obligation. But even under these divine command theories, not every single possible bad action requires a specific command forbidding it; a general command such as "love your neighbor as yourself" or the moral law written on our hearts (Rom. 2:14–15) is sufficient to create moral obligations for a host of specific actions.

act is good, God must necessarily command it" and "if an act is bad, God must necessarily forbid it." However, Craig isn't advocating for either of those necessary connections.

What, then, is the necessary connection between God's nature and his commands in Craig's divine command theory? Theists David Baggett and Jerry Walls agree that Craig is a bit vague at times when he writes about "God's commands' being necessary expressions of his nature" and that God's commands "flow necessarily from his moral nature."[14] They go on to explain that "at a minimum he means that God necessarily does not issue commands inconsistent with his essential goodness, a claim with which we wholeheartedly concur. But his language does not rule out a more ambitious reading instead: All of God's commands are a necessary result of God's nature."[15] They note that, while Craig's goal here is to avoid the arbitrariness horn of the Euthyphro dilemma, his explanation could be interpreted as meaning that all of God's commands are a necessary result of his nature.

Baggett and Walls explain that they're "very open to the truth of a great many obligations being necessary truth, but . . . remain unconvinced that they must all sport this modal status."[16] For instance, there's good reason to think, at least for some commands, that God could have commanded differently without violating his moral nature. Presumably he could have commanded people to tithe 11 percent instead of 10 percent, and this would not have violated his moral nature.[17] The key point is that, of all the possible alternatives he could have commanded, God was necessarily limited to command only those that would be consistent with his moral nature. In other words, God's nature places necessary constraints on which commands he does in fact issue. When God issues a command, it necessarily cannot be inconsistent with his moral nature. Thus, God's nature places necessary constraints on which commands he can issue.

This notion is not unreasonable nor implausible, especially if it's indeed the case that God does exist. Many theists have argued that it's reasonable, coherent, and plausible to suppose that a divine person is perfectly morally good such that they necessarily cannot do or command anything that would be inconsistent with their morally perfect nature. In his book on the coherence

---

14. Baggett and Walls, *Good God*, 119–20. Both of these quotes are from Craig, *Goodness without God*, 73 and 30, respectively.
15. Baggett and Walls, *Good God*, 119.
16. Baggett and Walls, *Good God*, 120.
17. Baggett and Walls, *Good God*, 120.

of theism, Richard Swinburne summarizes his position on this matter as follows: "That there can be a person who is by nature morally perfectly good in our sense seems evidently a coherent claim. . . . He always does the good because that is his nature."[18]

I've previously written about this issue, proposing that Baggett and Walls's first suggestion above is correct, that Craig intended only to mean that God necessarily issues commands consistent with his essential goodness.[19] Unfortunately, in his response to what I wrote, Wielenberg misunderstood Baggett and Walls's position, as well as mine. He began his response by correctly explaining that the main issue under consideration here is whether or not Craig is committed to what he called N-commands, commands such that God necessarily issues them because of his nature.[20] Next, he attempted to summarize Baggett and Walls's two interpretations of Craig's view as follows:

(C1) God's nature necessarily precludes his issuing certain commands, but there are no N-commands.

(C2) All divine commands are N-commands.

However, he then incorrectly suggested that Baggett and Walls interpreted Craig as holding C2 and that I interpreted Craig as holding C1. Instead, Wielenberg suggested that the most plausible interpretation of Craig's view is as follows:

(C3) God's nature necessarily precludes his issuing certain commands, and some (but not all) divine commands are N-commands.

I agree that C3 is the correct interpretation of Craig's view, but it should be noted again that Wielenberg was mistaken when he suggested Baggett and Walls interpreted Craig as holding C2 and that I interpreted Craig as holding C1. He concluded by noting that C3 will not enable theists to avoid his argument here because it implies there are still "some N-commands and, as far as I can see, Craig has not adequately explained the necessary connection between such commands and God's nature."[21] I will now propose such an explanation.

---

18. Swinburne, *Coherence of Theism*, 204.
19. Johnson, "Fortifying the Petard."
20. Wielenberg, "Reply," 373.
21. Wielenberg, "Reply," 374.

A Multitude of Relationships Between God's Nature and His Commands

As I discussed above, not all of God's commands share the same relationship to his moral nature. In this rest of this chapter I'll use my divine love theory to shed light on this topic by classifying the various relationships between God's nature and his various commands. What I'm proposing here concerning the different relationships between God's nature and his different commands is inspired by, though not necessarily always in agreement with, Duns Scotus's moral theology. My account is merely inspired by Duns Scotus and thus should be judged not on its accuracy to Duns Scotus but on how much it lines up with reality.

First, some of God's commands have little to no relationship with, or connection to, his moral nature. For the present classification system, I'll call these neutral commands. Though God's nature places constraints on which commands he issues, not all of God's commands are necessary given his moral nature. For example, as noted above, God could have commanded the Israelites to tithe 11 percent instead of 10 percent, and this would not have violated his moral nature. Neutral commands, such as a hypothetical case where God commands people to drive on the right side of the road instead of the left, are not necessitated by his moral nature. A command such as this is morally neutral in the sense that the action being commanded, driving on the right, is not good or evil in and of itself. Thus, it wouldn't be necessary for God to command people to drive on the right; he could command people to drive on the left instead, and doing so wouldn't violate his moral nature. God necessarily cannot command things that would be inconsistent with his moral nature, but beyond this constraint God has the freedom to command or forbid such neutral actions.

It's worth exploring possible reasons why God would give such neutral commands. Though these commands aren't necessary given his nature, it would seem reasonable that he gives such neutral commands out of good motivations, such as the well-being of those he's commanding. For instance, though driving on the right side (or the left side) is morally neutral in and of itself, it seems reasonable to imagine God being motivated to command this out of a desire for people's well-being, knowing that there would be fewer accidents if everyone drove on the same side.

Many of God's commands to the Israelites in the Old Testament seem to be of this sort, morally neutral in and of themselves but commanded by God out of good motivations for the well-being of his people. Certainly we don't know all of God's motivations, but many of the Old Testament commands seem to have served the purpose of providing safety and standardization for that particular society. This would help explain how God could rescind many of the Old Testament laws for people living today without violating his moral character, for such commands are not based on his nature. It would be as though God had commanded people to drive on the right side of the road at one time in history but now commands that they drive on the left side. This understanding is helpful in responding to those who claim that, by rescinding some of the Old Testament laws, Christianity implies that all of morality is culturally relative.

Another reason God may command a morally neutral action is to teach people about deeper moral principles. For instance, it's easy to imagine God commanding people to shake hands when they meet one another. Since shaking hands is morally neutral in and of itself, he could instead have commanded them to bow or greet one another with a kiss. His command to greet one another with a handshake may somewhat flow from his nature though, in the sense that human persons made in his image have value and thus it's good to respect people by acknowledging them when you meet them.

So why would God command people to greet one another in a specific way, if there are many other neutral ways that would also be acceptable? It may be the case that God, like a good parent, would want to instruct his children to greet people in a specific way as a teaching tool to help them learn about respecting people. He could teach them about respect by commanding them to shake hands or to bow when they meet people, and either would accomplish the same goal. The actual greeting practice is neutral, but commanding a specific greeting could be a useful way of helping people learn a deeper moral principle, the principle of respecting others. Parents in America often teach their children to respect others this way—look them in the eye and shake their hand—because the physical act of shaking hands is easier for a child to understand than the abstract notions of respecting and valuing people. However, when they become adults and understand the deeper moral principle of respecting people, they may go about greeting people in other ways. Many of the neutral Old Testament commandments served this purpose, to teach people about deeper moral principles.

Second, some of God's commands are based more on human nature than God's nature. For the present classification system, I'll call these human nature–based commands. These commands, like neutral commands, have little to no relationship with, or connection to, God's nature. Duns Scotus's moral theology will be helpful here in understanding and explaining this type of command.

The central idea in Duns Scotus's moral theology is that God's ultimate purpose in creating human beings was that they would become co-lovers with the three persons of the Trinity, that they would be brought into the loving fellowship that previously consisted only of the Father, Son, and Holy Spirit. Entering into this loving fellowship is the ultimate end, goal, purpose, and telos of every human being. Hare, in explicating Duns Scotus's theology, writes, "Human beings are by nature such that they are fulfilled, or they reach their end, by loving God."[22] Thus God's commands, including the ones I'm calling here human nature–based commands, serve the purpose of giving human beings a successful path to their proper end—that is, to be loving persons and fully enter into the loving fellowship of the Trinity.

Duns Scotus maintained that commands of this second type, human nature–based commands, are not necessary given God's nature. What about commands against murder or against having sex with someone who is not your spouse? Some may be hesitant to think of these as nonnecessary, given God's nature, but clearly they're based more on human nature than God's nature for God cannot die and is not sexual. Furthermore, God could have created humans with different natures—for example, as asexual beings like angels, or to come back to life thirty seconds after we die and feel great pleasure from the experience. At a minimum, it's unclear how creating us differently in these areas would cause us to be less "created in his image" in a morally pertinent way. Thus, I'm proposing here that it was possible for God to have created us with a different nature, say, coming back to life thirty seconds after we die; and if he did, then "thou shalt not murder" would not apply the way it does now. Commands such as "thou shalt not murder" are contingent and relative in the sense that they're relative to the way God created our natures; if God had created us to be different in these ways, then presumably God would have issued different commands.

Some natural law theorists, as I discussed in chapter 5, maintain that all moral obligations are based on human nature and thus would see all of God's commands as human nature–based commands. Duns Scotus and I respectfully disagree. While human nature plays a large and important part of morality, there are other, and more ultimate, aspects of morality—namely, God's trinitarian nature. As I argued in chapter 5, it's God's triune nature, not human nature, that is the absolute core foundation of morality and not relative in any sense. The core foundation of morality must be something that cannot be relative, and so, for instance, morality cannot ultimately be based on human nature because God could have created us with a different nature. This is opposed to those natural law theorists who maintain that all of morality is based on human nature.

---

22. Hare, *God's Command*, 101.

What's even more controversial than proposing that human nature–based commands aren't necessary, given God's nature, is Duns Scotus's proposal that human nature–based commands aren't necessary, even given that human nature is what it is. This is in direct opposition to most natural law theorists, possibly including Aquinas, who claim that once God decided on and then fixed human nature to be what it is, then God's commands based on human nature would automatically be fixed and necessary given such a nature. Evans notes that on some interpretations of Aquinas, "once God has decided to create a world in which the created objects, including humans, have the natures they have, then his commands for that world are determined. Of course God could have given humans different commands on such a view, but in order for him to do so, he would have to create different natures for some things, thereby changing what is good for them."[23]

Duns Scotus disagreed with such natural law theorists and argued that, while commands of this type fit extremely well with human nature, they're still contingent in that God could have commanded otherwise, given the same fixed human nature. In other words, though these commands provide a very proper and successful path for human beings to reach their final end of becoming a loving person and joining the loving fellowship of the Trinity, God could have commanded other paths, even without changing human nature.[24] Robert Prentice explains that, according to Duns Scotus, "it is possible that there could be another system of precepts which would lead man to union with God and to his last end. "[25] Thus Duns Scotus argued that commands of this type are contingent, even given our fixed human nature, in the sense that God could have commanded a different path for human beings. Hare carefully explains that what "Scotus is denying is that the route that God prescribes is the only possible route [to humans' final end], and so is mandatory for God to prescribe. He is not denying that the route fits our nature, or that once God has prescribed the route, it is necessary for us to follow it."[26] Duns Scotus argued that this position helped explain how it was appropriate for God, at times, to make exceptions to

---

23. Evans, *God and Moral Obligation*, 34. On this page Evans notes that natural law theorist John Finnis seemed to suggest this view of Aquinas but that natural law theorist Jean Porter argued that Aquinas believed God has some discretion with respect to commands of this type because human nature underdetermines the moral law.

24. Duns Scotus, *Will and Morality*, 202.

25. Prentice, "Contingent Element," 277.

26. Hare, *God and Morality*, 99.

commands of this type, such as murder in the case of Abraham and Isaac and adultery in the case of Hosea and Gomer.[27]

It could be that Duns Scotus and natural law theorists are both partially correct on this point. Maybe it's the case that some human nature–based commands are necessary, given our fixed human nature, and some are contingent, given our fixed human nature. In other words, we can make a distinction within this second category of commands and understand some as necessary (given human nature, they could not be otherwise) and some as contingent (given human nature, they could be otherwise). We might not be able to know for sure which commands are which, but conceptually we can understand there may be some of each. Regardless, none of these human nature–based commands are necessary, given God's moral nature, for that's true only of the third type of commands.

The third and final type of commands is what Wielenberg calls N-commands, commands such that God necessarily issues them because of his nature. For my present classification system, I'll call these necessary commands.[28] Duns Scotus maintained that with commands of this type, "God cannot make them false."[29] Prentice notes that, according to Duns Scotus, unlike commands based on human nature, "precepts of this kind . . . contain a truth which God cannot make false by any exercise of His will."[30]

I propose that the only necessary moral commands that aren't relative in any sense, and which God must issue, given his nature, are the two greatest

---

27. Prentice, "Contingent Element," 277. See also Duns Scotus, *Will and Morality*, xiv.
28. Duns Scotus, *Will and Morality*, 202. Though Duns Scotus explained these various types of commands similarly to how I'm explaining them here, he used different terms to classify them. What I'm calling here necessary commands, he called "natural law in a strict sense," and what I'm calling here human nature–based commands, he called "natural law in an extended sense." Since Duns Scotus used the term *natural law* to mean something quite different from what most natural law theorists mean when they use the term, using his terms of classification can cause confusion. Most natural law theorists use the term *natural law* to refer to moral truths that are based on, or true because of, human nature, whereas Duns Scotus used the term *natural law* to mean moral truths that can be known immediately once one understands the terms in the particular moral truth statement. The terms of classification used are not at all as important as the explanation of the various classification categories. I could have labeled the three categories of commands here A, B, and C for that matter, or purple, red, and black. The category labels themselves are merely names that, though useful for purposes of summarization and communication, are ultimately incidental. Too much ink has been wasted throughout history arguing over, and clearing up confusion concerning, the use, definition, and assignment of various category labels and terms. Instead, the focus should be on explanation of what someone means when they use a particular label or term, not on the label or term itself.
29. Duns Scotus, *Will and Morality*, 199.
30. Prentice, "Contingent Element," 262.

commandments: "'You shall love the Lord your God with all your heart, and with all your soul, and with all your mind.' This is the great and foremost commandment. The second is like it, 'You shall love your neighbor as yourself.' On these two commandments depend the whole Law and the Prophets" (Matt. 22:37–40). Evans agrees with my proposal when he writes that "some of what God commands he commands necessarily. . . . I think the most plausible candidates for divine commands that have this character of necessity are the command to love God and the command to love our neighbors as ourselves, with the 'neighbor' understood as including all human beings."[31]

To love God and love others are very broad commands that, by themselves, provide little direction for human beings. Hence the purpose of the second type of commands, those based on human nature. These human nature–based commands are important because they provide the form for how humans are to express this love and are based on how God created human nature. Certainly, how to love a being, or the form the love should take, would greatly depend on what that being is like. Since love is simply unselfish care for another, God created human nature in a certain way such that, given human nature, certain things humans do toward each other are loving and kind while other things they do toward each other are unloving and selfish. For example, God created humans to be sexual but designed them such that this sexuality could be expressed lovingly and kindly in the context of marriage or it could be expressed unlovingly and selfishly through rape.

Thus, these two types of commands, human nature–based commands and necessary commands, are complementary to one another but differ in their necessity, given God's moral nature. Hare explains that "the commandments that tell us *to* love . . . have the kind of necessity . . . [that] the commandments that tell us *how* to love . . . do not."[32] The necessary commands to love others provide the broad direction, irrespective of human nature, whereas human nature–based commands instruct us on how to be loving, given that God created human nature to be a certain way. Hare elaborates: "Scotus is not saying that love of the neighbor is contingently commanded . . . but that the form in which this love is to be shown is contingent."[33]

One of the reasons that loving God and loving others are the two greatest commands is that they summarize, and are necessitated by, the core foundation

---

31. Evans, *God and Moral Obligation*, 143.
32. Hare, *God's Call*, 67 (emphasis added).
33. Hare, *God's Call*, 68.

of morality—that is, God's triune nature. These commands flow necessarily from God's triune nature in that he could not command otherwise. In the next section I'll explain why God's triune nature results in him necessarily giving these two commands. But first it will be helpful to summarize my proposed classification system of various relationships between God's nature and his various commands.

1. Neutral commands: These commands are not connected to, or based on, God's nature or human nature. Possible examples include driving on the right side of the road or tithing 10 percent instead of 11 percent.

2. Human nature–based commands: These commands are connected to, or based on, not God's nature but human nature. Once God decided to create human nature to be a certain way, it's possible some of these commands were necessary (couldn't be otherwise), given human nature, while others, though still based on human nature, were contingent (could be otherwise). Thus:

   a. Some of these commands might be necessary, given human nature. Possible examples include commands concerning murder and sex.

   b. Some of these commands might be contingent, given human nature. Possible examples include commands concerning private property such as ownership and stealing.[34]

3. Necessary commands: These commands are such that God necessarily issues them because of his nature. He could not command otherwise. Possibly the only commands in this category are to love God and to love others.

The Necessary Relationship Between God's Nature and His Necessary Commands

In this section I'll attempt to provide what Wielenberg has asked for, an explanation of the relationship between God's nature and necessary commands, what Wielenberg calls N-commands—that is, commands that God must necessarily issue because of his nature.

By providing this explanation, I will refute his accusation that theists also posit unexplained necessary connections, allowing theists then to be consistent in criticizing his model for positing unexplained necessary connections. Thus,

---

34. For a discussion on how commands concerning private property may be contingent, even given our fixed human nature, see Hare, *God's Call*, 69.

I'll argue here, using facets of my divine love theory developed in chapter 4, that God's triunity explains how God's nature relates to his necessary commands.

Wielenberg has pointed out that, in order to explain the relationship between God's nature and his necessary commands, it's not enough to merely list some of God's character traits. He writes, "It might be thought that such a list provides the materials for explaining the connections between the divine nature and at least some N-commands. Consider the following: because God is loving, He necessarily commands that we love one another. This claim has a certain ring of plausibility to it, but notice that it posits a logically necessary connection between being loving and issuing the command that we love one another."[35] He states that unless theists provide an explanation for this necessary connection, they cannot critique his model for having unexplained necessary connections. I will now attempt to provide such an explanation. My basic argument is summarized in the following premises:

1. Since the persons of the Trinity necessarily love each other—that is, they necessarily love God and love others (themselves)—God is necessarily loving.
2. Because God is necessarily loving, when he creates humans, he must command "what is best" for them.
3. The "best for humans" is the ultimate good.
4. If good is that which resembles God in a morally pertinent sense, then the ultimate good is resembling God in the ultimate way.
5. Resembling God in the ultimate way is loving God and loving others, because the ultimate good in God is the inner-trinitarian loving relationships.
6. Therefore, God must necessarily command humans to love God and love others, which are the only two necessary commands.

First of all, it seems reasonable to assert that God is necessarily loving (premise 1); Hare also claims that "even God is required (by God's justice) to love God."[36] In addition, in chapter 4 I defended the idea that something is good if it resembles God in a morally pertinent sense (premise 4). Since our loving God and loving others analogously resembles the triune God in that within the Trinity the three divine persons are loving God and loving others (i.e., themselves),

---

35. Wielenberg, "Inconsistency in Craig's Defence," 70.
36. Hare, God's Call, 66.

we can conclude that humans loving God and loving others is morally good. But why think that resembling God in this way is the ultimate way to resemble him (premise 5)? Because, as I argued in chapter 4, the love between the persons of the Trinity is the ultimate moral good in that it's the very core and foundation of all of morality.

Hare, reflecting Duns Scotus's theology, comes to similar conclusions. He argues, "God is not required to create us. But if God does create us, the requirement of [his] justice is that we be created such that [a loving] union with God is our final end."[37] He also explains that "Scotus thinks that God necessarily loves God, and then wills to have co-lovers. . . . Moreover God necessarily orders these creatures towards himself, the primary good."[38] Similarly, while explaining Duns Scotus's theology, Allan Wolter writes, "Man is destined to be perfected by union with the Trinity, because God, as a perfect lover, wills that what he loves be loved by others."[39] In other words, because God is love, he necessarily must instruct humans toward what would be the greatest good for them (premise 2). In addition, loving God is the greatest good for them because, since good is that which resembles God, loving God resembles him more than anything else. Hare also argues that the "command to love the neighbor would also be . . . [neces- sary], since we are necessarily commanded to love God, and to love the love of God, and therefore to love the neighbor's love of God."[40]

It may be helpful to look at the situation from the opposite angle. While considering the impossibility of the alternative—God commanding us to hate— Duns Scotus writes that "just as no act is better formally than to love God, so no act is formally worse than to hate God."[41] God could not have commanded us to hate him or hate others because that would contradict his own triune nature. Alvin Plantinga concurs: "It is an essential property of God not to command hate instead of love. There aren't any possible worlds in which God commands hate rather than love."[42] Hare argues, on the basis of the work of William of Ockham, that it would be incoherent for God to "command us not to love God . . . because [such a command] cannot be disobeyed; this is because to disobey it is already to love God . . . [because] loving God entails obedience."[43] In other

37. Hare, *God's Call*, 66.
38. Hare, *God's Call*, 99.
39. Wolter, introduction to *Duns Scotus*, 13.
40. Hare, *God's Command*, 110.
41. Duns Scotus, *Will and Morality*, 302.
42. A. Plantinga, "Naturalism," 269.
43. Hare, *God's Command*, 56.

words, God could not command us to hate him because we would have to love him to obey such a command, for obedience is just *how* we love God.

With this explanation of the necessary connection between God's nature and his necessary commands now in hand, it would no longer be inconsistent to criticize Wielenberg's model for positing unexplained necessary connections. Though Wielenberg might not consider the explanation I've provided here adequate, at a minimum I believe I've shown that my proposed necessary connection between God's nature and his necessary commands is more plausible than Wielenberg's proposed necessary connection between natural properties and nonnatural properties.

CHAPTER 10

CONCLUSION TO PART THREE

In this section I focused on the metaphysics of Wielenberg's model and critiqued it for having a bloated ontology. Two primary facets of his model lead many, including Wielenberg himself, to conclude that his model is ontologically excessive—his *sui generis* moral properties, or brute ethical facts, and his proposed making relationship between nonmoral and moral properties.

I began chapter 8 by looking at various metaphysical concerns that atheists have had with models like Wielenberg's. I noted that Wielenberg, as an atheist who is a moral realist, finds himself in a difficult situation in which he must battle on two fronts—against atheists who are moral nonrealists and against theists who are moral realists. These two fronts, though they disagree on the existence of God, agree that theism provides a better explanation for objective morality than atheism does. Many atheists are turned off by Wielenberg's model in particular because of its extravagant ontological claims and by the fact that he often borrows concepts from theism to explain and defend his theory.

Next, I evaluated Wielenberg's proposed brute ethical facts. First, I noted that Wielenberg has put forth no evidence for the existence of these facts. Instead, his strategy is to begin by assuming they exist and then argue that they provide the best explanation for the existence of objective morality. He claims his approach is similar to the moral argument that many theists make for God's existence. However, I pointed out, first, that theists have a multitude of arguments and evidence for God, whereas Wielenberg gives little to no such evidence for his proposed brute ethical facts. Second, I argued that Wielenberg's proposed brute ethical facts do not serve as a satisfying ontological stopping point. In fact, many, including Plato himself, have argued that the most likely explanation, or source, for such abstract objects, if in fact they do exist, is a theistic God. An infinite, personal causal being seems to be a more reasonable and plausible ultimate ontological stopping point than Wielenberg's brute ethical facts. Third, I argued that Wielenberg was incorrect in his suggestion that his model could still work without abstract objects because, with no God and now no abstract objects, there's nothing left to provide a standard or foundation for objective morality.

Finally, in chapter 8 Wielenberg's proposed making relationship was evaluated and found wanting. He claims that certain natural properties—namely, our cognitive faculties—robustly cause, or make, moral properties to be instantiated. First, I argued that this proposal, at a minimum, is problematic because it seems arbitrary, given atheism and evolution, to pick a particular adaptive ability (i.e., cognitive faculties) and claim that somehow it's more special than other adaptive abilities such that it instantiates moral properties. Also, cognitive faculties are not universally equal among human beings. Infants and the mentally handicapped, for example, have substantially less cognitive ability, and thus Wielenberg's model seems to indicate they have less moral rights, a horrendous implication indeed. Second, his proposed making relationship imputes highly speculative metaphysical causal powers to natural properties, adding to the ontological bloatedness of his model.

In chapter 9 I further developed my divine love theory in response to Wielenberg's accusation that theistic models, like his model, posit unexplained necessary connections. To summarize, P1 is Wielenberg's summary of a critique often leveled at his model by theists—"P1: Any approach to metaethics that posits logically necessary connections without adequately explaining why such connections hold is unacceptable."[1] The unexplained necessary connection that some theistic critics of Wielenberg's theory have pointed out is the connection in his proposed making relationship between nonmoral properties and moral properties. He in turn has argued that unless theists can adequately explain their own proposed necessary connection between God's

---

1.   Wielenberg, *Robust Ethics*, 11.

nature and his commands, they "cannot consistently wield P1 as a weapon against nontheist approaches to ethics."[2]

In my attempt to provide such an explanation, I explained that there are different relationships between God's nature and his various commands. Some of God's commands are not based on his nature or human nature but are neutral; some are based more on human nature than his nature; and some are based, and necessarily so, on his nature. Only the last type, which Wielenberg has called N-commands, required an explanation in order to address Wielenberg's accusation.

The explanation I gave to address this accusation was my proposal that God's triunity explains the necessary relationship between God's nature and his two necessary commands to love God and love others. Since within God there are loving relationships between the persons of the Trinity, it seems reasonable that God would necessarily command those he created in his image to resemble him analogously by also loving God and loving others.

---

2.   Wielenberg, "Reply," 375.

PART 4

THE LUCKY COINCIDENCE OBJECTION

CHAPTER 11

AN EVOLUTIONARY DEBUNKING ARGUMENT

Introduction to the Lucky Coincidence Objection

Both theists and atheists have presented epistemological concerns about moral theories like Wielenberg's.[1] Even Wielenberg himself admits, "It is not only theistic philosophers who have found robust normative realism to be problematic. A number of contemporary non-theist philosophers charge that robust normative realism runs into trouble when it comes to accounting for human moral knowledge."[2] One of the most common epistemological concerns about such models is as follows: Granting, for the sake of argument, that there are such things as objective moral truths, and assuming, as Wielenberg does, that they are causally inert, it would be quite a lucky coincidence if our moral beliefs happened to match up with these objective moral truths. Call this the lucky coincidence objection.

---

1.   Portions of this chapter and portions of chapter 12 were previously published in Adam Lloyd Johnson, "Debunking Nontheistic Moral Realism: A Critique of Erik Wielenberg's Attempt to Deflect the Lucky Coincidence Objection," *Philosophia Christi* 17, no. 2 (2015): 353–68.
2.   Wielenberg, *Robust Ethics*, 85.

Proponents of evolutionary debunking arguments point out that this objection is amplified for a person if she believes our moral beliefs have developed contingently through a haphazard evolutionary process. In other words, if God doesn't exist and evolution is true, then it is unlikely our moral beliefs reliably correspond with objective moral truth—again, assuming there is such a thing. These proponents claim that our moral beliefs are merely human constructs that nature selected because they increased our prospects for survival and reproduction. As the television show *Survivor* has entertainingly illustrated, a group that works together well—which involves moral aspects such as fairness, reciprocity, and self-sacrifice—is better able to outwit, outplay, and outlast a group that does not. Similarly, as the story is often told, there was an evolutionary advantage to groups that adopted moral principles; working together well, they could better compete against other groups in the battle for scarce resources.[3]

Noted atheist and evolutionary debunking argument proponent Michael Ruse writes, "Darwinian theory shows that in fact morality is a function of (subjective) feelings, but it shows also that we have (and must have) the illusion of objectivity. . . . In a sense, therefore, morality is a collective illusion foisted upon us by our genes."[4] He also writes,

> The position of the modern evolutionist . . . is that humans have an awareness of morality . . . because such an awareness is of biological worth. Morality is a biological adaptation no less than are hands and feet and teeth. . . . Considered as a rationally justifiable set of claims about an objective something, ethics is illusory. I appreciate that when somebody says "Love thy neighbor as thyself," they think they are referring above and beyond themselves. . . . Nevertheless . . . such reference is truly without foundation. Morality is just an aid to survival and reproduction . . . and any deeper meaning is illusory.[5]

Other proponents of evolutionary debunking arguments include Joshua Greene, Peter Singer, Sharon Street, and Richard Joyce.[6]

---

3. Haidt, *Righteous Mind*, 189–220. See also Wilson, *Consilience*, 282.
4. Ruse, *Taking Darwin Seriously*, 253.
5. Ruse, *Darwinian Paradigm*, 261–69.
6. Greene, *Moral Tribes*; Singer, "Ethics and Sociobiology"; Street, "Darwinian Dilemma"; Joyce, *Evolution of Morality*, 184.

In chapter 4 of his book *Robust Ethics*, Wielenberg defends his view against three well-known evolutionary debunking arguments. Of these three, the one by Sharon Street is most similar to the one that I'll present below. She writes,

> Allowing our evaluative judgments to be shaped by evolutionary influences is analogous to setting out for Bermuda and letting the course of your boat be determined by the wind and tides: just as the push of wind and tides on your boat has nothing to do with where you want to go, so the historical push of natural selection on the content of our evaluative judgments has nothing to do with evaluative truth. . . . Of course it's *possible* that as a matter of sheer chance, some large portion of our evaluative judgments ended up true, due to a happy coincidence between the realist's independent evaluative truths and the evaluative directions in which natural selection tended to push us, but this would require a fluke of luck that's not only extremely unlikely, in view of the huge universe of logically possible evaluative judgments and truths, but also astoundingly convenient to the realist.[7]

Street's concern is that if there are such things as objective moral truths, then it would be quite the lucky coincidence if our moral beliefs corresponded to them, given that such beliefs developed haphazardly through an evolutionary process that selected for survival and reproduction, not for an ability to know truth. If evolution works as many claim, if it is driven by accidental random mutations (which Wielenberg affirms)[8] as well as chance changes in the environment (climate changes, meteorites, etc.), then it would be a lucky coincidence if it just so happened to shape our moral judgments such that they matched up with what atheistic moral realists claim are timeless, independent, objective moral truths.

The lucky coincidence objection would lose much of its bite if moral facts and properties somehow played a causal role in forming our moral beliefs. However, most proponents of theories similar to Wielenberg's robust normative realism reject the idea that objective moral truth has such causal power. For instance, Wielenberg explains, "An important feature of my view is that while many of the non-moral properties upon which moral properties D-supervene can produce causal effects, the moral properties themselves are epiphenomenal—they have no causal impact on the rest of reality. That aspect of moral properties makes the

---

7.   Street, "Darwinian Dilemma," 121–22.
8.   Wielenberg, *Robust Ethics*, 51, 56.

question of how we could have knowledge of them particularly pressing."[9] While discussing the difficulty of explaining why we should think objective moral facts and our moral beliefs correspond, Wielenberg reminds his readers that robust normative realists like himself are "hamstrung in this task by the fact that there is no causal connection between moral facts and moral beliefs."[10] He sums up this objection remarkably well when he notes that "if moral facts do not explain the moral beliefs of human beings, then those beliefs being correct would involve a lucky coincidence that is incompatible with genuine knowledge."[11]

Atheistic moral realists, including Wielenberg, have tried to refute evolutionary debunking arguments because these arguments aim to show that our moral convictions are the result of an accidental random process, rendering such convictions arbitrary and potentially meaningless. These realists maintain that morality is objectively real and that we can have true moral knowledge, even if atheism and evolution are true.[12] My purpose in this section is to argue that Wielenberg is unsuccessful in his attempts to deflect the major concern raised by evolutionary debunking arguments—namely, that if evolution and atheism are true, it would be a lucky coincidence if our moral beliefs reliably corresponded to objective moral truth. In order to make this case, here in chapter 11, I'll present an evolutionary debunking argument using Alvin Plantinga's evolutionary argument against naturalism as a base. In chapter 12, I'll reply to Wielenberg's four attempts to respond to evolutionary debunking arguments and deflect this lucky coincidence objection. In chapter 13, I'll use my divine love theory to answer Wielenberg's accusation that theistic models also have lucky coincidences.

Throughout these remaining chapters I encourage you to consider, in light of this lucky coincidence objection, whether my divine love theory is a superior explanation compared to Wielenberg's theory when it comes to how and why our moral beliefs match up correctly with objective moral truth. If we think our moral beliefs do correspond correctly with objective moral truth, which theory is a more plausible explanation of how this correspondence has come about? It seems to me that a personal, infinite, triune God, as the source and coordinator of all things, provides a much more plausible explanation for why our moral beliefs correctly match up with objective moral truth.

---

9. Wielenberg, *Robust Ethics*, 13–14.
10. Wielenberg, *Robust Ethics*, 155.
11. Wielenberg, *Robust Ethics*, 153.
12. See Martin, *Atheism, Morality, and Meaning*; Sinnott-Armstrong, *Morality without God?*; Enoch, *Taking Morality Seriously*; Huemer, *Ethical Intuitionism*; Shafer-Landau, "Evolutionary Debunking."

The Historical Background of Evolutionary Debunking Arguments

Charles Darwin may have been the first to recognize that if evolution and athe-ism were true, then this would result in a crushing blow against the confidence we have in our cognitive faculties, including our moral intuitions. For instance, he began to doubt the reliability of his own cognitive faculties when he became convinced humans had come about through an evolutionary process. In 1881 he wrote to W. Graham, in response to his *Creed of Science*, "You have expressed my inward conviction, though far more vividly and clearly than I could have done, that the Universe is not the result of chance. But then with me the horrid doubt always arises whether the convictions of man's mind, which has been developed from the mind of the lower animals, are of any value or at all trustworthy. Would any one trust in the convictions of a monkey's mind, if there are any convictions in such a mind?"[13]

Darwin may have thought this doubt applied only to subjective religious beliefs and not to more objective scientific beliefs, but as I'll show, there's no good reason to make such a distinction. Even if someone did hold to such a distinction, moral beliefs, because of their subjectivity, are more similar to reli-gious beliefs than scientific beliefs and hence should clearly come under the purview of Darwin's doubt. Darwin himself recognized that his theory of evolu-tion had such implications for morality. For example, in his 1876 autobiography he wrote, "Pleasurable sensations . . . stimulate the whole system to increased action. Hence it has come to pass that most or all sentient beings have been developed in such a manner, through natural selection, that pleasurable sensa-tions serve as their habitual guides. We see this in the pleasure from exertion, even occasionally from great exertion of the body or mind,—in the pleasure of our daily meals, and especially in the pleasure derived from sociability, and from loving our families."[14] According to Darwin, then, natural selection developed within us the subjective experience of pleasure and correlated it with behav-iors that led to greater chances for survival and reproduction. It's important to note that Darwin described sociability and family love, both key aspects of morality, as behaviors that natural selection associated with pleasure because they increased our chances for survival and reproduction. It seems, then, that Darwin believed his theory of evolution explained how moral beliefs developed,

---

13. Darwin, *Charles Darwin*, 64.
14. Darwin, *Charles Darwin*, 60.

but what's not clear from this passage is whether he concluded morality was therefore not objectively true.

It may be telling, though, that in a letter to a student in 1873 he wrote, "The impossibility of conceiving that this grand and wondrous universe, with our conscious selves, arose through chance, seems to me the chief argument for the existence of God; but whether this is an argument of real value, I have never been able to decide. . . . The safest conclusion seems to me that the whole subject is beyond the scope of man's intellect; but man can do his duty."[15] It seems as though Darwin realized his theory of evolution, combined with an agnosticism toward the existence of God, could lead to a breakdown of our moral beliefs. Evidently this is why he reminded his student that even if evolution and atheism were true we can, and presumably should, still do our duty.

Maybe we can be thankful that Darwin resisted what he saw as a potential implication of his theory—that is, the rejection of objective morality. But there were plenty who came after Darwin who fully embraced this conclusion. Jacques Monod, Nobel Prize winner and one of the founders of molecular biology, wrote, "Man at last knows that he is alone in the unfeeling immensity of the universe, out of which he emerged only by chance. His destiny is nowhere spelled out, nor is his duty."[16] As Monod aptly put it, if atheism and evolution are true, then our *duty* is merely a subjective experience that arose accidently by chance and was then selected for by nature.

Even though the basic framework of evolutionary debunking arguments might be as old as the theory of evolution itself, most contemporary versions follow Gilbert Harman's approach in his 1977 work *The Nature of Morality*.[17] For example, Richard Joyce specifically acknowledges his argument's connection with Harman's.[18] Wielenberg notes, "Harman was perhaps the first contemporary philosopher to outline a case against moral knowledge based on the claim that human moral beliefs can be explained without appealing to any moral truths. . . . Many epistemological evolutionary debunking arguments can be understood as variations on Harman's basic idea."[19] Since Harman, evolutionary debunking arguments have grown in popularity, in part because of the rise of sociobiology, now commonly called evolutionary psychology, which began with E. O. Wilson's 1975 work *Sociobiology: The New Synthesis*.

---

15. Darwin, *Charles Darwin*, 57.
16. Monod, *Chance and Necessity*, 180.
17. Harman, *Nature of Morality*.
18. Joyce, *Evolution of Morality*, 184.
19. Wielenberg, *Robust Ethics*, 147.

An Evolutionary Debunking Argument Based on Plantinga's Evolutionary Argument Against Naturalism

I'll use Plantinga's evolutionary argument against naturalism as the basis for my evolutionary debunking argument because, first, his argument is about the reliability of our cognitive faculties, which, as Wielenberg points out, is the crux of all evolutionary debunking arguments.[20] Second, because I'm a theist like Plantinga, I agree with him that our cognitive faculties, including those that produce our moral beliefs are, for the most part, reliable.[21] Plantinga's position is in contrast to atheists who usually use evolutionary debunking arguments to argue that our moral intuitions really are unreliable. However, I'll argue here that only *if* atheism and evolution were true, then our cognitive faculties would be unreliable. Third, Plantinga's evolutionary argument is broad in that it applies not just to moral intuitions but to all cognitive faculties; for this reason it's a more consistent position than those of atheists who often apply evolutionary debunking arguments only to moral and religious beliefs while maintaining that our cognitive faculties provide us with reliable beliefs in other areas.

Telling such an evolutionary story as described above is a common tactic employed by atheists, including Wielenberg, to try to explain away religious beliefs as false. In an effort to brush off C. S. Lewis's argument for God's existence from human desire for, and belief in, ultimate joy, Wielenberg writes of such desires that "evolutionary psychology . . . predicts that human beings will tend to hold a number of false beliefs."[22] As I'll show below, Wielenberg has spent a considerable amount of time trying to defend his assertion that we have true moral beliefs from evolutionary debunking arguments. Clearly he didn't realize his inconsistency in affirming evolutionary debunking arguments to dismiss the reliability of our religious beliefs while rejecting such arguments when it comes to the reliability of our moral beliefs. Russ Shafer-Landau rightly points out the inconsistency of applying evolutionary debunking arguments to only some of our beliefs: "If we are required to suspend judgment about all perceptual beliefs—as we must, if required to do so in the moral case—then we will most likely not be in a position to confirm the reliability of our perceptual faculties. We must presuppose the truth of at least some central, widely uncontroversial perceptual beliefs in order to get the confirmation of our perceptual faculties off the ground. But if we are allowed such

---

20. Wielenberg, *Robust Ethics*, 163.
21. A. Plantinga, *Where the Conflict Really Lies*, 313, 326, 335.
22. Wielenberg, *God and the Reach of Reason*, 118–19.

liberties in the perceptual realm, then we should be given similar license for morality. And then the debunking game is up."[23]

In order to construct an evolutionary debunking argument based on Plantinga's evolutionary argument against naturalism, let me first summarize the first three premises of his argument:[24]

1. The probability of our cognitive faculties being reliable, given atheism and evolution, is low.
2. If someone believes atheism and evolution, and sees that the probability of our cognitive faculties being reliable, given atheism and evolution, is low, then they have a defeater for their belief that our cognitive faculties are reliable.
3. If someone has a defeater for the reliability of their cognitive faculties, then they have a defeater for any belief produced by their cognitive faculties.

This argument can be applied explicitly to our moral beliefs as follows:

4. Our moral beliefs are produced by our cognitive faculties.
5. Therefore, if someone believes atheism and evolution, then they have a defeater for their belief that their moral beliefs are reliable.

Given atheism and evolution, there's no good reason to think our moral intuitions point to, or are connected with, moral truth that exists beyond our own subjective preferences. If the origination of our moral beliefs can be explained by their evolutionary survival value, then what reason is there to think they also happen to be objectively true? Surely there's no objective evidence for them; all we have to go on is our subjective intuitions, and there's no reason to think those are reliable, given atheism and evolution.

The first premise of Plantinga's argument is the most crucial. What is it about the evolutionary process that leads people to believe that it would not produce reliable cognitive faculties? Plantinga explains that, according to materialists, beliefs have two properties.[25] First, every belief has a physical property—

---

23. Shafer-Landau, "Evolutionary Debunking," 23.
24. A. Plantinga, *Where the Conflict Really Lies*, 314. Though Plantinga's argument uses naturalism in place of atheism, I use atheism here because, as explained previously, Wielenberg is not a naturalist.
25. A. Plantinga, *Where the Conflict Really Lies*, 321.

that is, the neuro-physiological process that occurs in the brain. Second, every belief also has a mental property that is the content of the belief. If someone believes that their coffee is hot, then the content of such a belief is "the coffee is hot." The content is true if it corresponds to reality and false if it does not. Materialists differ in their understandings of how a belief's content is related to its physical neuro-physiological properties. Reductive materialists claim that a belief's content *just is* the neuro-physiological properties, whereas nonreductive materialists claim a belief's content is *determined by* the neuro-physiological properties. In either case it's the neuro-physiological properties that cause the particular content of each belief we have.

The neuro-physiological properties also cause our behavior. This happens when, according to contemporary science, "neurons send a signal through effector nerves to the relevant muscles, causing those muscles to contract and thereby causing behavior."[26] The key point to premise 1 is that, if evolution works like contemporary scientists claim, nature selects for neuro-physiological properties on the basis of the *behavior* it causes, not on the basis of the *belief* it causes. The *right* type of behavior that nature selects for is of course the adaptive behavior that leads to greater chances for survival and reproduction. Thus, as long as a certain combination of neuro-physiological properties causes the right type of behavior, the content of the belief caused by such neuro-physiological properties makes no difference. Whether the content of a belief caused by some neuro-physiological properties is true or false is irrelevant because the only thing that matters to natural selection is whether those neuro-physiological properties cause the right behavior. According to this conclusion, then, our cognitive faculties were developed to produce the right behavior, not true beliefs. Therefore, if atheism and evolution are true, then the probability that our cognitive faculties are reliable, that they produce mostly true beliefs, is low.

It may be tempting to think that behavior would be more adaptive if it was associated with true beliefs. Plantinga uses the example of a zebra and a lion to illustrate this objection: Would not a zebra's behavior be more adaptive if its cognitive faculties produced true beliefs about the lion's presence and its tendency to eat zebras?[27] Plantinga gives two strong responses to this objection. First, he makes a distinction between true beliefs and accurate indicators. Indicators are devices that somehow track either an organism's internal processes or its external environment. While accurate indicators would certainly lead to

---

26. A. Plantinga, *Where the Conflict Really Lies*, 337.
27. A. Plantinga, *Where the Conflict Really Lies*, 328.

better adaptive behavior, it's important to recognize that indicators do not need true beliefs, or any beliefs at all, in order to work correctly. Plantinga offers the following examples:

> Anaerobic marine bacteria (so the story goes) contain magnetosomes, tiny internal magnets that indicate magnetic north; in the oceans of the northern hemisphere, this direction is down, toward the oxygen-free depths. These indicators are connected with the propulsion devices of the bacteria in such a way as to cause these creatures, which can't flourish in the oxygen-rich surface water, to move towards the deeper water. But this in no way requires that the bacteria form *beliefs*. . . . In the human body there are indicators for blood pressure, temperature, saline content, insulin level, and much else; in these cases neither the blood, nor its owner, nor anything else in the neighborhood ordinarily holds beliefs on the topic.[28]

In addition, one can easily think of many situations where false beliefs are associated with indicators that lead to adaptive behavior. For example, my cats are often frightened by the sight, and especially by the sound, of our vacuum. Presumably my cats have all sorts of false beliefs about the dreaded vacuum. If atheism and evolution are true, then their indicators, and the skittish behavior associated with them, were selected by nature because it helped keep cats out of the mouths of predators. This is an example of how the evolutionary process produced adaptive behavior that's associated with accurate indicators but false beliefs. The important thing to note is that the behavior is what nature selects for, regardless of the content of the belief. Similarly, assuming atheism and evolution, it would be reasonable to conclude that we also possess many beliefs not because they're true, but because they were associated with adaptive behavior.

Second, according to both reductive and nonreductive materialists, beliefs do not cause behavior. As explained above, if materialism is true, it must be the case that the physical neuro-physiological process causes both the behavior *and* the content of a belief. The content of the belief does not enter the causal chain between the physical neuro-physiological process and the resulting behavior.[29] As long as the neuro-physiological process causes the right adaptive behavior, it doesn't matter what belief content the neuro-physiological process also happens to cause.

---

28. A. Plantinga, *Where the Conflict Really Lies*, 328–29.
29. A. Plantinga, *Where the Conflict Really Lies*, 339.

If atheism and evolution are true, then we have good reason to worry about the reliability of our cognitive faculties, including those that produce our moral beliefs. If God does not exist and evolution is how we came to be, then the most plausible explanation for our moral beliefs is that they were selected by nature because they increased our chances for survival and reproduction. Because of the random process of evolution, and because nature selects for correct behavior, not true belief, evolutionary debunking arguments show that it would be extremely lucky if evolution happened to shape our moral beliefs so that they matched up with objective moral truth.

CHAPTER 12

ATTEMPTS TO DEFLECT THE LUCKY
COINCIDENCE OBJECTION

I acknowledge that Plantinga's evolutionary argument against naturalism has generated substantial controversy. His argument is cogent only to the extent that it can overcome the main objections that have been lodged against it in the literature.[1] However, since my purpose is to evaluate Wielenberg's model, I'll focus here on responding to his attempts to deflect it.

Wielenberg recognized that his readers may "be worried that [his] view entails that we are remarkably lucky" and referred such readers to the final section of his book, "How Lucky Are We?"[2] In this section he responds to two lucky coincidence objections. The first, he explains, is that "my model implies that many of our moral beliefs are 'Gettiered,' in that their being true depends on a kind of luck that is incompatible with knowledge. . . . The second

---

1.   For an introduction to these main objections, and Plantinga's responses to them, see Beilby, *Naturalism Defeated?*
2.   Wielenberg, *Robust Ethics*, 156.

worry is that because my account entails lots of lucky coincidences and other meta-ethical theories don't entail such coincidences, my theory has a weakness that those other theories lack."[3] In this chapter I'll address four of Wielenberg's attempts to deflect these lucky coincidence objections, and I'll argue that none of them are successful.

Wielenberg's Response to Plantinga's Evolutionary Argument Against Naturalism

Wielenberg wrote an article concerning Plantinga's evolutionary argument against naturalism in which he presents two critiques.[4] First, he argues that Plantinga's first premise (the probability of our cognitive faculties being reliable, given atheism and evolution, is low) should be rejected in light of the substantial evidence that our cognitive faculties *are* reliable. He admits that if *all we knew* was that some creatures developed by way of an evolutionary process, then "it would be unreasonable for us to believe that the cognitive faculties of such creatures are reliable."[5] However, he claims that we know much more than that; for instance, we know these creatures have reliable cognitive faculties. He writes, "I have all sorts of evidence for the reliability of my faculties. For example, most of my perceptual beliefs about medium-sized physical objects turn out to be true; such beliefs are deliverances of perception, so perception seems to be reliable. I know all sorts of things, and I wouldn't know these things if I weren't reliable."[6]

In a similar vein, he argues that even if Plantinga's first premise was granted, this still shouldn't lead to the second premise (if someone believes atheism and evolution are true, and sees that the probability of our cognitive faculties being reliable, given atheism and evolution, is low, then they have a defeater for their belief that our cognitive faculties are in fact reliable). Again, because we have so much evidence that our cognitive faculties are reliable, even if we came to see that the probability of this, given atheism and evolution, is low, we would have to conclude that, though it was unlikely, evolution must have indeed pulled it off and produced for us reliable cognitive faculties.

In his second critique of Plantinga's evolutionary argument against naturalism, Wielenberg argues that we don't know enough about how evolution worked to confidently assert Plantinga's first premise (the probability of our cognitive faculties being reliable, given atheism and evolution, is low). He admits there

---

3.   Wielenberg, *Robust Ethics*, 167.
4.   Wielenberg, "Alethically Rational Naturalist."
5.   Wielenberg, "Alethically Rational Naturalist," 85.
6.   Wielenberg, "Alethically Rational Naturalist," 90.

are cases where, despite having lots of good evidence for the reliability of his cognitive faculties, a person could become convinced concerning certain claims about his origin that would require him to doubt the reliability of his cognitive faculties. However, the theory of evolution doesn't meet this threshold because it's missing too much crucial information. Wielenberg explains, "While a typical reflective naturalist [atheist] believes that he has an understanding of some of the basic principles of evolution, he also believes that there are important causal factors of the actual process of evolution that led to the development of human cognitive faculties here on earth of which he is unaware."[7] To summarize, the less we know about how the actual evolutionary process took place, the less confidence we should place in Plantinga's first premise.

Wielenberg argues that, because our knowledge about how the evolutionary process formed our cognitive faculties is so incomplete, it should not undercut the vast amount of positive evidence we have for the reliability of our cognitive faculties. Therefore, we should place less confidence in Plantinga's first premise and more confidence in the evaluation of our own cognitive faculties. Wielenberg concludes, "It would take a lot of information about one's origin—it takes a developed, detailed, fleshed-out scenario that is not missing any crucial information, before the grounds for doubt are serious enough to annihilate or undercut all one's evidence for the reliability of one's faculties."[8] In other words, the evidence that our cognitive faculties are reliable is much greater than the evidence for Plantinga's first premise.

In response to Wielenberg's first critique, that we have a lot of evidence for the reliability of our cognitive faculties, it's important to note that Plantinga isn't arguing about how things actually *are*, but how things *would be* if evolution and atheism were true. As noted above, because Plantinga doesn't believe atheism is true, he doesn't face the implications of his argument and so can safely maintain our cognitive faculties are reliable. He writes, "Of course we all commonsensically assume that our cognitive faculties are for the most part reliable, at least over a large area of their functioning. . . . I don't mean to argue that this natural assumption is false; like everyone else, I believe that our cognitive faculties *are*, in fact, mostly reliable."[9] He even points out that this belief in the reliability of our cognitive faculties is properly basic.[10] However, the scenario under question is how things *would be* if atheism and evolution were true. Plantinga notes that

---

7. Wielenberg, "Alethically Rational Naturalist," 91.
8. Wielenberg, "Alethically Rational Naturalist," 93.
9. A. Plantinga, *Where the Conflict Really Lies*, 326.
10. A. Plantinga, *Where the Conflict Really Lies*, 341.

"in this context we can't just assume, of course, that if N&E [atheism and evolution], N [atheism] including materialism, were true, then things would still be the way they are."[11] If someone is convinced their cognitive faculties are reliable, and comes to see the probability of having reliable cognitive faculties is low given atheism and evolution, then this would be a good reason to doubt evolution or atheism or both. As noted above, raising doubts about the evolutionary process is the route Wielenberg takes in his second critique, but maybe what should be doubted instead is his atheism.

Regardless, there's a greater problem with Wielenberg's first critique. If someone believes atheism and evolution, and then comes to see that the probability of their cognitive faculties being reliable is low in this scenario, it wouldn't be possible for them to use arguments or evidence to try to prove their cognitive faculties are reliable. Any such attempt would fail because, to even begin such a move, they'd have to first assume their cognitive faculties were reliable, which is the very issue under consideration.[12] As Plantinga points out, "any such procedure would therefore be viciously circular."[13] In attempting such a strategy, one would be utilizing the very cognitive faculties under question in order to evaluate their reliability. Thus, it does Wielenberg no good in this context to try to argue for, or provide evidence of, the reliability of our cognitive faculties.

In response to Wielenberg's second critique, that we do not know enough about how evolution worked, it should be noted that Plantinga's argument is based on what contemporary scientists have reported about the process of evolution. He makes it clear that his argument applies only to someone who believes that atheism and evolution are true. Therefore, the hypothetical person in Plantinga's argument *does* believe what contemporary scientists currently say about the evolutionary process that developed our cognitive faculties. If someone *does not* believe evolution is true, or believes there are a lot of holes in the theory like the skeptic Wielenberg describes, then this argument doesn't apply to that person. Certainly there are various aspects about the theory of evolution that many do not find very credible; Plantinga himself has concerns with it.[14] Regardless, the force of Plantinga's argument depends not on whether the contemporary theory of evolution is true but on how much credibility a person attributes to it. The fact is that evolutionary scientists do claim to understand how evolution worked, and many atheists are confident that they're correct.

---

11. A. Plantinga, *Where the Conflict Really Lies*, 336.
12. A. Plantinga, *Where the Conflict Really Lies*, 346.
13. A. Plantinga, *Where the Conflict Really Lies*, 341.
14. A. Plantinga, *Where the Conflict Really Lies*, 225–64.

In fact, the theory of evolution is, for many atheists, a key part of their belief system. It's only to this type of atheist that Plantinga's argument applies.

In his article Wielenberg presents several hypothetical scenarios about someone finding out how he originated and then claims these scenarios more accurately reflect the position an atheist finds himself or herself in when considering evolution. In the first scenario, the hypothetical person discovers that he came about "by some process or other and [has] no idea at all what the process may be."[15] Each consecutive scenario increases the amount of information the person knows about how he originated. The fifth and final scenario, the one Wielenberg claims most resembles the situation of a reflective atheist, is as follows:

> I believe I was created by a certain machine. I believe that the machine operates according to certain principles, and I understand all or most of these principles. I cannot make a very good estimate of the probability of such a machine producing cognitively reliable creatures, but I suspect the probability is relatively low. I cannot make a very good estimate of the probability in question because I believe that whether or not a given being is cognitively reliable depends on the initial condition of the machine at the start of the creation process and I have no idea what the initial conditions of the machine were at the start of the process that created me. Now I realize that all the creatures around me were created in this machine as well. I further notice that the vast majority of them are cognitively reliable.[16]

The problem with this scenario is that it *does not* represent the typical atheist. It may represent how Wielenberg understands evolution, but most atheists believe they understand fairly well how evolution played out. It seems the more scientific or educated an atheist is, the louder he claims he can explain how evolution produced us.[17] Plus, it's the very cornerstone of their explanation—that nature selects for the ability to survive and reproduce, not the ability to know truth—that has led many, including Thomas Nagel, Barry Stroud, Patricia Churchland, and even Charles Darwin himself, to doubt the reliability of our cognitive faculties.[18]

---

15. Wielenberg, "Alethically Rational Naturalist," 87.
16. Wielenberg, "Alethically Rational Naturalist," 95.
17. Dawkins, *Selfish Gene*.
18. See quotes by these contemporary thinkers pointing out their doubts about our cognitive faculties in A. Plantinga, *Where the Conflict Really Lies*, 315.

With respect to our moral beliefs in particular, naturalist Joshua Greene, whom Wielenberg describes as one of the central figures in contemporary moral psychology,[19] and whose work Wielenberg highly praises,[20] writes, "I view science as offering a 'behind the scenes' look at human morality. Just as a well-researched biography can, depending on what it reveals, boost or deflate one's esteem for its subject, the scientific investigation of human morality can help us to understand human moral nature, and in so doing change our opinion of it. . . . Understanding where our moral instincts come from and how they work can . . . lead us to doubt that our moral convictions stem from perceptions of moral truth rather than projections of moral attitudes."[21] I'm contending here that Greene, Darwin, Dawkins, Nagel, Stroud, and Churchland more closely represent the typical atheist than Wielenberg's hypothetical so-called reflective atheist.

In this section I've argued that Wielenberg's attempt to deflect the lucky coincidence objection by critiquing Plantinga's evolutionary argument against naturalism fails for two reasons. First, his argument that we have a lot of evidence for the reliability of our cognitive faculties fails because it's viciously circular; one has to use the very cognitive faculties under question in order to evaluate their reliability. Second, his argument that we don't know enough about how evolution worked to confidently assert Plantinga's first premise fails because Plantinga's argument, by definition, applies only to those who claim to know enough about how evolution worked. In addition, many, if not most, atheists confidently claim to know enough about how evolution worked such that they should, if they're consistent, confidently assert Plantinga's first premise (the probability of our cognitive faculties being reliable, given atheism and evolution, is low).

Wielenberg's Third Factor Model

The second way Wielenberg attempts to address the lucky coincidence objection is by proposing that a third factor—namely, our cognitive faculties—explains why there's a correspondence between objective moral truth and our moral beliefs. He uses this third factor model to try to show why it's not a lucky coincidence that moral truth and moral beliefs correspond; they correspond because they both stem from our cognitive faculties. He summarizes this idea as follows: "There is a necessary connection between the cognitive faculties and moral rights [those who have such cognitive faculties necessarily have moral rights]. Those

---

19. Wielenberg, *Robust Ethics*, 110.
20. Wielenberg, *Robust Ethics*, 123.
21. Greene, "From Neural 'Is' to Moral 'Ought.'"

very cognitive faculties also generate moral beliefs, including the relevant beliefs about rights. The connection between the cognitive faculties and beliefs about moral rights is causal. In this way, the relevant cognitive faculties are responsible for both moral rights and beliefs about those rights, and so the cognitive faculties explain the correlation between moral rights and beliefs about those rights."[22] In other words, he posits that our cognitive faculties do more than generate our moral knowledge; they also instantiate ontologically our moral rights and obligations in the first place. Thus, our cognitive faculties, as a third factor, explain why there's a match between our moral beliefs and objective moral truth. Wielenberg writes, "The presence of the very cognitive faculties that cause (or at least causally contribute to) my belief that I have certain rights also entails that I have those very rights. . . . Certain non-moral features of the world [our cognitive faculties] both entail certain moral facts and causally contribute to the presence of moral beliefs that correspond to those moral facts."[23] Thus he argues that there's a correlation between our beliefs about moral rights and the fact that we do indeed have these rights in that both stem from a third factor, our cognitive faculties.[24] He notes that "if these claims are correct, then we have explained the 'remarkable fact' [that moral properties and moral beliefs correspond]. . . . It seems to me that if we can explain why (i) x causes y and (ii) x entails z, then we have explained why y and z tend to go together."[25]

To summarize, Wielenberg claims that human cognitive faculties do two things: they make objective moral properties be instantiated, and they generate our moral beliefs. Because moral properties and moral beliefs both stem from the same thing, our cognitive faculties, this secures a correlation between them while also allowing for the fact that moral properties themselves are causally inert. Wielenberg argued that if this is in fact the case, then "it is not at all unlikely that moral beliefs and moral facts will correspond."[26] He goes on to use his third factor model to try to deflect criticism from several prominent evolutionary debunking arguments from Gilbert Harman, Michael Ruse, Sharon Street, and Richard Joyce.[27]

In this section I'll argue that Wielenberg's third factor model fails to rebut the lucky coincidence objection. Assuming, for the sake of argument, that

---

22. Wielenberg, *Robust Ethics*, 145.
23. Wielenberg, *Robust Ethics*, 153–54.
24. Wielenberg, *Robust Ethics*, 56.
25. Wielenberg, *Robust Ethics*, 156.
26. Wielenberg, *Robust Ethics*, 154.
27. Wielenberg, *Robust Ethics*, 146–64.

cognitive faculties do necessarily make moral properties to be instantiated (see the concerns I raised about this proposed making relationship in chapter 8), the correspondence between moral properties and moral beliefs breaks down because, while his proposed making relationship between cognitive faculties and moral properties is necessary, his proposed relationship between cognitive faculties and moral beliefs is contingent. There's no good reason to think that beings with cognitive faculties like ours would come to have the same moral beliefs we do. We can easily imagine beings with similar cognitive faculties as our own but with radically different moral beliefs.

As I noted earlier, this point is amplified if one believes, as most atheists do, that our cognitive faculties and moral beliefs came about haphazardly through a random evolutionary process. Wielenberg himself doesn't take a position on whether all our moral beliefs can be explained in evolutionary terms, but he is "sympathetic to the view that at least *some* of our moral beliefs can be given evolutionary explanations."[28] In particular, he sketches an evolutionary explanation of how we came to have our beliefs about moral rights.[29]

The reason that beings with cognitive faculties like ours may not have the belief that they have moral properties such as rights is that the causal connection between cognitive faculties and moral beliefs is contingent, not necessary. That Wielenberg's model still includes contingency—that is, the contingency in the relationship between our cognitive faculties and our moral beliefs—leaves his model open to the lucky coincidence objection because, as Wielenberg himself admits, where there's contingency, there's luck.[30] Thus he doesn't eliminate the lucky coincidence objection with his third factor model, but only moves it somewhere else as he attempts to sweep contingency under the rug.

Wielenberg describes this making relationship between cognitive faculties and moral properties, the first part of his third factor model, as a necessary relationship, that it obtains in all possible worlds.[31] However, he proposes that the second part, the relationship between cognitive faculties and our moral beliefs, is contingent. Wielenberg admits that "because the basic ethical facts are necessary truths, if there is any luck in the correspondence between our psychological dispositions and moral reality, it must lie entirely on the psychological side of the equation."[32] His proposed correspondence between moral properties and moral

---

28. Wielenberg, *Robust Ethics*, 148.
29. Wielenberg, *Robust Ethics*, 135–44.
30. Wielenberg, *Robust Ethics*, 167.
31. Wielenberg, *Robust Ethics*, 36, 145, 156.
32. Wielenberg, *Robust Ethics*, 167.

beliefs breaks down because of this difference in causal necessity between the first and second parts of his third factor model.

Consider the following refutation by analogy. If Wielenberg's model works in the realm of moral knowledge, then it should also work in other realms of knowledge generated by our cognitive faculties, realms such as science and mathematics. Let us consider his third factor in the context of Fermat's Last Theorem.[33] For the purpose of this analogy, it's sufficient to note that Fermat's Last Theorem is a mathematical theorem proposed by Pierre de Fermat in 1637. He claimed he had developed a proof of this theorem, but such a proof was never found in any of his writings. Despite numerous attempts by mathematicians, there were no published successful proofs of this theorem until 1994. If we insert Fermat's Last Theorem into Wielenberg's third factor model, the two parts of the model would be as follows:

1. Our cognitive faculties make the property of "being able to prove Fermat's Last Theorem" to be instantiated.
2. Our cognitive faculties cause us to believe we can prove Fermat's Last Theorem.

It's easy to imagine beings like us who have the cognitive faculties that make them able to prove Fermat's Last Theorem, but who do not have the belief that they can. Similarly, it's easy to imagine beings like us who have cognitive faculties that make them have moral properties such as rights and obligations (assuming the first part of Wielenberg's model, his proposed making relationship, is correct), but who do not have the belief that they have such properties. Our imagination isn't even necessary, for there are in fact such people—that is, humans who do not think they, or others, have moral rights and obligations. The reason that beings with cognitive faculties like ours may not believe that they have moral properties is that the causal connection between cognitive faculties and moral beliefs is contingent, not necessary.

To summarize, I've argued in this section that Wielenberg doesn't avoid the lucky coincidence objection with his third factor model because he doesn't eliminate contingency; he only moves it to a different location in an attempt to sweep it under the rug. There is still contingency in his third factor model— namely, in the second part, his proposed relationship between our cognitive faculties and our moral beliefs. And where there's contingency, there's luck.

---

33. This particular refutation by analogy was suggested by Greg Welty.

Wielenberg's Proposal That the Laws of Nature Are Necessary

The issue we're considering is how much of a lucky coincidence it is in Wielenberg's model for our moral beliefs to match up with objective moral truth. Wielenberg understands that because his model, even with his third factor approach, still contains contingency, it remains vulnerable to this lucky coincidence objection. Therefore, in an attempt to remove all contingency, he spends the last few pages of his book *Robust Ethics* asking readers to entertain the idea that the laws of nature are metaphysically necessary. By "necessary" he means that something must be the case in all possible worlds, whereas something is "contingent" if it's possible for it not to be the case.[34] If the laws of nature were necessary in this sense, he argues, then any being with cognitive faculties like ours would necessarily have moral beliefs similar to ours.[35] Wielenberg makes this move because he understands that eliminating all contingency is the only way to ultimately rebut the lucky coincidence objection.

Wielenberg seems to agree with theists that there must be a necessary foundation of some sort for objective morality. Both sides, then, theists and atheists, recognize that contingent things are not enough; there must be something necessary that provides the stability needed for morality to be objective as opposed to just a subjective, accidental human belief. Theists argue that God provides such a necessary foundation, whereas Wielenberg asks his readers here to consider that the laws of nature are necessary.

In his attempt to deflect the lucky coincidence objection made by theists who argue that the existence of God is the best explanation for why our moral beliefs correspond to moral truth, Wielenberg writes, "The question of whether God's existence would decrease how lucky we would have to be to possess moral knowledge depends on the modal status of the laws of nature."[36] He considers two possible scenarios. First, if the laws of nature are metaphysically necessary, then it would not matter if God doesn't exist. He writes, "If there is no God but the laws of nature are metaphysically necessary, then the fact that there is no God to put in place just the right laws for moral knowledge to arise doesn't make us any luckier to have moral knowledge than we would be if God did exist because the laws of nature couldn't have been any different from what they are."[37] He

---

34. Wielenberg (*Robust Ethics*, 36) explains that he adopted these from A. Plantinga, *Nature of Necessity*, 44–45.
35. Wielenberg, *Robust Ethics*, 166–75.
36. Wielenberg, *Robust Ethics*, 174.
37. Wielenberg, *Robust Ethics*, 174.

argues, "Consequently, to make the case that the truth of theism would make our possession of moral knowledge less lucky than atheism, one would need to make the case that the laws of nature are not metaphysically necessary."[38]

Wielenberg seems to ignore the fact that the inverse is also true: to make the case that the truth of atheism would make our possession of moral knowledge *no more lucky* than if theism were true, which is what Wielenberg is trying to do, one would need to make the case that the laws of nature are metaphysically necessary. But Wielenberg makes no such attempt. Certainly one can speculate that the laws of nature are metaphysically necessary, but such an assertion is notoriously difficult to prove, as Wielenberg himself admits.[39]

Also, even if some of the laws of nature are metaphysically necessary, this would not mean that the evolutionary path that led to human beings was necessary. Therefore, Wielenberg has to go even further and speculate that the evolutionary process that led to the development of human beings may itself have been necessary in some sense. He summarizes this possibility as follows: "These considerations are hardly decisive, but I think they do indicate that it is a mistake simply to assume that it is nomologically possible for us (or other beings) to have evolved to m-possess radically different moral principles than the ones we actually possess. For all we know, m-possessing the DDE [a particular moral principle] is an inevitable outcome of the evolutionary process that made us capable of forming moral judgments in the first place."[40] Wielenberg is forced into this remarkable speculation because he realizes that if the evolutionary process that supposedly produced human beings was contingent, if it could have occurred differently, then our cognitive faculties could be different, which in turn may have resulted in vastly different moral beliefs. Charles Darwin himself recognized this when he wrote,

> If . . . men were reared under precisely the same conditions as hive-bees, there can hardly be a doubt that our unmarried females would, like the worker-bees, think it a sacred duty to kill their brothers, and mothers would strive to kill their fertile daughters; and no one would think of interfering. Nevertheless, the bee, or any other social animal, would gain in our supposed case . . . some feeling of right or wrong, or a conscience. For

---

38. Wielenberg, *Robust Ethics*, 174.
39. Wielenberg, *Robust Ethics*, 69.
40. Wielenberg, *Robust Ethics*, 172. On page 99 Wielenberg explained that "a person m-possesses (morphologically possesses) a moral principle when that principle guides their moral beliefs even though they aren't consciously aware of the principle itself."

each individual would have an inward sense of possessing certain stronger or enduring instincts, and others less strong or enduring. . . . In this case an inward monitor would tell the animal that it would have been better to have followed the one impulse rather than the other. The one course ought to have been followed, and the other ought not; the one would have been right and the other wrong.[41]

Fellow moral robust realist David Enoch agrees that "it is indeed true that had the causal forces shaping our intellectual and other normative faculties been very different, had they 'aimed' at things that are of no value at all or that are of disvalue, we would have been systematically mistaken in our normative beliefs. And we are indeed epistemically lucky that this (presumably) isn't the case. . . . So yes, some brute luck may remain."[42] He goes on to call the fact that our moral beliefs do line up with objective moral truth a miracle, albeit, in his estimation, a small miracle. After presenting a third factor model similar to Wielenberg's, he concludes his discussion as follows: "Let me not give the impression that this suggested way of coping with the epistemological challenge is ideal. Indeed, because of the (perhaps) remaining small miracle perhaps Robust Realism does lose some plausibility points here."[43]

As for Wielenberg's speculative solution that our evolutionary path might have been necessary, he explains that the amount of lucky coincidence involved in having moral beliefs that are correlated with objective moral truth depends on the answer to this question: "To what extent do the actual laws of nature permit the emergence of species of beings that m-possess moral principles radically different from the moral principles we m-possess?"[44] He begins his answer to this question with the following hypothetical claim, which he calls Extreme Specificity (ES): "The actual laws of nature entail that any being capable of forming moral beliefs at all m-possess all and only the principles included in Moral Truth."[45] He argues that if the laws of nature are metaphysically necessary in this regard, then "there is no luck at all involved in the fact that Bart [a hypothetical person he uses as an example] m-possesses moral

---

41. Darwin, *Descent of Man*, 100–101.
42. Enoch, *Taking Morality Seriously*, 173.
43. Enoch, *Taking Morality Seriously*, 175.
44. Wielenberg, *Robust Ethics*, 167.
45. Wielenberg, *Robust Ethics*, 168. Moral Truth is the set of all necessarily true general moral principles, which, as has been noted, are what he claims are brute ethical facts.

principles that correspond with moral reality rather than m-possessing radically different (and false) moral principles."[46]

Wielenberg is clear that he doesn't believe Extreme Specificity is true; he admits that "we simply lack the knowledge required to warrant a clear and confident answer" concerning Extreme Specificity, but he does suggest that "we may be relatively close to ES—or at least, closer to ES than some philosophers have suggested."[47] He even postulates that "for all we know, m-possessing the DDE [a particular moral principle] is an inevitable outcome of the evolutionary process that made us capable of forming moral judgments in the first place."[48] He understands that the closer we are to Extreme Specificity in the actual world, the smaller amount of luck is entailed by our having moral beliefs that correspond to objective moral truth. He concludes his book by stating, "As far as I can tell, a certain degree of agnosticism is called for with respect to just how lucky we are to have moral knowledge on a view like mine."[49]

Anticipating how some would respond to this speculation, Wielenberg preemptively argues that just because one can think of other ways evolution could have played out doesn't mean that those ways are actually possible. He explains his point as follows: "One might be tempted to argue that the fact that it is easy to imagine the laws of nature being different than they are is an indication of their metaphysical contingency. However, theists typically maintain that God's existence is metaphysically necessary; yet it is easy to imagine the nonexistence of God. Therefore, theists cannot consistently appeal to the conceivability of different laws of nature to support the metaphysical contingency of the actual laws of nature."[50] In response, it should be noted that the supposed evolutionary tree would seem to say that evolution not only could have but in fact did sprout off in many directions, leading to wildly different organisms. In addition, since Wielenberg is the one suggesting that the laws of nature and the evolutionary path that led to human beings may be necessary, the onus is on him to provide evidence for this claim.

In addition, Wielenberg himself inconsistently affirms that human beings were produced by an evolutionary process that was accidental and thus *contingent*. He writes, "Evolutionary processes have endowed us with certain unalienable rights and duties. Evolution has given us these moral properties by giving us

---

46. Wielenberg, *Robust Ethics*, 168.
47. Wielenberg, *Robust Ethics*, 169.
48. Wielenberg, *Robust Ethics*, 172.
49. Wielenberg, *Robust Ethics*, 175.
50. Wielenberg, *Robust Ethics*, 174 (emphasis added).

the non-moral properties that make such moral properties be instantiated. And if, as I believe, there is no God, then it is in some sense an *accident* that we have the moral properties that we do."[51] He also writes, "Contemporary atheists typically maintain that human beings are *accidental*, evolved, mortal, and relatively short-lived."[52]

Realizing the implications of these statements, Wielenberg explains in a footnote that, in the context of evolution, "accidental" should not be understood as a result of entirely random processes because "according to contemporary evolutionary theory, evolutionary processes are not, contrary to popular mischaracterizations, entirely chance-driven. Rather, they are driven by a combination of chance and necessity; see Mayr 2001, 119–20."[53] It's important to note that Mayr actually states that chance rules at the first step of evolution, with the production of variation through random mutation, and that determinism comes in only during the second step through nonrandom aspects of survival and reproduction based on a particular species' fixed, or determined, environment.[54] Thus, if evolution worked as many claim, that it was driven by accidental random mutations, which Wielenberg agrees to,[55] as well as chance changes in the environment, such as the success of other organisms, climate changes, meteorites, and so on, then it's very difficult to think that evolution had to *necessarily* produce human beings just the way they are.

Lastly, the suggestion that the laws of nature are metaphysically necessary comes dangerously close, at least for an atheist such as Wielenberg, to another line of reasoning—fine-tuning arguments for the existence of God.[56] Wielenberg recognizes this when he explains that if it's metaphysically necessary that any being capable of forming moral beliefs at all possesses only true moral beliefs, then "there is no luck at all involved in the fact that Bart [a hypothetical person he uses as an example] m-possesses moral principles that correspond with moral reality rather than m-possessing radically different (and false) moral principles."[57] Recognizing that this may be seen as a hint of fine-tuning, he writes in a footnote, "Perhaps Bart is lucky to exist at all, but that is a separate

---

51. Wielenberg, *Robust Ethics*, 56 (emphasis added).
52. Wielenberg, *Robust Ethics*, 51 (emphasis added).
53. Wielenberg, *Robust Ethics*, 51.
54. Mayr, *What Evolution Is*, 120–21.
55. Wielenberg, *Robust Ethics*, 51, 56.
56. Collins, "Teleological Argument."
57. Wielenberg, *Robust Ethics*, 168.

issue—one that connects with so-called 'fine-tuning' arguments, a topic I cannot engage in here."[58]

The important point is that the fine-tuning debate has sparked a lot of discussion over the past couple of decades, instigating a whole host of arguments for and against it. The fine-tuning argument itself and the most common argument against it, the argument for a proposed multiverse, are both based on the strong intuition that the laws of nature are not necessary but contingent. Wielenberg's suggestion that the laws of nature are metaphysically necessary would thus effectively rebut the prominent positions on both sides of the fine-tuning debate. At the very least, this should give one pause in accepting Wielenberg's speculative proposal that the laws of nature are metaphysically necessary. Whether one believes that God exists or not, it seems much more plausible that if he does exist, he exists necessarily—that is more plausible than the idea that the laws of nature are necessary.

Wielenberg's Accusation That Theism Also Has Lucky Coincidences

Wielenberg summarizes the lucky coincidence objection well when he explains that he's "assuming that there is significant overlap between the moral principles we m-possess and those included in Moral Truth[,] and . . . the issue before us is how lucky must we be in order for this overlap to exist."[59] Earlier he admits that if "there is no God, then it is in some sense an accident that we have the moral properties that we do."[60] He also acknowledges that his "view undoubtedly entails that certain elements of the universe (the actual laws of nature and basic ethical facts) fit together in a nifty and perhaps amazing way."[61] Elsewhere Wielenberg even admits that "there is . . . one view that might seem to require much less luck for moral knowledge than my view does. That view is our old friend theism."[62] He then quotes Derek Parfit, another advocate of robust normative realism: "God might have designed our brains so that, without causal contact, we can reason in ways that lead us to reach true answers to mathematical questions. We might have similar God-given abilities to respond to reasons, and to form true beliefs about these reasons."[63]

---

58. Wielenberg, *Robust Ethics*, 168.
59. Wielenberg, *Robust Ethics*, 169.
60. Wielenberg, *Robust Ethics*, 56.
61. Wielenberg, *Robust Ethics*, 175.
62. Wielenberg, *Robust Ethics*, 173.
63. Parfit, *On What Matters*, 2:493.

Wielenberg notes that many theists have suggested to him that theism seems "to require much less luck for moral knowledge than . . . [his] view does."[64] For instance, Adams explains that "if we suppose that God directly or indirectly causes human beings to regard as excellent approximately those things that are Godlike in the relevant way, it follows that there is a causal and explanatory connection between facts of excellence and beliefs that we may regard as justified about excellence, and hence that it is in general no accident that such beliefs are correct when they are."[65] Mark Linville has even suggested a specific "moral fine-tuning argument. . . . Certain of our moral beliefs—in particular, those that are presupposed in all moral reflection—are truth-aimed because human moral faculties are designed to guide human conduct in light of moral truth."[66] In response, Wielenberg argues that while it may *seem* that theism requires less luck for moral knowledge than his view, on further inspection this is actually not the case. He claims that theists should not criticize his model for having lucky coincidences because their view of objective morality also includes similar unexplained lucky coincidences. In this section I will challenge Wielenberg's claim.

To begin, consider his second possible scenario concerning the modal status of the laws of nature: "Suppose for the sake of argument that (i) if God exists then the laws of nature are contingent and are determined by God and that . . . (ii) there can be lucky coincidences involving only necessary truths. Given these assumptions, it might be suggested that my view involves a large number of unexplained coincidences between necessary truths[,] . . . that theism does not involve such coincidences, and that this is an advantage of theism over my view."[67] Wielenberg responds to this objection by first admitting his view does have unexplained coincidences: "For example, on my view it is a coincidence that the DDE [a certain moral principle] is necessarily true and that the laws of nature that generate beings that reason in accordance with the DDE are necessarily true."[68] But he claims that theists should not criticize this, because "there is reason to believe that the theistic account of moral knowledge . . . will also involve unexplained coincidences between necessary truths. Back in chapter two . . . I suggested that Adams's theistic meta-ethical theory implies that there are a number of brute ethical facts."[69]

64. Wielenberg, *Robust Ethics*, 173.
65. Adams, *Finite and Infinite Goods*, 70.
66. Linville, "Moral Argument," 5.
67. Wielenberg, *Robust Ethics*, 174.
68. Wielenberg, *Robust Ethics*, 174–75.
69. Wielenberg, *Robust Ethics*, 175.

It's necessary to consider Wielenberg's argument in chapter 2 of his book because it's a crucial part of his response to the theist's lucky coincidence objection and explains the connection he makes between this objection and brute ethical facts. In chapter 2, while trying to explain the ontological existence of morality, Wielenberg appeals to brute ethical facts as an important part of his model. He writes, "Such facts are the foundation of (the rest of) objective morality and rest on no foundation themselves. To ask of such facts, 'where do they come from?' or 'on what foundation do they rest?' is misguided. . . . They come from nowhere, and nothing external to themselves grounds their existence; rather, they are fundamental features of the universe that ground other truths."[70] Similar to his strategy in chapter 4, here in chapter 2 Wielenberg maintains that theists should not criticize his view for appealing to brute ethical facts because they do so as well. He explains that "[theists] and I are all committed to the existence of basic ethical facts. If this is right, then none of us can reasonably criticize the approach of the other on the grounds that it posits values with no external foundation."[71]

Wielenberg specifically points to Adams's model as an example, claiming that his "divine command theory relies on ethical claims for which no further explanation is provided. . . . Adams provides no explanation for them. Within his system, they are brute ethical facts."[72] In other words, "God's ability to impose obligations by way of His commands depends on the truth of certain ethical facts that are not themselves grounded in God. . . . Both sides appeal to ethical claims for which they provide no foundation."[73] Thus Wielenberg maintains, "Adams's theistic view and my non-theistic view have the same basic structure: some ethical claims are taken as substantive, metaphysically necessary, and brute."[74] He believes this should "put to rest once and for all the demand that non-theists ground all of their ethical claims. Neither a theist . . . nor an adherent of non-theistic robust normative realism can satisfy this demand. . . . On both types of views, the bottom floor of objective morality rests ultimately on nothing."[75]

It's important to understand what Wielenberg has claimed here. He has claimed that all theistic moral theories include brute ethical facts and then has

---

70. Wielenberg, *Robust Ethics*, 38.
71. Wielenberg, *Robust Ethics*, 46.
72. Wielenberg, *Robust Ethics*, 53–54.
73. Wielenberg, *Robust Ethics*, 54.
74. Wielenberg, *Robust Ethics*, 43.
75. Wielenberg, *Robust Ethics*, 55.

attempted to show in particular that Adams's model includes brute ethical facts. But what does he mean by brute ethical facts? If all he means to say is that all theistic moral theories have explanatory ultimates, then, yes, that's true. In chapter 8 above I affirmed, in agreement with Wielenberg, that there must be an ultimate ontological stopping point. Wielenberg posits brute ethical facts, akin to Platonic abstract objects, as the ontological ultimate, whereas theists posit God as the ontological ultimate. In chapter 8 I made my case that God is a more satisfactory ontological ultimate than Wielenberg's brute ethical facts. In addition, I explained that there is a vast difference between theists proposing necessary facts about God as a concrete object—that he exists, that he has a certain moral nature, that he is triune, and so on—and Wielenberg's proposal that there are necessary brute ethical facts that exist abstractly on their own. In the former, it is God, a concrete object, who is the ontological ultimate, not facts about him. Most theists, including me, do not claim that these necessary facts about God are ontologically ultimate but that these facts are simply descriptions of what the ontological ultimate (i.e., God) is like. This is vastly different than Wielenberg's proposal that certain brute ethical facts exist abstractly on their own as ontological ultimates.

However, Wielenberg has gone further than merely claiming that all theistic moral theories have an explanatory ultimate. In this context, when Wielenberg says all theistic theories have brute ethical facts, he actually means that they all have ethical facts that, as seen in the quotes from his book included in the previous few paragraphs, "have no external foundation," "come from nowhere," and have "nothing external to themselves [grounding] their existence"; "ultimately there is no explanation for their existence," and they "are not grounded in God."

Of course Wielenberg is comfortable with having such ethical facts in his model because he affirms them as abstract objects that can exist on their own. His argument here, though, is that theists cannot criticize his model for having such ungrounded ethical facts because he claims all theistic models also affirm such ethical facts that are not grounded in God but exist on their own in this abstract sense. If some ethical facts are not grounded in God but exist on their own in this abstract sense, then why couldn't all moral facts exist this way? His point is well taken that, in such a scenario, God becomes unnecessary for objective morality.

Thus the pertinent question is: Do all theistic moral theories, and Adams's in particular, contain such ethical facts that are not grounded in God? By explaining that Wielenberg attributes such ungrounded ethical facts to Adams only because he misunderstood his moral theory, I will show how his attempt here to deflect the theist's lucky coincidence objection is unsuccessful. Wielenberg is mistaken when he writes that Adams's "divine command theory relies on ethical claims for which no further explanation is provided," and that the ethical facts in Adams's model "are not themselves grounded in God."[76]

Wielenberg claims that Adams's ungrounded ethical facts include the following: "(i) only good social *relationships* can generate morally good reasons to obey commands; (ii) the better the *character* of the commander, the more reason there is to obey his or her commands; and (iii) the better the *command* itself, the more reason there is to obey it."[77] It's understandable how Wielenberg misunderstood Adams here and concluded that he was proposing these as ungrounded ethical facts considering the way Adams presented them as three general moral truths and then applied them to our relationship with God. However, Wielenberg failed to note that, in this section of his book, Adams was specifically discussing the second part of his model, the part that only grounds the nature of moral obligation, not moral value, which is the first part of his theory.

As I explained in chapter 4, a theory of moral obligation has to do only with grounding our moral duties, whereas a theory of moral value attempts to provide the metaphysical grounds for what is morally good. After Adams discusses these three ethical facts that Wielenberg summarizes, he notes that a "theory of the nature of obligation is not a theory of the nature of value. Obligation and value have different roles in an ethical system. . . . The goodness of *actions, relationships, personal characteristics, and demands* that is invoked in the present discussion of the nature of obligation can be assumed to be faithful imaging of God, as explained in chapter 1."[78] There, in chapter 1, Adams wrote that "if God is the Good itself, then the Good is not an abstract object but a concrete (though not a physical) individual."[79] In other words, in Adams's model these three ethical facts are not ungrounded, as Wielenberg claims, but are in fact grounded in God's moral nature. Adams explains further:

> I assume that the character and commands of God satisfy certain conditions. More precisely, I assume that they are consistent with the divine nature having properties that make God an ideal candidate, and the salient candidate, for the semantically indicated role of the supreme and definitive Good. . . . Divine command theory, as I conceive it, is a theory of the nature

---

76. Wielenberg, *Robust Ethics*, 53–54.
77. Wielenberg, *Robust Ethics*, 53 (emphasis added).
78. Adams, *Finite and Infinite Goods*, 245 (emphasis added).
79. Adams, *Finite and Infinite Goods*, 14.

of obligation only, and not of moral properties in general. In particular, it is not a theory of the nature of the good, but presupposes a theory of the good. . . . For in articulating the necessary conditions on the characteristics of a God whose commands are to constitute the standard of moral obligation, and in developing the related reasons for accepting divine commands as such a standard, I make full use of the account of the nature of the good that I have given in part I.[80]

Wielenberg is mistaken; theists do not believe that some ethical facts are ungrounded, existing on their own, and ultimately resting on nothing. No, most theists, including Adams and me, claim that all ethical facts are grounded in God. Adams writes that "anything we can plausibly regard as moral obligation must be grounded in a relation to something of real value. . . . The goodness of finite things consists in fragmentary and multidimensional resemblance to a supreme Good [i.e., God]."[81] With Wielenberg's model the story ends with brute ethical facts, but with theism all ethical facts are ultimately grounded in God and rest on him as their foundation.

Thus, going back now to Wielenberg's response to the theist's lucky coincidence objection in chapter 4 of his book, he claims that, according to theism, "morality depends on some coincidences between certain divine facts and various basic ethical facts. For example, on Adams's view the fact that we have powerful reasons to fulfill our moral obligations depends on the following pair of necessary truths: (i) there is a good God; and (ii) we have reason to obey commands issued by good agents."[82] He exclaims that these two "necessary truths coincide in just the way required to generate reasons to fulfill our moral obligations—how convenient! Therefore, there is a plausible case to be made that the unexplained necessary coincidences worry has equal force against my view and a theistic approach to meta-ethics, and hence there is no advantage for the theistic approach here."[83] Wielenberg claims, first, that Adams's model has ethical facts that are not grounded in God and, second, that it's a lucky coincidence these ungrounded ethical facts match up with God's moral nature. However, since, as has been shown, Adams's model does not have such ungrounded ethical facts, Wielenberg's lucky coincidence accusation concerning Adams's model falls flat.

---

80. Adams, *Finite and Infinite Goods*, 250.
81. Adams, *Finite and Infinite Goods*, 232–33.
82. Wielenberg, *Robust Ethics*, 175.
83. Wielenberg, *Robust Ethics*, 175.

To summarize, Wielenberg argues that the theist's lucky coincidence objection to his theory doesn't carry weight because theism also involves lucky coincidences between the goodness of God and certain ungrounded ethical facts. But as I've shown, his response is unsuccessful because he misunderstood Adams's model. According to theists, these are not two separate issues: Wielenberg's (ii), that we have reason to obey commands issued by good agents, is not a separate ungrounded ethical fact but is itself grounded in (i), the goodness of God. One final quote from Adams's explanation will be helpful to clear up Wielenberg's confusion:

> The goodness that I have thus ascribed to God's *commands*, to God's personal *characteristics*, and to God's *relationship* to us is the goodness whose nature I discussed in previous chapters—a goodness of which God is the standard. . . . The order of presentation is significant here. . . . A theory of the good for which God is the constitutive standard of excellence need not presuppose moral obligation, but my theory of moral obligation does presuppose my theory of the good. It is only a God who is supremely excellent in being, in commanding, and more generally in relating to us, whose commands can plausibly be regarded as constituting moral obligation.[84]

A correct understanding of Adams's theistic model takes the force out of this fourth attempt of Wielenberg's to deflect the theist's lucky coincidence objection. There is no lucky coincidence between (i) and (ii) within theism because (ii), that we have reason to obey commands issued by good agents, is not an ungrounded ethical fact but is grounded in (i), the goodness of God. Thus, the theist's lucky coincidence objection to Wielenberg's model still stands.

I've argued here that Wielenberg is incorrect in his account of theistic moral theories. I've also argued that not all theistic moral theories have ungrounded ethical facts. Specifically, Wielenberg claims that Adams's model includes unexplained lucky coincidences between certain divine facts and some ethical facts that Wielenberg thinks are ungrounded. I cleared up this confusion by showing where Adams explains that these ethical facts are actually grounded in God and thus that Adams's theory doesn't include the lucky coincidence Wielenberg claims it does. Thus Wielenberg is unsuccessful in his attempt to deflect the lucky coincidence objection by claiming theism is vulnerable in this regard too. If atheism and evolution are true, then it would

---

84. Adams, *Finite and Infinite Goods*, 255 (emphasis added).

be an extremely lucky coincidence if our moral beliefs reliably corresponded with objective moral truth. On the other hand, a triune God, as the source of all things, provides a more plausible explanation for why our moral beliefs match up correctly with objective moral truth.

CHAPTER 13

THEISTIC MORAL THEORIES
AND LUCKY COINCIDENCES

Grounds for the Moral Goodness of Obeying God

The theistic moral theory that Wielenberg critiques most is Robert Adams's. As I discussed above, one of his primary criticisms is that he claims Adams's theory, just like Wielenberg's own theory, entails lucky coincidences. In particular, he argues that Adams's model includes lucky coincidences between God's goodness and certain supposed ungrounded ethical facts. He claims this is representative of all theistic models, that they all inevitably posit moral truths that are not grounded in God but exist as ungrounded ethical facts. Insofar as my divine love theory is similar to Adams's, Wielenberg's criticisms apply to it as well. Above I argued that his critique of Adams's model in this regard is incorrect, but in this chapter I'll show how my divine love theory more fully rebuts Wielenberg's accusation that all theistic moral theories have lucky coincidences and ethical facts that are not grounded in God.

Remember that ungrounded ethical facts play a large and important role in Wielenberg's model. He maintains that theists cannot consistently criticize him for appealing to ungrounded ethical facts because they do so as well. He goes on to claim that all theistic moral theories must ultimately, either explicitly or implicitly, entail such ungrounded ethical facts; hence theistic models fail in trying to ground all objective moral truths in God. He argues that since theistic models include ungrounded ethical facts, this makes his nontheistic model more plausible. If theists have at least some ungrounded ethical facts in their models, they must agree it's possible for such moral truths to exist on their own without any foundation. If some moral truths can exist without a foundation, why not all of them? In such a scenario God becomes unnecessary for the existence of objective morality.

Wielenberg writes that the divine command theorist's "explanation of the origin of our moral duties depends on an ungrounded ethical fact, namely that if the Good commands you to do something, then you are morally obligated to do it. The atheist might well ask: what is the grounding for *this* ethical claim?"[1] In other words, what grounds the truth that it's morally good to obey God? On the same page Wielenberg argues that Adams's model is susceptible to this attack by noting that Adams's particular "divine command theory relies on ethical claims for which no further explanation is provided. . . . Adams provides no explanation for them. Within his system, they are brute ethical facts."[2]

A brief side note is required here. The question I'm dealing with at this point is: What grounds the ethical fact that it's *good* to obey God's commands? However, Wielenberg's critique raises an additional question: Why are we *obligated* to obey God's commands? I addressed this issue at the end of chapter 4, but I'll summarize it here again to give some context. Basically, it seems there's one obligation that doesn't come from God's commands—the obligation to obey God's commands. Critics claim it's circular, or results in an infinite regress, if one claims this obligation comes from God's command as well. The two questions (What grounds the ethical fact that it's good to obey God's command? and Why are we obligated to obey God's command?) are related in that Wielenberg claims the theist, in answering either of them, ultimately has to appeal to ungrounded brute ethical facts. Thus, to avoid this accusation, it's not enough to explain why it's good to obey God, which is what I'll attempt to do for the rest of this

---

1.   Wielenberg, *Robust Ethics*, 53.
2.   Wielenberg, *Robust Ethics*, 53–54.

chapter, for one could then ask what obligates us to do what God commands in the first place.

Let me first address this other issue—the issue of what grounds the ethical fact that we *should* obey God's commands—before we move on to the issue of what grounds the ethical fact that it's *good* to obey God's commands. As I noted in chapter 4, John Hare, drawing on Duns Scotus's moral theology, has provided the best answer to the question "Why are we obligated to obey God's commands?"

> It is necessarily true, Scotus holds, that God is to be loved. We know this just by knowing the terms "God" and "to be loved." This is because we know that, if God exists, God is supremely good, and we know that what is supremely good is to be loved. It is also true that we know that to love God is at least to obey God. . . . Loving God is not simply to repeat God's will in our will, because there are things God wills that God does not will for us to will. So what we are to repeat in our wills is God's will for our willing. But willing what God wills for our willing is obedience. So it is necessarily true not just that God is to be loved, but that God is to be obeyed. If I justify the claim that the moral demand is a proper demand upon me by saying that God's command makes things obligatory, I am not terminating the justification in something that *itself* requires justification, except in as far as I have to justify the claim that God exists. This means that divine commands do not generate *all* our obligations, because there is one important exception, namely the obligation to obey divine commands. But this is not a troubling exception once one accepts the necessary truths (if God exists) that God is to be loved and that God is to be obeyed.[3]

Basically, our obligation to obey God's commands comes from the necessary truth that God should be loved. If God should be loved, and obeying God's commands is one of the primary ways we love him, then we should obey his commands. "God should be loved" generates our moral obligation to obey his commands because obeying God's commands is how we go about loving him. As I explained at the end of chapter 9, because God is love, he necessarily must command humans toward what would be the greatest good for them—that is, a loving relationship with him. Loving God is the greatest good for humans

---

3.   Hare, *God's Command*, 17–18.

because, since good is that which resembles God, loving God resembles him more than anything else.

If our moral obligation to obey God's commands ultimately stems from the fact that God should be loved, then someone may well ask, "What grounds the truth that God should be loved?" Quite simply, God does. God is the ultimate ontological ground of this truth. "God should be loved" is not an ungrounded abstract ethical fact but is itself grounded in God. As I argued in chapter 8, God is the ultimate ground and ontological stopping point for everything. Yes, we can list reasons *why* God should be loved—he is supremely good, he created us, he loved us first, and so on—but these are all merely facts about God. These true facts themselves are not the ultimate ontological stopping point; the ground for these facts about God is God himself because he is the ultimate ontological stopping point that these facts are merely describing.

Hare affirms my line of reasoning here when he notes, in the long quote above, that God's existence—that is, God himself—is what terminates this regress of moral obligation. God himself, a concrete being that exists as three divine persons in loving relationship with each other, is the ultimate stopping point that needs no further explanation. Yes, there are brute facts that describe God—he exists, he's triune, and so on—but God is the thing that's ultimate, not facts about him. Facts about God merely describe who and what he is like, and thus these facts are grounded in him. Such facts, which are grounded in a concrete being in the sense that they merely describe him, are radically different from Wielenberg's proposed brute ethical facts that exist ungrounded on their own without a concrete foundation.

To summarize, I'm proposing that there are true facts that describe what God is like and how the three divine persons treat each other—they love each other, respect each other, care for each other, and want what's best for each other unselfishly. However, these facts merely describe who and what God is and how the trinitarian persons act toward each other, and then we use the term *good* to describe these ways in which God is like. As Adams explains, God *is* the Good. These facts about God are not the ultimate stopping point, but God himself, as a necessary concrete being, is the ultimate stopping point. This situation is similar to when children are told that God made the universe, but then they ask, "Well, then who made God?" If Christianity is true, and I believe it is, then God wasn't made, but everything else was made by him. God is the ultimate ontological stopping point that ends the infinite regress in terms of where things came from, both with the physical universe and with moral obligation; both are ultimately grounded in him.

Let's return now to the matter at hand: What grounds the ethical fact that it's *good* to obey God's commands? As discussed above, Wielenberg identifies the following supposed ungrounded ethical facts in Adams's model: "(i) only good social *relationships* can generate morally good reasons to obey commands; (ii) the better the *character* of the commander, the more reason there is to obey his or her commands; and (iii) the better the *command* itself, the more reason there is to obey it."[4] Wielenberg's suggestions that theistic models include ungrounded ethical facts ("it's morally good to obey God" and Adams's supposed three brute ethical facts) are related in that both of them have to do with moral obligation. In both cases Wielenberg is claiming that there are key truths concerning moral obligation within theistic models that have no foundation or grounding. Thus, his concern may be summarized as follows: How is the theistic theory of moral obligation grounded in the theistic theory of moral good? In other words, what grounds the truth that it's morally good to obey God? Wielenberg's claim is that in fact in theistic models it's not grounded, but here I'll show how it is grounded in God within my divine love theory.

In particular I'll argue that the specific ungrounded ethical facts that Wielenberg claims to find in Adams's model are actually not ungrounded but are grounded in God's triunity. As noted above, Adams himself explicitly stated that the second part of his model (moral obligation) is grounded in the first part of his model (moral value). However, while Adams noted *that* these specific ethical facts are grounded in God, he didn't give a thorough explanation as to *how* they are so grounded. Here I'll expand on Adams's model by adding to it important truths concerning God's triunity in order to show more explicitly *how* God is the ground of these specific ethical truths. If this argument is successful, then it will show that Wielenberg is incorrect in his claim that all theistic models entail ungrounded ethical facts, and thus theists are not inconsistent when criticizing Wielenberg for positing unexplained lucky coincidences and ungrounded ethical facts.

Human Obedience as Imaging the Triune God

My goal in this section is to show more specifically how the second part of Adams's model (moral obligation) is grounded in the first part (moral value), and ultimately grounded in God, by adding to his model important truths concerning God's triunity. First, consider the possibility that moral obligation (humans should obey God) is grounded in moral value (good is what resembles

---

4.   Wielenberg, *Robust Ethics*, 53 (emphasis added).

God) as follows: Our human moral obligation to obey God is grounded in the Good (God as Trinity) because God exists analogously as a fellowship of persons, a fellowship that itself includes obedience. Therefore, when humans obey God, this very obedience is imaging, or resembling, God, and hence it's morally good according to the first part of Adams's model. If God exists analogously as a fellowship of persons, a fellowship that includes obedience, then there's a sense in which humans' obedience to God does resemble the Godhead and hence is morally good. Thus the moral truth that it's good to obey God is not an ungrounded ethical fact with no foundation, as Wielenberg claims, but rests on the foundation of God's triunity.

The key here is to understand how obedience itself exists within the Trinity, such that human obedience to God resembles the obedience found within the triune God. If the Trinity exists analogously as a fellowship of persons where, for instance, God the Son obeys God the Father, then, when we obey God, we are actually resembling the Godhead in a morally pertinent sense. Remember that Wielenberg's primary critique, as summarized above, is the question of what grounds the truth that it's morally good to obey God. I'm arguing here that the truth "It's morally good to obey God" is not an ungrounded ethical fact that has no foundation but is grounded in God's triunity, in that "obeying God" is "good" because it resembles God's inner-trinitarian relationships.

To summarize, I'm arguing that ultimately something is morally good if it resembles God in a morally pertinent sense. In addition, if God exists as a Trinity that is analogously like a fellowship of persons that includes obedience among the persons, even if we do not fully understand all the details about how this obedience works, then human obedience to God resembles God and is therefore morally good. Certainly, in God's creation of human beings, there are ways that the relationship between humans and God is different from the relationship between the persons of the Trinity. However, it may be the case that the obedience of the Son to the Father within the Trinity is similar enough to the relationship between humans and God such that human obedience to God resembles the obedience of the Son to the Father, and this resemblance could be enough such that, since it resembles God, it is morally good. If this is correct, then the truth that it's morally good for humans to obey God is grounded in God.

What about the three moral facts within Adams's model that Wielenberg claims are ungrounded ethical facts? Remember that these three facts have to do with moral obligation; here again is Wielenberg's accurate summary of them: "(i) only good social *relationships* can generate morally good reasons to obey commands; (ii) the better the *character* of the commander, the more reason there is to obey his or her commands; and (iii) the better the *command* itself, the more reason there is to obey it."[5] Below are three passages from Adams's work where he claims *that* these aspects of moral obligation (the second part of his model) are grounded in moral value (the first part of his model). After each passage I'll explain how adding important truths concerning God's triunity helps explain *how* this is the case. First, Adams writes,

> The goodness that I have thus ascribed to God's *commands*, to God's personal *characteristics*, and to God's *relationship to us* is the goodness whose nature I discussed in previous chapters—a goodness of which God is the standard. . . . The order of presentation is significant here. . . . A theory of the good for which God is the constitutive standard of excellence need not presuppose moral obligation, but my theory of moral obligation does presuppose my theory of the good. It is only a God who is supremely excellent in *being*, in *commanding*, and more generally in *relating to us*, whose commands can plausibly be regarded as constituting moral obligation.[6]

By considering the relationships between the persons of the Trinity, we can more readily see *how* God is the standard of goodness for these three things. God's triunity is the standard, ground, and foundation of these three things because, according to this first proposal, within the Trinity there are good *relationships*, excellent personal *characteristics*, and *commands* that are obeyed.

Second, Adams explains his position as follows:

> I assume that the character and commands of God satisfy certain conditions. More precisely, I assume that they are consistent with the divine nature having properties that make God an ideal candidate, and the salient candidate, for the semantically indicated role of the supreme and definitive Good. . . . Divine command theory, as I conceive it, is a theory of the nature of obligation only, and not of moral properties in general. In particular, it is not a theory of the nature of the good, but presupposes a theory of the good. . . . For in articulating the necessary conditions on the characteristics of a God whose commands are to constitute the standard of moral obligation, and in developing the related reasons for accepting divine commands

---

5.   Wielenberg, *Robust Ethics*, 53 (emphasis added).
6.   Adams, *Finite and Infinite Goods*, 255 (emphasis added).

as such a standard, I make full use of the account of the nature of the good that I have given in part I.[7]

God is the ideal candidate for the role of the supreme and definitive Good that can be resembled by humans because, according to this first proposal, within God as Trinity these three things exist—good *relationships*, excellent personal *characteristics*, and commands that are *obeyed*. Thus, if this first proposal is correct, when humans obey God, the very act of their obedience resembles God and thus is morally good.

Third, Adams writes that a "theory of the nature of obligation is not a theory of the nature of value. Obligation and value have different roles in an ethical system. . . . The goodness of *actions, relationships, personal characteristics, and demands* that is invoked in the present discussion of the nature of obligation can be assumed to be faithful imaging of God, as explained in chapter 1."[8] The second part of Adams's model, the part that deals with moral obligation (relationships, personal characteristics, and commands), is grounded in the first part of his model (humans are good when they faithfully image the Good—i.e., God) because *relationships*, personal *characteristics*, and *commands* are aspects of God's triunity that can be imaged by humans in their relationship to God.

My argument can be summarized as follows:

1. If something resembles God, it is good.
2. Our obedience to God analogously resembles the triune God.
3. Therefore, our obedience to God is good.

In this section I've entertained the proposal that premise two can be derived as follows:

a. There is obedience of the Son to the Father within the Trinity.
b. Human obedience to God is sufficiently similar to the obedience of the Son to the Father such that there is an analogous resemblance between these two instances of obedience.
c. Therefore premise two: our obedience to God analogously resembles the triune God.

---

7.   Adams, *Finite and Infinite Goods*, 250.
8.   Adams, *Finite and Infinite Goods*, 245 (emphasis added).

Call this the "human obedience resembles the Son's obedience" proposal. In the next few sections I'll explore two alternative ways of deriving premise two.

Concerns with Social Trinitarianism

Some may have concerns with the trinitarian ideas I've presented so far in this chapter. As I discussed in chapter 5, the two main camps in trinitarian theology are classical trinitarians and social trinitarians.[9] Most classical trinitarians may be uncomfortable with the way I've described the Trinity in this chapter. I presented the proposal above first (human obedience resembles the Son's obedience) because it most simply illustrates how I'm trying to respond to Wielenberg's critique. Now that you the reader understands what I'm trying to do, I'll elaborate on and slightly adjust key trinitarian aspects within my argument. By doing so I'll show that the argument I'm presenting in this chapter, in response to Wielenberg's accusation that theistic models also have ungrounded ethical facts, doesn't entail, or in any way require, social trinitarianism or obedience within the Trinity. If I'm successful, then both social trinitarians and classical trinitarians should be able to support my argument here.

Below I'll explore the three trinitarian claims I made in the previous section, each roughly corresponding to one of the three summary statements encapsulating Adams's three points that Wielenberg claims are brute ethical facts. After each claim I'll discuss how classical trinitarians can affirm such a claim. The important issue at the heart of all three claims is that a particular aspect of "God as Trinity" is *analogously similar* to an aspect of the relationship between God and humans—that is, *similar enough* that humans can resemble this aspect of God and thus would be "morally good" as defined in the first part of Adams's model.

The first claim is that the relationships within the Trinity are analogously like the relationships between God and humans. This roughly corresponds to Adams's first point that only good relationships can generate morally good reasons to obey commands. Though classical trinitarians understand God to be a single divine subject, most of them, as I showed in chapter 5, also affirm that there are loving relationships between the persons of the Trinity and that this same love is extended analogously from the Trinity to humans.

While classical trinitarians are rightfully leery about positing too much of a resemblance between the divine life and human life, they do acknowledge there is some resemblance. For example, Lewis Ayres writes that although "the divine

---

9.   For a good introduction, see Sexton, *Two Views on the Doctrine of the Trinity.*

life is unique . . . Christ himself calls us to the task [of drawing parallels between the divine life and ours] at John 17:20–21. . . . Thinking about the relationship between the divine life and ours *as if* we were dealing with two distinct and separated realities is a mistake."[10] The verses Ayres mentions here show Jesus explicitly pointing out the connection between God's inner-trinitarian relationships and the relationship between God and humans. Jesus prays that his disciples "may all be one; even as You, Father, are in Me and I in You, that they also may be in Us, so that the world may believe that You sent Me" (17:20–21). He continues, "The glory which You have given Me I have given to them, that they may be one, just as We are one; I in them and You in Me, that they may be perfected in unity, so that the world may know that You sent Me, and loved them, even as You have loved Me . . . for You loved Me before the foundation of the world" (17:22–24). Note how Jesus draws attention to the similarity between the Father's love for the Son and the Father's love for humans. Further, because he says the Father's love for the Son existed before the foundation of the world, it cannot be that this inner-trinitarian love was limited merely to the time of Jesus's incarnation—that is, what some refer to as the economic Trinity.

For examples of classical trinitarians who affirm that relationships within the Trinity are analogously like the relationships between God and humans, consider Ayres's assertion that Augustine "consistently founds the unity of God in the Father's eternal act of giving rise to a communion in which the mutual love of the three constitutes their unity of substance."[11] Elsewhere Ayres writes that

> our main focus should be the character of the individual and multiple inter-relationships between the divine three. The manner in which the divine love is performed by the Father as eternally giving all that he is, by the Son eternally receiving and eternally being the giver of life, by the Spirit as drawing us into unity as the body of Christ, the different ways in which the divine love is performed here provide us with a matrix of points of departure for our meditation and prayer. Attention to any of the ways in which the life of divine love is performed draws us—I hope—first, constantly toward a confession of our own failure to act in love and hence in unity.[12]

---

10. Ayres, "As We Are One," 110–11.
11. Ayres, *Nicaea and Its Legacy*, 319.
12. Ayres, "As We Are One," 112.

Also consider the classical theologian Anselm, who, speaking to God, writes, "You are so simple that there cannot be born of You any other than what You are. This itself is the Love, one and common to You and to Your Son, that is the Holy Spirit proceeding from both. For this same Love is not unequal to You or to Your Son since Your love for Yourself and Him, and His love for You and Himself, are as great as You and He are."[13] But is this love within the Trinity something that humans can participate in as well? Anselm thinks so. While discussing how all good human desires will ultimately be fulfilled in heaven, he writes, "If it is friendship, they will love God more than themselves and one another as themselves, and God will love them more than they love themselves because it is through Him that they love Him and themselves and one another, and He loves Himself and them through Himself."[14]

Lastly, consider the beautiful way classical trinitarian Thomas F. Torrance draws out the connection and similarities between the loving relationships within God and the loving relationship humans can have with God:

> To the fellowship of love which God establishes with us through the incarnation of his beloved Son in space and time there corresponds an eternal Fellowship of Love within God himself. The Freedom in which God enters into communion with us is grounded in and flows from the Freedom of the Father, the Son and the Holy Spirit in their love for one another. The communion which God eternally is in the mutual indwelling of the three Divine Persons within the relations of his one Being, he is toward us and with us and for us in his saving presence and loving activity in history. This is what the doctrine of the Holy Trinity supremely means, that God himself is Love.[15]

There may be some classical trinitarians who will not affirm this first claim, that the relationships within the Trinity are analogously like the relationships between God and humans. Karl Rahner is one possible example; he writes that there is "properly no mutual love between Father and Son, for this would presuppose two acts."[16] One is hard pressed to understand how he could come to such a position considering the verses from John 17 discussed above where Jesus refers to the loving relationship he had with his Father before the foundation of the

---

13. Anselm, *Proslogion*, in *Major Works*, 100.
14. Anselm, *Proslogion*, in *Major Works*, 102.
15. T. Torrance, *Christian God*, 162.
16. Rahner, *Trinity*, 106.

world. Regardless, even Rahner was inconsistent in his position on this; earlier in the same book, he writes that the "Father gives himself to us too as Father, that is, precisely because and insofar as he himself, being essentially with himself, utters himself and in this way communicates the Son as his own, personal self-manifestation; and because and insofar as the Father and the Son (receiving from the Father), welcoming each other in love, drawn and returning to each other communicate themselves in this way, as received in mutual love, that is, as Holy Spirit."[17]

The second claim I presented above is that the persons of the Trinity have moral characteristics analogously similar to moral characteristics that humans can have. This corresponds to Adams's second point that the better the character of the commander, the more reason there is to obey his or her commands. This claim isn't as controversial to classical trinitarians because the idea that there are attributes of God that can be shared by humans, often referred to as communicable attributes, is a common part of most Christian theologies. The Bible is replete with verses that encourage us to be more like God in a morally pertinent sense, as I noted in chapter 4. Here are just two powerful examples: "Therefore be imitators of God, as beloved children; and walk in love, just as Christ also loved you and gave Himself up for us, an offering and a sacrifice to God as a fragrant aroma" (Eph. 5:1–2). While discussing moral issues in the Sermon on the Mount, Jesus told his followers that they "are to be perfect, as your heavenly Father is perfect" (Matt. 5:48).

Thus, it's evident that humans can resemble God in a morally pertinent sense because there are some analogous similarities between God and humans made in his image. Social trinitarians tend to think this similarity has to do with the fact that God and "humans made in his image" are both persons but classical trinitarians are uncomfortable using the term *person* in that way because they believe the church fathers used this term to speak of the persons of the Trinity in a completely different sense than what we use the term *person* for today when referring to human beings.[18] Regardless, social trinitarians and classical trinitarians agree that there's enough analogous similarities between God and humans such that it's possible for humans to resemble God in a morally pertinent sense, even if they wouldn't use the same term (i.e., person) to refer to those similarities, and even if it's not possible to nail down exactly what those similarities are.

---

17. Rahner, *Trinity*, 35.
18. Holmes, "Response to Thomas H. McCall," 143.

For an example of a classical trinitarian affirming this point, consider Ayres's summary of Gregory of Nyssa: "Nyssa describes the soul's imitation of the divine through imagining a shaping of the soul's life or activity such that it eventually displays nothing but the activity of love. This activity both transforms the soul into a perfect image (achieving its natural end) *and* draws the soul into union with the life of God."[19] Also consider classical trinitarian Torrance's comment that "God does not will to exist for himself alone and does not wish to be without us, but has in his eternal purpose of love freely created a universe, within which he has placed human beings made after his own image and likeness in order that he may share his love with them and enable them to enjoy his divine fellowship."[20]

The third claim I mentioned in this section is that there are commands, and obedience to these commands, between the persons of the Trinity that are analogously like commands, and obedience to these commands, between God and humans. This loosely corresponds to Adams's third point that the better the command itself, the more reason there is to obey it. This third claim is basically the doctrine of eternal functional subordination, the idea that the Son is subordinate to the Father's authority not only in the incarnation (the economic Trinity) but in all eternity past (the immanent Trinity). Of the three claims, this one is certainly the most controversial, and the majority of classical trinitarians wholeheartedly reject it. It's worth noting that some social trinitarians also reject this doctrine; for example, Thomas McCall rejects it because, like many classical trinitarians, he believes it results in an ontological difference between the Son and the Father, thus making the Son of a different essence than the Father.[21]

Recently there's been a firestorm of debate concerning eternal functional subordination within evangelicalism. McCall summarizes the controversy well: "Some influential evangelical theologians want to deny 'ontological' or 'essential' subordination while also insisting that the Son's function (or 'economic') subordination is eternal. Some evangelicals have received this proposal with enthusiasm; others have expressed grave concern about it."[22] I'll summarize these concerns below and then, assuming eternal functional subordination is false, present two alternatives which, if true, will allow us to still affirm premise two in

---

19. Ayres, *Nicaea and Its Legacy*, 306.
20. T. Torrance, *Christian God*, 207.
21. McCall, *Which Trinity? Whose Monotheism?*, 175–88.
22. McCall, *Which Trinity? Whose Monotheism?*, 175. For lists of theologians both for and against eternal functional subordination, see Whitfield, introduction, 5.

my argument above—namely, that our obedience to God analogously resembles the triune God.

Concerns with Eternal Functional Subordination

The first problem many have with eternal functional subordination is that it results in God having multiple wills. Emerson and Stamps ask, "If the persons are distinguished in terms of authority and submission, does this not require distinct wills in the Godhead?"[23] They note that "the traditional doctrine of the Trinity has maintained that the three persons share one divine will . . . using 'will' here to denote a volitional *faculty*."[24] Whether volitional faculties are associated with natures or with persons, corresponding to either one or three wills in the Godhead respectively, has been an ongoing debate among Christians for centuries. Regardless, even if one is adamant that wills are associated with natures, and thus there's only one will in the Godhead, Ware explains how it's still possible for the divine persons to be in relationships of authority and submission:

> While each possesses the same volitional capacity, each can also make use of that volitional capacity in distinct yet unified ways, according to his distinct hypostatic identity and mode of subsistence. . . . One could also speak of these as three hypostatically distinct expressions of that one divine will or even three distinguishable acts of willing, which together bring to light the fullness of that one unified will. . . . This way of understanding the will of God—one volitional capacity of nature with distinct expressions or inflections of willing from each of the three divine persons—is akin to how we should understand, for example, the intratrinitarian love of God.[25]

While arguing against eternal functional subordination, classical trinitarians Emerson and Stamps say almost the exact same thing as Ware when they explain how there could be relationships of love in the Trinity even though there's only one will in the Godhead: "We can say that while there is only one divine will, there are three modes of subsistence (or existence) in that one will. . . . The will is identical, but the three persons subsist in it according to their distinct personal modes."[26] Regardless of the term used for the distinction under consideration here between the persons of the Trinity (will, volition, expressions of

---

23. Emerson and Stamps, "On Trinitarian Theological Method," 118.
24. Emerson and Stamps, "On Trinitarian Theological Method," 119.
25. Ware, "Unity and Distinction," 47.
26. Emerson and Stamps, "On Trinitarian Theological Method," 123.

willing, inflections of willing, or modes of subsistence), it's difficult to see why this distinction is large enough such that they can be in loving relationships with each other but not large enough for them to be in relationships of authority and submission.

The second problem many have with eternal functional subordination is that it stands at odds with some earlier theologians of the church. Emerson and Stamps complain that this doctrine "represents a novel and significant departure from the historic doctrine of the Trinity."[27] It's beyond the scope of this chapter to address this underlying issue—how much we should be concerned if our theological positions don't line up with some previous theologians, especially some of the church fathers. Even if a theological position is new, certainly it's not necessarily wrong merely because it arose more recently in history; further reflection often leads to greater discoveries and insight concerning truth and reality. As thankful as we are for previous theologians, it should be remembered that they, like all of us, were finite, imperfect, and susceptible to error. The theological work of those who have come before us is surely a treasure from which we have much to learn, but we are not bound to their positions.

Even if someone puts a tremendous amount of importance on the position of earlier theologians, it should be noted that some have attempted to provide evidence that a few early church theologians have argued for eternal functional subordination, or at least ideas similar to it. For example, Wayne Grudem claims to have documented that this position has been taught and affirmed throughout church history.[28] For example, Aquinas held that the Father had a special authority the Son and Spirit did not; he wrote that "although we attribute to the Father something of authority by reason of His being the principle, still we do not attribute any kind of subjection or inferiority to the Son. . . . In this way, Hilary says (De Trin. ix): By authority of the Giver, the Father is the greater; nevertheless the Son is not less to Whom oneness of nature is given."[29] Steven Boyer attempted to provide evidence that even some of the church fathers discussed the eternal obedience of the divine Son.[30] Ware points out some notable theologians on the classical trinitarian side, including Charles Hodge and James Petigru Boyce, who "have seen that this unique ontological distinction [the eternal relations of origin] entails an accompanying functional or operational distinctions which

---

27. Emerson and Stamps, "On Trinitarian Theological Method," 166.
28. Whitfield, introduction, 5.
29. Aquinas, *Summa Theologica*, 1:173.
30. Boyer, "Articulating Order."

also may rightly be included to distinguish the persons from another."[31] As for Hodge in particular, he maintained that the eternal functional subordination of the Son to the Father was tied directly to their eternal relations of origin. Ware summarizes Hodge's position as follows: "Because the Father begets the Son, it will be the Father who sends the Son and precisely not the Son sending the Father. Because the Spirit proceeds from the Father and the Son, the Spirit will be sent by the Father and the Son rather than sending either the Father or the Son. One distinction is ontological; the other functional. Yet both are eternally true since the operational subordination is expressive of the ontological mode of subsistence."[32]

As for more recent classical trinitarians who have affirmed ideas similar to eternal functional subordination, consider Karl Barth, well known for his decidedly anti-social trinitarianism because he understood God to be one divine subject and not three individual centers of consciousness. In spite of this, Barth described the Son's eternal relationship to the Father as one of willing subordination. He wrote that God is "both One who is obeyed and Another who obeys."[33] As a classical trinitarian, he admitted that this conclusion might come across as quite astonishing when he wrote, "We have not only not to deny but actually to affirm and understand as essential to the being of God the offensive fact that there is in God himself an above and a below, a prius and a posterius, a superiority and a subordination. And our present concern is with what is apparently the most offensive fact of all, that there is a below, a posterius, a subordination, that belongs to the inner life of God that there should take place within it obedience."[34] Barth went on to argue that this position of his did not result in the ancient heresy that Christ is ontologically inferior to the Father. In defending Barth against this charge, Darren Sumner writes that "for God, subordination entails no inferiority, no deprivation or lack, but is a way of being that possesses its own dignity. This is why the way of humility, the way of the Son of God into the far country, is at the same time his glory."[35] Because Barth's position is so similar to eternal functional subordination, some have even used Barth to argue for this doctrine.[36] However, Sumner argues that Barth's position is distinctly different from eternal functional subordination, distinct enough

---

31. Ware, "Unity and Distinction," 131.
32. Ware, "Unity and Distinction," 132.
33. Barth, *Church Dogmatics* IV/1, 201.
34. Barth, *Church Dogmatics* IV/1, 200–201.
35. Sumner, "Obedience and Subordination," 136.
36. Ware, "Equal in Essence," 35.

such that "Barth can be no happy ally [to those who advocate for eternal functional subordination]; his account of the obedience of the Son, of God's submission to God, is simply not compatible with the evangelical case for trinitarian subordination."[37] Assuming Sumner is correct about this, it seems that if one rejected eternal functional subordination but affirmed Barth's idea here, then he would be able to affirm that there is obedience within the Godhead, and thus could affirm the first proposal I offered above, namely, that "human obedience resembles the Son's obedience."

Lastly, some classical trinitarians themselves admit that eternal functional subordination may be found among earlier theologians. While describing Gregory of Nyssa's understanding of how the divine persons are differentiated, Ayres notes that some have detected in Gregory's work a subtle ontological inferiority of Son and Spirit to the Father. He argues that this is not the case but concludes his discussion with the following: "Of course, even if I am right [that in fact there is no ontological inferiority of the Son in Gregory's theology], this does not mean that there is no hierarchy in Gregory's account. It means we cannot assume the order and hierarchy in the Trinity to bring along an ontological subordinationism. The priority of the Father as cause—even if it is the priority of one who eternally gives rise to a mutuality of loving exchange—is in some sense still a priority."[38]

The third problem many have with eternal function subordination is that it makes too much of a distinction between the persons of the Trinity. Some classical trinitarians maintain that the only difference between the persons of the Trinity is their difference in origin: the Father is eternally unbegotten, the Son is eternally begotten from the Father (sometimes referred to as eternal generation), and the Spirit is eternally proceeding from the Father (some say the Father and the Son). For example, Emerson and Stamps note that "in the traditional doctrine of the Trinity, the persons share every property in common except for these relations of origin. To add to these traditional distinctions is to introduce a host of theological problems."[39]

It's worth addressing, among the host of theological problems Emerson and Stamps argue this position causes, the one they consider most troublesome. They argue that attributing different levels of authority among the divine persons results in an ontological difference between them because "authority has

---

37. Sumner, "Obedience and Subordination," 145.
38. Ayres, *Nicaea and Its Legacy*, 363.
39. Emerson and Stamps, "On Trinitarian Theological Method," 118.

traditionally been understood as an attribute of the shared divine nature, not a property of the persons."[40] In other words, if they have different levels of authority, then they must have different natures, which results in the Son being ontologically different than the Father. This is a common concern among those who reject eternal functional subordination. For example, Torrance argues that if the Son eternally submitted to the Father, then the persons of the Trinity would not be ontological equals, and thus eternal functional subordination undermines the full deity of the Son and the Spirit.[41]

In response to this concern, Bruce Ware, a leading proponent of eternal functional subordination, argues that "authority and submission describe merely the manner in which these persons relate to each other, not what is true of the nature of the Father or the Son."[42] He provides a fuller explanation as follows:

> Authority and submission are functional and hypostatic, not essential (i.e., of the divine essence) or ontological categories, and hence they cannot rightly be invoked as a basis of declaring one person's ontology (nature) greater and the other's lesser. Ontologically the Father and Son are fully and identically equal, but, as persons, they function in an eternal Father-Son relation, in which the Father always acts in a way that befits who he is as Father, and the Son always acts in a way that befits who he is as Son. Their Father-Son manner of relating (functioning) is seen (in part) in the authority of the Father and submission of the Son, as is evidenced by the vast array of the biblical self-revelation of the trinitarian persons. And, since the Father is eternal Father, and the Son eternal Son, this manner of relating is likewise eternal.[43]

Since both sides agree there are no ontological differences between the persons of the Trinity, what we have here is a case where some claim their opponent's position entails a nefarious implication, in this case that the Son is lesser ontologically than the Father, whereas those who hold the position reject that entailment. Who is correct? The difference hinges on whether authority and submission are properties of persons or natures. At the human level at least, it's difficult to see how they could be properties of natures, for, if that were the case, a human's nature would change every time she began or ended a relationship of authority

---

40. Emerson and Stamps, "On Trinitarian Theological Method," 118.
41. T. Torrance, *Christian God*, 180.
42. Ware, "Unity and Distinction," 52.
43. Ware, "Unity and Distinction," 52.

or submission. Certainly a human being's nature doesn't change when she moves from one country to another simply because she finds herself under the authority of a new government. However, if being divine necessarily entails having ultimate authority, and according to eternal functional subordination the Son doesn't have ultimate authority since he submits to the Father, then the result is that Jesus isn't fully divine. It's concerns like this that require us to explore alternatives to eternal functional subordination below.

Certainly those who affirm eternal functional subordination will be comfortable with this third claim that there are commands, and obedience to these commands, between the persons of the Trinity that are analogously like commands, and obedience to these commands, between God and humans. But what if eternal functional subordination is false? Since there is so much uncertainty regarding whether or not eternal functional subordination is true, I will now present two alternative aspects of the Trinity and, for each alternative, I'll consider how affirming it, instead of eternal functional subordination, will allow us to affirm the argument I've presented in this chapter. If either of these alternatives is true, if either corresponds to how the Trinity really is, then the argument I presented above will still be successful even if eternal functional subordination is false. One of my goals here is to show that both those who affirm and those who reject eternal functional subordination can affirm premise two of my argument above—namely, that there is *some* sense in which human obedience to God resembles God's triunity.

The First Alternative: The Son's Eternal Generation

The first alternative is eternal generation of the Son by the Father, sometimes referred to as the eternal begottenness of the Son. Most all theologians affirm that Christ obeyed the Father's commands—that is, was subordinate to the Father—in his incarnation (the economic Trinity), but many reject the notion that this reflects how things work in the eternal Trinity (the immanent Trinity). Unfortunately, this economic obedience is not strong enough for the argument I've presented here in this chapter because it's more of an "accidental" consequence of the incarnation and not an "essential" aspect of God's triunity. However, if the accidental economic obedience of the Son flows from something that *is* an essential aspect of God—that is, the Son's eternal generation—then my argument can utilize this truth instead of eternal functional subordination.

As for classical trinitarians who have made such a connection, consider Thomistic theologians Scott Swain and Michael Allen's position that "the obedience of the Son is the economic extension of his eternal generation to a

Spirit-enabled, creaturely life of obedience unto death."[44] To make their case, they argue from Scripture and reason that, because the mode of being (*modus essendi*) shapes the mode of acting (*modus agenda*), the Son's essential property of being generated from the Father determines his distinctive role as the Father's obedient Son. They explain that the "fact that the Son does not do His own will but the will of the Father who sent him is a consequence of his distinctive *modus agenda*, which follows from his distinctive *modus essendi*."[45] In addition, they argue that, in order for the revelation we receive in Christ to be valid, Jesus's economic obedience must be a reflection of his essential self. While they maintain it's necessary to distinguish "the Son's eternal generation, which is natural and necessary to His identity, from his saving mission, which is contingent to His identity,"[46] they are adamant concerning the linkage between the two. They conclude, "The eternal Son's receptivity in relation to the Father—expressed poignantly in the doctrine of eternal generation—provides the metaphysical and relational grounds for his free enactment of his proper activity in the divine economy, which is time and again characterized as obedience."[47]

Classical trinitarians Emerson and Stamps similarly affirm that Jesus's being sent on his economic mission by the Father proceeds from, and extends, the eternal relations of origin within the immanent Trinity.[48] Drawing on Augustine's theology, they argue that because Jesus's Sonship did not begin in his economic mission but is grounded in his eternal generation, there is a fittingness to the Son's being sent from the Father because the Son is eternally from the Father and not vice versa.[49] Standing firm against eternal functional subordination, they are quick to add that although the Son's economic mission flows from and reflects his eternal generation, his mission should not be collapsed back into the eternal relations of origin, "as if everything that obtained in the former (such as submission) must also obtain in the latter."[50] Regardless, because of the connection they see between Jesus's economic submission and his eternal generation from the Father, it seems as though this is a viable alternative to eternal functional subordination that can be used in my argument.

This first alternative to eternal functional subordination, the Son's eternal generation, can be used to affirm premise two in my argument: our obedience

---

44. Swain and Allen, "Obedience of the Eternal Son," 117.
45. Swain and Allen, "Obedience of the Eternal Son," 126.
46. Swain and Allen, "Obedience of the Eternal Son," 132.
47. Swain and Allen, "Obedience of the Eternal Son," 134.
48. Emerson and Stamps, "On Trinitarian Theological Method," 117.
49. Emerson and Stamps, "On Trinitarian Theological Method," 167.
50. Emerson and Stamps, "On Trinitarian Theological Method," 117.

to God analogously resembles the triune God. Remember that the basic form of the argument goes like this:

1. If something resembles God, it is good.
2. Our obedience to God analogously resembles the triune God.
3. Therefore, our obedience to God is good.

With the first alternative, premise two can be arrived at as follows:

a. When humans obey God, that analogously resembles the economic obedience of the Son to the Father.
b. The economic obedience of the Son to the Father is an extension of the eternal generation of the Son from the Father.
c. Thus there is an analogous resemblance relationship between humans' obedience to God and an essential aspect of God, the eternal generation of the Son from the Father.
d. Therefore, premise two: our obedience to God analogously resembles the triune God.

Call this the "human obedience resembles the Son's eternal generation" alternative.

The Second Alternative: Inner-Trinitarian Love

The second alternative is to replace obedience within the Trinity with mutual self-giving love between the persons of the Trinity. This inner-trinitarian love is similar to the mutual submission that takes place when people put the interests of others above their own. Thus, moral good and moral obligation are related in that inside the Good—that is, inside God—there are relationships of love and humans analogously resemble this love when they love God through their obedience to him.

First, is there self-giving love between the persons of the Trinity? Ayres, an ardent defender of classical trinitarianism, writes, "Scripture invites us to meditate on the priority of love as the constitutive feature of what it is to be a divine person in relationship. Whether we attend to the unity of Father and Son, to the manner in which Father shows all to the Son, or to the complex parallels between the Spirit as the love of God and the gift that draws us into unity, in every case the reality that we are drawn to contemplate is that of an eternally *self-giving love*."[51] Millard

---

51. Ayres, "As We Are One," 112 (emphasis added).

Erickson, in describing ideal human relationships, wrote that "the nature of such relationships, if they are to reflect the nature of the intratrinitarian relationships . . . would be one of unselfish love and submission to the other, seeking the welfare of the other over one's own."[52] In this alternative, then, love is what is fundamental, and mutual submission is how that love is expressed; the persons of the Trinity do not obey each other per se, but they do love each other and express that love by putting one another before themselves. Torrance writes, "The love of God revealed to us in the economic Trinity is identical with the Love of God in the ontological Trinity; but the Love of God revealed to us in the economic manifestation of the Father, the Son and the Holy Spirit in the history of our salvation, tells us that God loves us with the very same love with which he loves himself, in the reciprocal love of the three divine Persons for Each Other in the eternal Communion of the Holy Trinity."[53]

Consider also the twelfth-century thinker Richard of St. Victor. Stanley Grenz writes that Richard "provided what has been hailed as one of the most learned expositions of the doctrine of the Trinity in the Middle Ages. . . . Richard drew from, but then thoroughly recast, the analogy from love found in Augustine's work. . . . Richard's main line of reasoning begins with the idea of supreme goodness, which, he argued, must involve love."[54] Similarly, while explaining the Trinity, Erickson describes love as "the attractive force of unselfish concern for another person" and thus the "most powerful binding force in the universe."[55] Knowing that we resemble God when we love him and others elucidates Jesus's admonition that the greatest commandments are to love God and to love others, and that all the rest of the commandments rest on this foundation (Matt. 22:37–40).

With this second alternative, then, the human-to-God relationship images this self-giving love within the Trinity analogously in the sense that we are to love God via our obedience to him. Hence, at a minimum, our obedience to God is a means of expressing our love to him, but it might very well be that our obedience is equivalent to our love for him. The key here is to see the strong connection between our love for God and our obedience to him. Jesus emphasized this connection when he explained that loving God and obeying God are intertwined, if not one and the same: "He who has My commandments and keeps them is the one who loves Me; and he who loves Me will be loved by My Father, and I will love him and will disclose Myself to him. . . . If anyone

---

52. Erickson, *God in Three Persons*, 332–33 (emphasis added).
53. T. Torrance, *Christian God*, 165.
54. Grenz, *Rediscovering the Triune God*, 11.
55. Erickson, *God in Three Persons*, 221.

loves Me, he will keep My word; and My Father will love him, and We will come to him and make Our abode with him" (John 14:21, 23). This is reinforced throughout the New Testament, especially in 1 John where it's written, "Whoever keeps His word, in him the love of God has truly been perfected" (2:5), and, "This is the love of God, that we keep His commandments" (5:3). Jesus even made the connection that our loving and obeying God is parallel to the love and the economic obedience between him and the Father: "Just as the Father has loved Me, I have also loved you; abide in My love. If you keep My commandments, you will abide in My love; just as I have kept My Father's commandments and abide in His love" (John 15:9–10). Hence, when humans love God through obedience, this analogously resembles God's inner-trinitarian self-giving love that exists within God between the persons of the Trinity.

Hare, drawing on the theology of Duns Scotus, has provided a helpful explanation of this connection between our obedience to God and our love for God. He explains that "to love God is at least to obey God. There is scriptural warrant for this . . . but independently of Scripture it is plausible to say that to love God is at least to will what God wills for us to will."[56] Summarizing Duns Scotus, Hare describes the relation between love and obedience as follows: "To love God requires us to repeat in our wills God's will for our willing, and such a repetition is obedience."[57]

This connection between love and obedience is just a small part of Duns Scotus's overall theology, which I more fully described in previous chapters. Others have observed that the "lodestone of Scotus' theological vision is the idea of Divine Love, as understood both within the mutuality of the Trinitarian Persons and in God's relation to creation."[58] Duns Scotus proposed a relational understanding of obedience to divine commands in that God created us to be co-lovers with the persons of the Trinity. With that as our ultimate purpose, God then chose the best route for us to achieve this end and communicates this route to us through divine commands. Thus, Hare prefers to see these instructions from God not as commands but as callings that draw us into a greater and deeper loving union with God.[59]

This understanding of divine commands, that they flow not from a harsh motivation of authority and power but from a motivation of love, weakens the common accusation that divine command theories are mostly concerned with God's control

---

56. Hare, *God's Command*, 18.
57. Hare, *God's Command*, 39.
58. Duns Scotus, *Will and Morality*, ix.
59. Hare, *God's Command*, 40.

over us. For example, Linda Zagzebski, while arguing against Adams's divine command theory in favor of her divine motivation theory, complains that "one problem with this approach [i.e., Adams's] is that prima facie, making demands is not a loving thing to do. One thinks of a husband's demanding that his wife iron his shirt. . . . Most of us think there is something wrong with a relationship in which such demands are made. . . . Commands are harsh acts."[60] Though it's true we are morally accountable to God, as I explained toward the end of chapter 6, the final purpose of God's commands is not control and authority but a loving union between us and him.[61] God is a personal divine lover whose commands build a relationship of communication between us and him.[62] This relationship is not dictatorial but relational, guiding us to our ultimate end of being in a vibrant loving relationship with the three persons of the Trinity, being brought fully into their fellowship.[63] This is a profound shift away from viewing divine command theories as harshly authoritarian and upheld by the threat of punishment.

This second alternative to eternal functional subordination, inner-trinitarian love, can be used to affirm premise two of my argument: our obedience to God analogously resembles the triune God. Remember that the basic form of the argument goes like this:

1. If something resembles God, it is good.
2. Our obedience to God analogously resembles the triune God.
3. Therefore, our obedience to God is good.

With this second alternative, premise two can be arrived at as follows:

a. When humans obey God, that's the same as loving God.
b. There is love within God, in that persons of the Trinity love each other—that is, they love God.
c. The love of God involved in humans' obedience to God is analogously similar to the love between the persons of the Trinity such that there's a resemblance between these loves.
d. Therefore, premise two: our obedience to God analogously resembles the triune God.

---

60. Zagzebski, *Divine Motivation Theory*, 263–64.
61. Hare, *God's Call*, 52.
62. Hare, *God's Command*, 260.
63. Hare, *God's Call*, 119.

CHAPTER 13: THEISTIC MORAL THEORIES AND LUCKY COINCIDENCES   223

Call this the "human obedience resembles the inner-trinitarian love" alternative.

With these two alternatives to eternal functional subordination, nearly all theologians should be able to affirm the idea that our obedience to God is morally good because it analogously resembles the triune God. My reason for arguing for this idea was to respond to Wielenberg's accusation that all theistic models have ungrounded ethical facts as his model does. Specifically, Wielenberg argues that the theist's proposed fact "It is morally good to obey God" is an ungrounded ethical fact. Using my divine love theory, I've been able to show how this fact is not ungrounded within a theistic theory of morality but is actually grounded in God's trinitarian nature.

CHAPTER 14

CONCLUSION TO PART FOUR

In this section I focused on an epistemological objection to Wielenberg's godless normative realism—the lucky coincidence objection. To summarize, his model has a difficult time explaining how our moral beliefs could ever match up correctly with objective moral truths considering that, according to Wielenberg, these truths are causally inert. Because of this, critics of models like Wielenberg's have noted that it would be quite a lucky coincidence if our moral beliefs happened to correspond with objective moral truth. Evolutionary debunking arguments have shown this problem is exacerbated if, like Wielenberg, a person believes our moral beliefs came about haphazardly through an evolutionary process. In chapter 11, I presented an evolutionary debunking argument based on Alvin Plantinga's evolutionary argument against naturalism.

In chapter 12, I argued that Wielenberg was unsuccessful in his attempts to defend his model from this lucky coincidence objection. I addressed four of his responses to the lucky coincidence objection. First, Wielenberg pushed back against Plantinga's argument by appealing to the evidence we have for the reliability of our cognitive faculties and by questioning how much we really know about evolution. However, it's difficult to see how one could trust his own cognitive faculties to evaluate the reliability of such faculties when it is those very faculties that are under suspicion. In addition, it should come as no surprise that evolutionary debunking arguments apply only to those who believe in evolution. Obviously the less a person believes in evolution, the less force such arguments have on her. It should also be remembered that evolutionary debunking arguments only amplify the lucky coincidence objection, and hence, even if someone rejects evolution completely, they still haven't fully answered the lucky coincidence objection.

Second, Wielenberg suggested that moral truth and our moral beliefs correspond accurately because both are the result of the same third factor—our cognitive faculties. He speculated that moral properties and truths D-supervene (Wielenberg's proposed making relationship) on our cognitive faculties and that our moral beliefs are generated by our cognitive faculties. If both moral truth and our moral beliefs arise from the same thing, then it's not surprising that they would match up well. However, I showed that because his model still contains contingency, it continues to be vulnerable to the lucky coincidence objection. The contingency in this third factor model is found in the second part, the idea that cognitive faculties generate our moral beliefs, in that the same cognitive faculties can, and do, generate wildly different moral beliefs.

Third, in an effort to address this lingering contingency, Wielenberg proposed that the laws of nature, and even the evolutionary process that resulted in human beings, might be necessary. Whether or not the laws of nature are necessary has been debated among philosophers and scientists, but this is something that seems very difficult, if not impossible, to prove. What's worse for Wielenberg's strategy here is that it's hard even to fathom his suggestion that the human evolutionary path was necessary, especially considering, according to evolutionists, all the varying paths evolution took that resulted in a plethora of wildly different species.

Fourth, Wielenberg attempted to turn the tables and argued that lucky coincidences are found within theistic moral theories too, so theists can't critique his theory for having them. He specifically targeted Robert Adams's divine command theory and argued that it includes lucky coincidences between certain divine facts and some ethical facts, facts that Wielenberg claimed Adams did not ground in God and thus had no foundation. I showed that Wielenberg misunderstood Adams's model—what he thought were ungrounded ethical facts were actually facts about moral obligation that Adams specifically said were grounded in the first part of his model, the part having to do with moral value. Because these facts are grounded in God, there is no lucky coincidence between them and facts about God's goodness.

This last attempt by Wielenberg to deflect the lucky coincidence objection sparked a lengthy discussion in which I used my divine love theory to more fully answer Wielenberg's accusation that theistic moral theories also have lucky coincidences and ungrounded ethical facts. While Adams stated *that* the moral facts he posited concerning obligation were grounded in God as the source of moral value, my divine love theory more clearly shows *how* they are so grounded. Simply put, our obedience to God's commands is good because such obedience analogously resembles the relationships within the triune God, and, according to the first part of Adams's model and my divine love theory, good *just is* that which resembles God.

Because some theologians might be concerned with how the Trinity was described in my reply to Wielenberg in chapter 13, it was necessary for me to address these potential concerns and show that what I've proposed is not outside the bounds of what classical trinitarians affirm. However, the idea that the Son eternally obeys the Father is strongly opposed by classical trinitarians, as well as many social trinitarians. Therefore, I proposed two alternatives to eternal functional subordination that, if true, would allow those who reject eternal functional subordination to support the argument I presented in chapter 13.

The first alternative to eternal functional subordination I presented was the Son's eternal generation by the Father. Though those who reject eternal functional subordination believe the Son's obedience to the Father was only limited to the incarnation, most of them maintain that this economic obedience is closely connected back to his eternal generation. Thus, my argument was adjusted such that humans' obedience to God is good because it resembles these eternal relations of origin, relations that resulted in the Son's economic obedience.

The second alternative to eternal functional subordination I presented was the inner-trinitarian love between the divine persons. It was important in this alternative to establish that there is a strong resemblance relationship between this inner-trinitarian love and human obedience to God. In order to do this I explained that human obedience to God is, at most, equivalent to how humans love God and, at a minimum, a vital expression of their love for God. Regardless of which of these positions is correct, this human love/obedience to God is sufficiently similar to the love between the persons of the Trinity such that it's good when humans obey God's commands because this love/obedience resembles the loving relationships within the triune God.

CHAPTER 15

FINAL THOUGHTS

My goal in this work, as I stated at the beginning of chapter 3, was, first, to understand and then explain how God is the source and foundation of morality. I argued that the ultimate ground of objective morality is God's trinitarian nature as found in, and expressed among, the loving relationships between the divine persons of the Trinity. Second, I tried to show how this theory, which I call my divine love theory, is a more plausible explanation of objective morality than the leading atheistic theory, Wielenberg's godless normative realism. Certainly this is not the end of the discussion, but I hope I've been able to make some small contribution to this fascinating topic.

I recognize that this book might be difficult to classify. Is it about theology? Philosophy? Ethics? Metaethics? There's a sense in which all these subjects intersect in this work, so I suppose it could be considered interdisciplinary. While that might be an issue for some, it doesn't bother me for at least two reasons. First, there's a real danger in all of us becoming so specialized in our respective fields that we lose the ability to connect the dots between the various parts of our unified reality. If Christianity is true, and I believe it is, then we should expect to find connections between different subjects. The reason for this stems, once again, from God's triunity. If God, one unified being that exists as three diverse persons, is the source of everything, then we should expect to see unity and connectivity amidst the diversity of subjects because God's creation reflects aspects of himself.

Second, I've always found it a bit odd to strictly label and then categorize our various beliefs into different subjects. Take my beliefs about abortion: Are those moral, scientific, political, or religious beliefs? I have no desire to categorize these beliefs, but others may if they like. The way I understand it is that I have certain beliefs about reality, in this case abortion, and those beliefs are either true or false. I'd say the same thing about all of my beliefs, including my belief that there is a God, that Jesus is God, and that the Bible is from God. You may call those religious beliefs if you'd like, but as I understand it they're simply beliefs about reality that are either true or false.

This was driven home to me in a humorous way several years ago when I asked a local coffee shop if I could hang up a poster on their public bulletin board advertising an upcoming debate about the existence of God. The barista said they wouldn't allow this because they had a policy against hanging up religious material in their store. I explained that since both debaters had PhDs in philosophy, were both philosophy professors, and that the debate was taking place at a large public state university, this material therefore wasn't religious but philosophical. Lo and behold, as a result they allowed me to hang up the poster on their bulletin board! This is just one episode that reminded me how silly it can be to categorize our beliefs. Instead of using labels to dismiss certain beliefs we disagree with or to try to silence those advocating for them, let's just admit we all have beliefs about reality that are either true or false.

Though this book may be considered interdisciplinary, I think of it primarily as apologetic. Many academics have a negative attitude toward apologetics in general, and certainly toward the term *apologetics* in particular. Most likely this attitude stems from the fact that some Christian apologists are brashly overconfident, lacking in their academic credentials, research capabilities, or awareness of the literature, and tend to overstate their case by making stronger assertions than the evidence actually supports. However, Christian apologetics at its root is simply providing good reasons and evidence to believe that Christianity is true. There's a sense in which every scholar in every field tries to provide good reasons and evidence for things they've come to believe are true. You could even say that Erik Wielenberg provided an apologetic of his moral theory; that is, he tried to provide strong reasons and evidence for believing his theory is true. Therefore, I have no qualms about describing this book as primarily an apologetic for Christianity.

Even though some may look down upon contemporary apologetics, the practice of apologetics has a long, rich, intellectual history. There's a sense in which apologetics, providing good reasons and evidence to believe Christianity is true, was practiced by Jesus, his disciples, and early church leaders. However, it wasn't until the second century that entire books were devoted to Christian apologetics—two of the earliest were written by Quadratus and Aristides. Quadratus wrote to the Roman Emperor Hadrian, giving reasons to believe Christianity is true and defending Christian beliefs against various spurious charges. Philosopher Aristides also wrote his *Apology* to Emperor Hadrian, in which he provided several arguments for God's existence. After these two early works there were numerous apologetic books written in the second century to address criticisms by non-Christian philosophers and to appeal for tolerance to governmental leaders who were either actively persecuting Christians or considering whether or not they should. Justin Martyr was the most influential of these second-century apologists, and his philosophical works advocating for Christianity have been highly respected down through the centuries. After the second century, numerous well-known thinkers throughout history produced works of Christian apologetics—Origen, Augustine, Aquinas, Duns Scotus, Anselm, René Descartes, John Locke, Isaac Newton, Blaise Pascal, and Immanuel Kant, just to name a few.

The apologetic focus of this book has been the moral argument for God's existence. Like most theistic arguments, it begins with a certain phenomenon—the beginning of the universe, the design we see in the universe, or in this case objective moral truth—and then argues that God is the best explanation for that phenomenon. In this work I didn't take the time to argue for the premise that there is objective moral truth; after all, you can only tackle so much in one book. However, I recognize that some people reject objective moral truth, so it's important to be aware of arguments for that premise. As I noted previously, Christian writer C. Stephen Evans wrote that the most comprehensive and sophisticated case for objective morality can be found in atheist David Enoch's book *Taking Morality Seriously*.[1] In this book I merely argued that *if* there is objective moral truth, then the trinitarian God of Christianity is the best explanation of such truth.

Some think that the moral argument can be used to argue for the existence of a generic theistic god but not for the particular trinitarian God of Christianity.

---

1. C. Stephen Evans, *God and Moral Obligation* (Oxford: Oxford University Press, 2014), 166. See David Enoch, *Taking Morality Seriously: A Defense of Robust Realism* (New York: Oxford University Press, 2011).

They maintain this because they believe it's impossible to begin with objective moral truth and work deductively from that premise alone to arrive at the conclusion that the trinitarian God of Christianity exists. I agree such an attempt is untenable, but why think the moral argument, or any argument for God for that matter, has to follow such a strictly deductive approach? While it's true most arguments for God historically have been deductive, it seems to me just as feasible to craft abductive arguments for God's existence.

Consider again the simple example I used in chapter 3 to illustrate how abductive arguments work. In my example, a farmer experiences a larger bumper crop than he's ever seen. His friend Toni proposes that the best explanation for this is the ideal weather conditions they experienced over the last few months. His other friend Lenny proposes that the best explanation is that a local scientist developed a super-fertilizer and secretly put it on the farmer's crops to test its effectiveness. It would be difficult, if not impossible, for Lenny to build a strict deductive argument starting with the phenomenon alone, the bumper crop, which concluded that this local scientist is the source of the abundant harvest. No, instead he would, as we'd all expect, gather everything he could find about this supposed scientist and her work from various sources (newspaper articles, books, eyewitness reports, etc.) to build his theory and see how well it fits with the phenomenon under question, the bumper crop. This is the process we go through to arrive at most of our beliefs—what theory best matches up with the evidence? Lenny will be successful if he can show that his theory about the scientist, which he built at least somewhat from information apart from the phenomenon, best explains the bumper crop, and if it does then the farmer has good reason to believe this theory is true.

Similarly, the abductive form of the moral argument starts out with objective moral truth as the phenomenon. In this book I proposed a divine love theory to explain this phenomenon, a theory which I built at least somewhat from information apart from the phenomenon, namely the claims of Christianity that come from various sources such as general revelation (creation and reason) and special revelation (Scripture)—for example, the idea that God is one being yet three persons. I've been successful if I've shown that this theory best explains the phenomenon: objective moral truth. And if it does, then we now have even more reason to believe that Christianity is true.

BIBLIOGRAPHY

Adams, Robert Merrihew. *Finite and Infinite Goods: A Framework for Ethics*. New York: Oxford University Press, 1999.

————. "Moral Arguments for Theistic Belief." In *Rationality and Religious Belief*, edited by C. F. Delaney, 116–40. Notre Dame, IN: University of Notre Dame Press, 1979.

————. *The Virtue of Faith and Other Essays in Philosophical Theology*. New York: Oxford University Press, 1987.

Alston, William P. "Some Suggestions for Divine Command Theorists." In *Christian Theism and the Problems of Philosophy*, edited by Michael D. Beaty, 303–26. Notre Dame, IN: University of Notre Dame Press, 1990.

Anatolios, Khaled. *Retrieving Nicaea*. Grand Rapids: Baker Academic, 2011.

Anscombe, G. E. M. "Modern Moral Philosophy." *Philosophy* 33, no. 124 (1958): 1–16.

Anselm. *The Major Works*. Edited by Brian Davies and G. R. Evans. Oxford World's Classics. New York: Oxford University Press, 1998.

Aquinas, Thomas. *Summa Contra Gentiles Book One: God*. Translated by Anton Charles Pegis. Notre Dame, IN: University of Notre Dame Press, 1975.

————. *Summa Theologica*. Vol. 1. Translated by Fathers of the English Dominican Province. English Dominican Province Translation Edition. Notre Dame, IN: Christian Classics, 1981.

Aristotle. *The Basic Works of Aristotle*. Edited by Richard McKeon. New York: Modern Library, 2001.

Armchair Atheism (podcast). Episode 4, "Morality without God? with Erik Wielenberg." March 2, 2015. Video, 34:23. https://www.youtube.com/watch?v=XesENa4YJFs.

Audi, Robert. *Rationality and Religious Commitment*. New York: Oxford University Press, 2011.

Augustine. *On the Holy Trinity*. Translated by A. W. Haddan. New York: Kessinger Legacy Reprints, 2010.

Ayres, Lewis. "As We Are One: Thinking Into the Mystery." In *Advancing Trinitarian Theology*, edited by Oliver D. Crisp and Fred Sanders, 94–113. Grand Rapids: Zondervan, 2014.

_____. *Augustine and the Trinity*. New York: Cambridge University Press, 2010.

_____. *Nicaea and Its Legacy: An Approach to Fourth-Century Trinitarian Theology*. New York: Oxford University Press, 2004.

Baggett, David. "Psychopathy and Supererogation." In *A Debate on God and Morality: What Is the Best Account of Objective Moral Values and Duties?*, edited by Adam Lloyd Johnson, 131–48. New York: Routledge, 2021.

Baggett, David, and Jerry L. Walls. *God and Cosmos: Moral Truth and Human Meaning*. New York: Oxford University Press, 2016.

_____. *Good God: The Theistic Foundations of Morality*. New York: Oxford University Press, 2011.

Barr, Stephen M. *Modern Physics and Ancient Faith*. Notre Dame, IN: University of Notre Dame Press, 2003.

Barth, Karl. *Church Dogmatics*. Vol. II, part 2, *The Doctrine of God*. Edited by G. W. Bromiley and T. F. Torrance. Edinburgh: T&T Clark, 1957.

_____. *Church Dogmatics*. Vol. IV, part 1, *The Doctrine of Reconciliation*. Edited by G. W. Bromiley and T. F. Torrance. New York: T&T Clark, 2004.

Beilby, James, ed. *Naturalism Defeated? Essays on Plantinga's Evolutionary Argument against Naturalism*. Ithaca, NY: Cornell University Press, 2002.

Bonhoeffer, Dietrich. *Creation and Fall: A Theological Exposition of Genesis 1–3*. Edited by John W. de Gruchy. Translated by Douglas Stephen Bax. Dietrich Bonhoeffer Works 3. Minneapolis: Fortress, 1997.

Boyd, Craig A., and Raymond J. VanArragon. "Ethics Is Based on Natural Law." In *Contemporary Debates in Philosophy of Religion*, edited by Michael L. Peterson and Raymond J. VanArragon, 299–309. Malden, MA: Blackwell, 2004.

Boyer, Steven D. "Articulating Order: Trinitarian Discourse in an Egalitarian Age." *Pro Ecclesia* 18 (2009): 255–72.

Bridges, J. Thomas. "A Moderate-Realist Perspective on God and Abstract Objects." *Philosophia Christi* 17, no. 2 (2015): 277–85.

Budziszewski, J. *The Line through the Heart: Natural Law as Fact, Theory, and Sign of Contradiction*. Wilmington, DE: ISI Books, 2011.

Calvin, John. *Institutes of the Christian Religion*. Translated by Henry Beveridge. Peabody, MA: Hendrickson, 2008.

Carson, Thomas. *Value and the Good Life*. Notre Dame, IN: University of Notre Dame Press, 2000.

Clarke, W. Norris. *Person and Being*. Milwaukee: Marquette University Press, 1993.

Collins, Robin. "The Teleological Argument: An Exploration of the Fine-Tuning of the Universe." In *The Blackwell Companion to Natural Theology*, edited by William Lane Craig and J. P. Moreland, 202–82. Malden, MA: Wiley-Blackwell, 2012.

Copan, Paul. "Hume and the Moral Argument." In *In Defense of Natural Theology: A Post-Humean Assessment*, edited by James F. Sennett and Douglas Groothuis, 200–225. Downers Grove, IL: InterVarsity, 2005.

Copleston, F. C. *Greece and Rome*. Vol. 1 of *A History of Philosophy*. Westminster, MD: Newman, 1946.

Craig, William Lane. "Does the Problem of Material Constitution Illuminate the Doctrine of the Trinity?" *Faith and Philosophy* 22 (2005): 77–86.

———. "Erik Wielenberg's Metaphysics of Morals." *Philosophia Christi* 20, no. 2 (2018): 333–38.

———. *God Over All: Divine Aseity and the Challenge of Platonism*. New York: Oxford University Press, 2016.

———. *Is Goodness without God Good Enough? A Debate on Faith, Secularism, and Ethics*. Edited by Nathan L. King and Robert K. Garcia. Lanham, MD: Rowman & Littlefield, 2009.

———. "Reason Enough." In *God? A Debate between a Christian and an Atheist*, by William Lane Craig and Walter Sinnott-Armstrong, 53–80. Point/Counterpoint. New York: Oxford University Press, 2004.

———. *Time and Eternity: Exploring God's Relationship to Time*. Wheaton, IL: Crossway, 2001.

Craig, William Lane, and J. P. Moreland. *Philosophical Foundations for a Christian Worldview*. Downers Grove, IL: IVP Academic, 2003.

Darwin, Charles. *Charles Darwin: His Life Told in an Autobiographical Chapter, and in a Selected Series of His Published Letters*. Edited by Francis Darwin. London: Murray, 1902.

———. *The Descent of Man and Selection in Relation to Sex*. 2nd ed. New York: Appleton, 1909.

Davies, Brian. *The Reality of God and the Problem of Evil*. New York: Continuum International, 2006.

Dawkins, Richard. *River Out of Eden: A Darwinian View of Life*. New York: Basic Books, 1996.

———. *The Selfish Gene*. 30th anniversary ed. New York: Oxford University Press, 2006.

DePaul, Michael R. "Supervenience and Moral Dependence." *Philosophical Studies* 51 (1987): 425–39.

Doolan, Gregory. *Aquinas on the Divine Ideas as Exemplar Causes*. Washington, DC: Catholic University of America Press, 2008.

Draper, Paul. "Cosmic Fine-Tuning and Terrestrial Suffering: Parallel Problems for Naturalism and Theism." *American Philosophical Quarterly* 41, no. 4 (2004): 311–21.

Duns Scotus, John. *Duns Scotus on the Will and Morality*. Edited by William A. Frank. Translated by Allan B. Wolter. 2nd ed. Washington, DC: Catholic University of America Press, 1997.

Emerson, Matthew Y., and Luke Stamps. "On Trinitarian Theological Method." In *Trinitarian Theology: Theological Models and Doctrinal Application*, edited by Keith S. Whitfield, 95–128. Nashville: B&H Academic, 2019.

Enoch, David. "An Outline of an Argument for Robust Metanormative Realism." *Oxford Studies in Metaethics*, edited by Russ Shafer-Landau, 2:21–50. Oxford: Oxford University Press, 2007.

―――――. *Taking Morality Seriously: A Defense of Robust Realism*. New York: Oxford University Press, 2011.

Erickson, Millard J. *God in Three Persons: A Contemporary Interpretation of the Trinity*. Grand Rapids: Baker Books, 1995.

Evans, C. Stephen. *God and Moral Obligation*. Oxford: Oxford University Press, 2014.

―――――. "Moral Arguments for the Existence of God." *Stanford Encyclopedia of Philosophy*, revised June 29, 2018. https://plato.stanford.edu/entries/moral-arguments-god.

Finlay, Stephen. "Normativity, Necessity, and Tense: A Recipe for Homebaked Normativity." In *Oxford Studies in Metaethics*, edited by Russ Shafer-Landau, 5:57–85. Oxford: Oxford University Press, 2010.

FitzPatrick, William. "Robust Ethical Realism, Non-Naturalism, and Normativity." In *Oxford Studies in Metaethics*, edited by Russ Shafer-Landau, 3:159–205. Oxford: Oxford University Press, 2008.

Frank, William A. "Preface to This Edition." In *Duns Scotus on the Will and Morality*, by John Duns Scotus, edited by William A. Frank, translated by Alan B. Wolter, ix–xvi. 2nd ed. Washington, DC: Catholic University of America Press, 1997.

Gould, Paul M. "Introduction to the Problem of God and Abstract Objects." In *Beyond the Control of God? Six Views on the Problem of God and Abstract Objects*, edited by Paul M. Gould, 1–20. New York: Bloomsbury Academic, 2014.

Gould, Paul M., and Richard Brian Davis. "Modified Theistic Activism." In *Beyond the Control of God? Six Views on the Problem of God and Abstract Objects*, edited by Paul M. Gould, 51–80. New York: Bloomsbury Academic, 2014.

Greene, Joshua. "From Neural 'Is' to Moral 'Ought': What Are the Moral Implications of Neuroscientific Moral Psychology?" *Nature Reviews Neuroscience* 4 (2003): 846–49.

―――――. *Moral Tribes: Emotion, Reason, and the Gap between Us and Them*. New York: Penguin, 2013.

Grenz, Stanley J. *Rediscovering the Triune God: The Trinity in Contemporary Theology*. Minneapolis: Fortress, 2004.

Grotius, Hugo. *On the Rights of War and Peace: An Abridged Translation*. Edited and translated by William Whewell. Cambridge: John W. Parker, 1853.

Gruenler, Royce Gordon. *The Trinity in the Gospel of John: A Thematic Commentary on the Fourth Gospel*. Grand Rapids: Baker, 1986.

Haidt, Jonathan. *The Righteous Mind: Why Good People Are Divided by Politics and Religion*. New York: Pantheon, 2012.

Haines, David, and Andrew Fulford. *Natural Law: A Brief Introduction and Biblical Defense*. Lincoln, NE: Davenant, 2017.

Hanink, James G., and Gary R. Mar. "What Euthyphro Couldn't Have Said." *Faith and Philosophy* 4, no. 3 (1987): 241–61.

Hare, John. *God and Morality: A Philosophical History*. Malden, MA: Blackwell, 2009.

―――――. *God's Call: Moral Realism, God's Commands, and Human Autonomy*. Grand Rapids: Eerdmans, 2001.

————. *God's Command*. Oxford Studies in Theological Ethics. Oxford: Oxford University Press, 2015.

Harman, Gilbert. *The Nature of Morality: An Introduction to Ethics*. New York: Oxford University Press, 1977.

Hasker, William. "An Adequate God." In *Searching for an Adequate God: A Dialogue between Process and Free Will Theists*, edited by John B. Cobb Jr. and Clark H. Pinnock, 215–45. Grand Rapids: Eerdmans, 2000.

————. *Metaphysics and the Tri-Personal God*. New York: Oxford University Press, 2013.

Henry, Carl F. H. *God, Revelation, and Authority*. Vol. 5. Wheaton, IL: Crossway, 1999.

Holmes, Stephen R. "Response to Thomas H. McCall." In *Two Views on the Doctrine of the Trinity*, edited by Jason S. Sexton, 138–43. Counterpoints. Grand Rapids: Zondervan, 2014.

Howe, Richard. "Does Morality Need God in Order to Be Objective? The 'Yes and No' Answer of Thomism." Unpublished paper, 2015. http://www.richardghowe.com/index_htm_files/Morality.pdf.

Huemer, Michael. *Ethical Intuitionism*. New York: Palgrave Macmillan, 2005.

Huffling, Brian. "God Is Not a Moral Being and the Moral Argument Is Often Wrongheaded." Southern Evangelical Seminary and Bible College. February 12, 2018. https://ses.edu/god-is-not-a-moral-being.

Jenson, Robert W. "The Holy Spirit." In *Christian Dogmatics*, edited by Carl E. Braaten and Robert W. Jenson, 2:101–82. Philadelphia: Fortress, 1984.

————. *Systematic Theology*. Vol. 1. New York: Oxford University Press, 1997.

Johnson, Adam Lloyd. "Debunking Nontheistic Moral Realism: A Critique of Erik Wielenberg's Attempt to Deflect the Lucky Coincidence Objection." *Philosophia Christi* 17, no. 2 (2015): 353–68.

————. "Fortifying the Petard: A Response to One of Erik Wielenberg's Criticisms of the Divine Command Theory." *Philosophia Christi* 20, no. 2 (2018): 357–64.

Joyce, Richard. *The Evolution of Morality*. Cambridge, MA: MIT Press, 2007.

Kagan, Shelly. *The Limits of Morality*. Oxford: Clarendon, 1989.

Kant, Immanuel. *Critique of Practical Reason*. Translated by Mary Gregor. Cambridge Texts in the History of Philosophy. Cambridge: Cambridge University Press, 1997.

————. *Religion within the Bounds of Bare Reason*. Translated by Werner S. Pluhar. Indianapolis: Hackett, 2009.

Kilby, Karen. "Perichoresis and Projection: Problems with Social Doctrines of the Trinity." *New Blackfriars* 81 (2000): 432–45.

Leftow, Brian. *God and Necessity*. New York: Oxford University Press, 2012.

Linville, Mark. "Darwin, Duties, and the Demiurge." In *A Debate on God and Morality: What Is the Best Account of Objective Moral Values and Duties?*, edited by Adam Lloyd Johnson, 166–84. New York: Routledge, 2021.

————. "The Moral Argument." In *The Blackwell Companion to Natural Theology*, edited by William Lane Craig and J. P. Moreland, 391–448. Malden, MA: Wiley-Blackwell, 2012.

Lipton, Peter. *Inference to the Best Explanation*. 2nd ed. New York: Routledge, 2004.

MacIntyre, Alasdair. *After Virtue: A Study in Moral Theory*. 3rd ed. Notre Dame, IN: University of Notre Dame Press, 2007.

Mackie, J. L. *Ethics: Inventing Right and Wrong*. New York: Penguin, 1977.

_____. *The Miracle of Theism: Arguments For and Against the Existence of God*. New York: Oxford University Press, 1982.

Mann, William. *God, Modality, and Morality*. New York: Oxford University Press, 2015.

Martin, Michael. *Atheism, Morality, and Meaning*. Amherst, NY: Prometheus, 2003.

Mayr, Ernst. *What Evolution Is*. New York: Basic Books, 2001.

McCall, Thomas H. "Relational Trinity: Creedal Perspective." In *Two Views on the Doctrine of the Trinity*, edited by Jason Sexton, 113–37. Counterpoints. Grand Rapids: Zondervan, 2014.

_____. *Which Trinity? Whose Monotheism? Philosophical and Systematic Theologians on the Metaphysics of Trinitarian Theology*. Grand Rapids: Eerdmans, 2010.

McGinn, Colin. *Ethics, Evil, and Fiction*. Oxford: Oxford University Press, 1997.

Menuge, Angus. "Vindicating the Dilemma for Evolutionary Ethics: A Response to Erik Wielenberg." Paper presented at the Evangelical Philosophical Society Annual Meeting. Denver, CO, November 2018.

Menzel, Christopher. "Theism, Platonism, and the Metaphysics of Mathematics." *Faith and Philosophy* 4 (1987): 365–82.

Moltmann, Jürgen. *The Trinity and the Kingdom*. Minneapolis: Fortress, 1993.

Monod, Jacques. *Chance and Necessity: An Essay on the Natural Philosophy of Modern Biology*. New York: Knopf, 1971.

Moore, G. E. *Principia Ethica*. Edited by Thomas Baldwin. 2nd ed. Cambridge: Cambridge University Press, 1994.

Moreland, J. P. "Wielenberg and Emergence: Borrowed Capital on the Cheap." In *A Debate on God and Morality: What Is the Best Account of Objective Moral Values and Duties?*, edited by Adam Lloyd Johnson, 93–114. New York: Routledge, 2021.

Morris, Thomas V., and Christopher Menzel. "Absolute Creation." *American Philosophical Quarterly* 23 (1986): 353–62.

Murphy, Mark. "Divine Command, Divine Will, and Moral Obligation." *Faith and Philosophy* 15 (1998): 3–27.

_____. *God and Moral Law: On the Theistic Explanation of Morality*. New York: Oxford University Press, 2011.

_____. "No Creaturely Intrinsic Value." *Philosophia Christi* 20, no. 2 (2018): 347–56.

Nagel, Thomas. *Mind and Cosmos: Why the Materialist Neo-Darwinian Conception of Nature Is Almost Certainly False*. New York: Oxford University Press, 2012.

Nietzsche, Friedrich. *The Will to Power*. Translated by Walter Kaufmann and R. J. Hollingdale. New York: Random House, 1968.

Parfit, Derek. *On What Matters*. Vol. 2. New York: Oxford University Press, 2011.

Peppers-Bates, Susan. "Divine Simplicity and Divine Command Ethics." *International Philosophical Quarterly* 48, no. 3 (2008): 361–69.

Plantinga, Alvin. "Naturalism, Theism, Obligation and Supervenience." *Faith and Philosophy* 27, no. 3 (2010): 247–72.

_____. *The Nature of Necessity*. Oxford: Clarendon, 1974.

_____. *Where the Conflict Really Lies: Science, Religion, and Naturalism.* New York: Oxford University Press, 2011.

Plantinga, Cornelius, Jr. "Social Trinity and Tritheism." In *Trinity, Incarnation, and Atonement: Philosophical and Theological Essays,* edited by R. J. Feenstra and Cornelius Plantinga Jr., 21–47. Notre Dame, IN: University of Notre Dame Press, 1989.

Plato. *The Republic.* In *Six Great Dialogues.* Translated by Benjamin Jowett. Mineola, NY: Dover, 2007.

_____. *Theaetetus.* Vol. 12 of *Plato in Twelve Volumes.* Translated by Harold N. Fowler. Cambridge, MA: Harvard University Press, 1921.

_____. *Timaeus.* In *Plato: Timaeus and Critias.* Translated by Robin Waterfield. Oxford World's Classics. New York: Oxford University Press, 2008.

Poythress, Vern S. *Knowing and the Trinity.* Phillipsburg, NJ: P&R, 2018.

Prentice, Robert. "The Contingent Element Governing the Natural Law on the Last Seven Precepts of the Decalogue, According to Duns Scotus." *Antonianum* 42 (1967): 259–92.

Quinn, Philip. "An Argument for Divine Command Ethics." In *Christian Theism and the Problems of Philosophy,* edited by Michael Beaty, 289–302. Notre Dame, IN: University of Notre Dame Press, 1990.

_____. "Divine Command Theory." In *Guide to Ethical Theory,* edited by Hugh LaFollette, 57–73. Oxford: Blackwell, 1999.

_____. *Divine Commands and Moral Requirements.* Oxford: Clarendon, 1978.

Rachels, James. *Created from Animals: The Moral Implications of Darwinism.* New York: Oxford University Press, 1990.

Rahner, Karl. *The Trinity.* New York: Burns and Oates, 2001.

Ratzinger, Josef. *Introduction to Christianity.* New York: Herder & Herder, 1970.

Richard of St. Victor. *The Twelve Patriarchs; The Mystical Ark; Book Three of the Trinity.* Translated by Grover Zinn. New York: Paulist, 1979.

Richards, Jay Wesley. *The Untamed God.* Downers Grove, IL: InterVarsity, 2003.

Rodriguez-Pereyra, Gonzalo. "Nominalism in Metaphysics." *Stanford Encyclopedia of Philosophy,* revised April 1, 2015. https://plato.stanford.edu/entries/nominalism-metaphysics.

Ruse, Michael. *The Darwinian Paradigm: Essays on Its History, Philosophy and Religious Implications.* New York: Routledge, 1989.

_____. *Taking Darwin Seriously: A Naturalistic Approach to Philosophy.* New York: Blackwell, 1986.

Russell, Bertrand. "The Free Man's Worship." *Independent Review* 1 (1903): 415–24.

Sartre, J. P. *Existentialism and Human Emotions.* Translated by Bernard Frechtman and Hazel E. Barnes. Secaucus, NJ: Citadel, 1957.

Searle, John R. *Mind: A Brief Introduction.* New York: Oxford University Press, 2005.

Sexton, Jason S., ed. *Two Views on the Doctrine of the Trinity.* Counterpoints. Grand Rapids: Zondervan, 2014.

Shafer-Landau, Russ. "Evolutionary Debunking, Moral Realism and Moral Knowledge." *Journal of Ethics and Social Philosophy* 7, no. 1 (2012): 1–37.

_____. *Moral Realism: A Defence.* New York: Oxford University Press, 2003.

Singer, Peter. *Animal Rights and Human Obligations*. Englewood Cliffs, NJ: Prentice Hall, 1976.

————. "Ethics and Sociobiology." *Philosophy and Public Affairs* 11, no. 1 (1982): 40–64.

Sinnott-Armstrong, Walter. *Morality without God?* New York: Oxford University Press, 2009.

————. "There Is No Good Reason to Believe in God." In *God? A Debate between a Christian and an Atheist*, by William Lane Craig and Walter Sinnott-Armstrong, 31–52. Point/Counterpoint. New York: Oxford University Press, 2004.

Street, Sharon. "A Darwinian Dilemma for Realist Theories of Value." *Philosophical Studies* 127 (2006): 109–66.

Stump, Eleonore. "Francis and Dominic: Persons, Patterns, and Trinity." *American Catholic Philosophical Quarterly* 74 (2000): 1–25.

Sumner, Darren O. "Obedience and Subordination in Karl Barth's Trinitarian Theology." In *Advancing Trinitarian Theology*, edited by Oliver D. Crisp and Fred Sanders, 130–46. Grand Rapids: Zondervan, 2014.

Swain, Scott, and Michael Allen. "The Obedience of the Eternal Son." *International Journal of Systematic Theology* 15, no. 2 (2013): 114–34.

Swinburne, Richard. *The Christian God*. Oxford: Oxford University Press, 1994.

————. *The Coherence of Theism*. 2nd ed. Oxford: Oxford University Press, 2016.

————. *The Existence of God*. 2nd ed. Oxford: Clarendon, 2004.

Taylor, Richard. *Ethics, Faith and Reason*. Cambridge, MA: Harvard University Press, 1985.

Torrance, Alan J. *Persons in Communion: Trinitarian Description and Human Participation*. Edinburgh: T&T Clark, 1996.

Torrance, Thomas F. *The Christian Doctrine of God: One Being, Three Persons*. Edinburgh: T&T Clark, 1996.

————. *The Christian God: One Being Three Persons*. New York: Bloomsbury T&T Clark, 2016.

van Roojen, Mark. *Metaethics*. Routledge Contemporary Introductions to Philosophy. New York: Routledge, 2015.

Wainwright, William J. *Religion and Morality*. Burlington, VT: Ashgate, 2005.

Ware, Bruce A. "Equal in Essence, Distinct in Roles: Eternal Functional Authority and Submission among the Essentially Equal Divine Persons of the Godhead." In *The New Evangelical Subordinationism? Perspectives on the Equality of God the Father and God the Son*, edited by Dennis Jowers and H. Wayne House, 13–38. Eugene, OR: Wipf & Stock, 2012.

————. "Unity and Distinction of the Trinitarian Persons." In *Trinitarian Theology: Theological Models and Doctrinal Application*, edited by Keith S. Whitfield, 17–62. Nashville: B&H Academic, 2019.

Welty, Greg. "Theistic Conceptual Realism." In *Beyond the Control of God? Six Views on the Problem of God and Abstract Objects*, edited by Paul M. Gould, 81–96. New York: Bloomsbury Academic, 2014.

_____. "Truth as Divine Ideas." *Southwestern Journal of Theology* 47, no. 1 (2004): 56–68.

Whitfield, Keith S. Conclusion to *Trinitarian Theology: Theological Models and Doctrinal Application*. Edited by Keith S. Whitfield. Nashville: B&H Academic, 2019.

_____. Introduction to *Trinitarian Theology: Theological Models and Doctrinal Application*. Edited by Keith S. Whitfield. Nashville: B&H Academic, 2019.

Wielenberg, Erik. "Erik Wielenberg's Opening Speech." In *A Debate on God and Morality: What Is the Best Account of Objective Moral Values and Duties?*, edited by Adam Lloyd Johnson, 39–47. New York: Routledge, 2021.

_____. *God and the Reach of Reason: C. S. Lewis, David Hume, and Bertrand Russell*. New York: Cambridge University Press, 2008.

_____. "How to Be an Alethically Rational Naturalist." *Synthese* 131, no. 1 (2002): 81–98.

_____. "In Defense of Non-Natural, Non-Theistic Moral Realism." *Faith and Philosophy* 26, no. 1 (2009): 23–41.

_____. "An Inconsistency in Craig's Defence of the Moral Argument." *European Journal for Philosophy of Religion* 4, no. 4 (2012): 65–74.

_____. "Objective Morality and the Nature of Morality." *American Theological Inquiry* 3, no. 2 (2010): 77–84.

_____. "Questions and Answers." In *A Debate on God and Morality: What Is the Best Account of Objective Moral Values and Duties?*, edited by Adam Lloyd Johnson, 80–90. New York: Routledge, 2021,

_____. "Reply to Craig, Murphy, McNabb, and Johnson." *Philosophia Christi* 20, no. 2 (2018): 365–75.

_____. *Robust Ethics: The Metaphysics and Epistemology of Godless Normative Realism*. New York: Oxford University Press, 2014.

Wilson, Edward O. *Consilience: The Unity of Knowledge*. New York: Vintage, 1998.

_____. *Sociobiology: The New Synthesis*. Cambridge, MA: Belknap Press of Harvard University Press, 1975.

Wolter, Allan B. Introduction to *Duns Scotus on the Will and Morality*. By John Duns Scotus. Edited by William A. Frank. Translated by Allan B. Wolter. 2nd ed. Washington, DC: Catholic University of America Press, 1997.

Yandell, Keith. "Response to Scott A. Shalkowski." In *Beyond the Control of God? Six Views on the Problem of God and Abstract Objects*, edited by Paul M. Gould, 155. New York: Bloomsbury Academic, 2014.

Yarnell, Malcolm B., III. "From God to Humanity: A Trinitarian Method for Theological Anthropology." In *Trinitarian Theology: Theological Models and Doctrinal Application*, edited by Keith S. Whitfield, 63–94. Nashville: B&H Academic, 2019.

Zagzebski, Linda. *Divine Motivation Theory*. Cambridge: Cambridge University Press, 2004.

Zizioulas, John D. *Being as Communion: Studies in Personhood and the Church*. Crestwood, NY: St. Vladimir's Seminary Press, 1985.